MW00425490

A CHRONOLOGICAL TOUR THROUGH THE BIBLE

RON RHODES

HARVEST HOUSE PUBLISHERS
EUGENE, OREGON

Cover by Dugan Design Group, Bloomington, MN

A Chronological Tour Through the Bible
Copyright © 2018 Ron Rhodes
Published by Harvest House Publishers
Eugene, Oregon 97408
www.harvesthousepublishers.com

ISBN 978-0-7369-6433-3 (pbk.)
ISBN 978-0-7369-6434-0 (eBook)

Library of Congress Cataloging-in-Publication Data

Names: Rhodes, Ron, author.
Title: A chronological tour through the Bible / Ron Rhodes.
Description: Eugene : Harvest House Publishers, 2018.
Identifiers: LCCN 2018006856 (print) | LCCN 2018016429 (ebook) | ISBN 9780736964340 (ebook) | ISBN 9780736964333 (pbk.)
Subjects: LCSH: Bible--Chronology. | Bible--Criticism, interpretation, etc.
Classification: LCC BS637.3 (ebook) | LCC BS637.3 .R46 2018 (print) | DDC 220.6/1--dc23
LC record available at https://lccn.loc.gov/2018006856

Printed in the United States of America

18 19 20 21 22 23 24 25 26 / VP-SK / 10 9 8 7 6 5 4 3 2 1

To my grandson –
Carter Choisnet,
with affection

ACKNOWLEDGMENTS

There is not a day that passes that I am not thankful to God for my wife Kerri and our two grown children, David and Kylie. Life is rich because of these three wonderful people. I am blessed!

I also continue to be thankful for the opportunity of working with Bob Hawkins Jr., president of Harvest House Publishers, and his fine staff of friendly professionals. What a great team to work with!

Most importantly, I am grateful to the Lord Jesus for the opportunity to serve Him through the written word. There is nothing I'd rather be doing.

CONTENTS

A ONE-YEAR CHRONOLOGICAL TOUR THROUGH THE BIBLE

Thank you for joining me on this exciting journey through the Bible. You are in for a spiritually uplifting time. My hope and prayer is that as you go through *A Chronological Tour Through the Bible*, you will...

- experience a growing love for the Word of God,
- grow in your understanding of God's redemptive plan for humanity,
- grow in your knowledge of—and appreciation for—the wondrous salvation God has provided for you personally,
- experience more intimacy with God—*with Jesus*—than ever before,
- grow in your faith and trust in God, especially in the midst of life's troubles, and
- gain an eternal perspective so that you will see life's problems and difficulties from heaven's vantage point.

I pray you will gain the same blessings I did as I journeyed through Scripture chronologically!

The Blessings of a Chronological Approach

You might be wondering about the benefits of studying the Bible chronologically. My answer to that is that the Bible is a divinely inspired book—or, more accurately, collection of books—that tells the true story of human redemption. Taking a chronological approach helps us to understand this redemption drama in the order that it unfolded in ancient times. That helps us to understand the drama *in context*. It helps us to understand the drama in *real history*. And those are good things!

The Challenges of a Chronological Approach

There are notable challenges in taking a chronological approach to studying the Bible. To start, let's recognize that the ancients were not as concerned about precise chronological order as we are today. Sometimes the ancients organized material in a book according to a particular purpose, not according to a day-by-day calendar of events.

We must also admit that even though the Scriptures are inerrant, human attempts at Bible chronology are not! Some Bible scholars have different opinions on the precise order that events took place in the Bible. My personal view is that so much study has been done on all this through the years that it's now possible to put together a chronology with a strong confidence that we are "in the ballpark." It seems to me that we are all fairly certain on the big picture of Bible chronology. It is primarily the finer details that generate the most debate. The chronology reflected in this book is, in my studied opinion, one that makes good sense of the biblical data.

The Old and New Testaments

The word *Testament* carries the idea of covenant, or agreement. The Old Testament focuses on the old covenant between God and the Israelites. According to that covenant (the Sinai covenant), the Jews were to be God's people and were to be obedient to Him, and in return God would bless them (Exodus 19:3-25). The various books of the Old Testament provide information related to this old covenant and its outworking in Jewish history. Of course, Old Testament history reveals that Israel failed repeatedly, and continually violated the covenant.

The Old Testament as a body of literature is the "entire Bible" of the Jews, but only "Part One" of the Christian Bible. It is interesting to note that Jews do not like the designation *Old Testament* because of the implication that there must be a New Testament (which they reject). To them, the books that constitute the Old Testament comprise the entire Word of God.

Christians, however, answer that even in Old Testament times, the prophets began to speak of a new covenant that would focus not on keeping external laws but on an inner reality and change in the human heart (Jeremiah 31:31). Unlike the old covenant, the new covenant was to make full provision for the forgiveness of sins. This new covenant is the focus of the New Testament (see 1 Corinthians 11:25; 2 Corinthians 3:6; Hebrews 8:13).

While some Christians have minimized the importance of the Old Testament, its teachings are actually quite relevant to our daily lives. "Such things were written in the Scriptures long ago to teach us" (Romans 15:4). Speaking of things that happened to people in Old Testament times, the apostle Paul said: "These things happened to them as examples for us. They were written down to warn us who live at the end of the age" (1 Corinthians 10:11). So, fellow believer, drink richly of both the Old and New Testaments.

The New Testament is a collection of 27 books composed over a 50-year period by a number of different authors. The primary personality of the New Testament is Jesus Christ. The primary theme is salvation in Jesus Christ, based on the new covenant. The New Testament tells us all about Jesus and the new covenant. (More on all this later.)

How to Use this Book

As you begin each daily Bible study, it is wise to pray:

> *Lord, I ask You to open my eyes and enhance my understanding so that I can grasp what You want me to learn today (Psalm 119:18). I also ask You to enable me, by Your Spirit, to apply the truths I learn to my daily life, and be guided moment by moment by Your Word (Psalm 119:105; 2 Timothy 3:15-17). I thank You in Jesus's name. Amen.*

There are 365 days' worth of Bible studies in this book—one for each day of the year. These 365 daily studies are categorized under nine eras of time:

Era 1: Beginnings (the undated past–1800 BC)

Era 2: The Birth of Israel (1800–1406 BC)

Era 3: Possessing the Promised Land (1406–1050 BC)

Era 4: The United Monarchy (1050–930 BC)

Era 5: The Kingdom Divided (930–586 BC)

Era 6: Living in Exile (586–538 BC)

Era 7: The Return from Exile (538–6 BC)

Era 8: The Coming of Jesus Christ (6 BC–AD 30)

Era 9: The Early Church (AD 30–95)

These eras give us a framework that makes it easier to approach the Bible from a chronological perspective. They help us to see the big picture so that the finer details in each biblical book make better contextual sense.

You will notice that each chapter has a descriptive heading to let you know the topic of each day's study. Immediately following, I state the exact Bible passage(s) we'll explore that day. That gets us off to a quick start.

After you read each passage (or set of passages), you will find these very brief but helpful sections:

- *Key concept*—a broad thematic statement about today's Scripture reading
- *The big picture*—a short summary of the most important aspects of today's Bible reading
- *Transformational truth*—a Bible principle to apply to your life
- *A verse for meditation*—for personal reflection
- *A question to ponder*—to motivate self-examination

Each of these sections are necessarily brief. After all, this book has 365 chapters, which means each chapter needs to be very short—in essence, a micro-chapter. But these short chapters are strategically designed to give you maximum benefit as you read Scripture and allow it to transform your life.

Following are a few tips to help you get the most out of this book:

1. If a particular day's Scripture reading involves more than one Bible book, I always place the most important book first. (It is important in the sense of providing the backdrop for my main lesson for that day.) In some cases, the second or third Bible book listed may contain only supplementary material. For example, the Scripture readings for Day 3 are Genesis 4–6 and 1 Chronicles 1:1-4. The primary passage is Genesis 4–6, while 1 Chronicles 1:1-4 contains a short list of Adam's descendants. My advice is that on any given day, pay primary attention to the first book listed (and possibly the second book) in the Scripture reading assignment, and then quickly peruse through the remaining books—especially if they are books like 1 and 2 Chronicles, or 1 and 2 Kings. These latter books typically contain supplementary historical data—much like we might include in a footnote in modern literature.

2. The books written by Old Testament prophets typically set forth constantly recurring themes—such as unrepentant sin, judgment, a call to repentance, restoration, and/or the survival of a remnant. Don't be surprised at such repetition. Just keep in mind that prophets were often contemporaries of other prophets, and so common themes amongst them are understandable because they were all dealing with the same problems.

3. You probably wouldn't be surprised to learn that it is very difficult to divide the Bible into 365 daily readings, in chronological order, while at the same time making an effort to avoid breaking right in the middle of a good Bible story. I say this only to let you know that while most Bible readings are midrange in length, there are some on the shorter side and others on the longer side. Everything ultimately makes better sense this way.

And now it's time for you to grab your favorite Bible so we can begin our journey! Please allow me to pray for you:

> *Lord, please enable my reader—by the power of Your Spirit—to understand and apply important spiritual truths from each book of the Bible. Please excite them with Your Word. Please instill in them a sense of awe for You, and for the salvation You have provided us. I thank You in Jesus's name. Amen.*

ERA 1: BEGINNINGS
THE UNDATED PAST – 1800 BC

Genesis • Job • Selections from 1 Chronicles

Today we'll get oriented on the era titled "Beginnings." Did you know that Genesis derives its name from the first three words of the book, "In the beginning"? *Genesis* means "beginning." *Genesis is the book of beginnings.*

Besides addressing God's creation of the universe and humankind (Genesis 1–2), the book also details the fall of humankind and the consequences of that fall (3), the lives of Adam and his family (4–5), Noah and the worldwide flood (6–10), the judgment that took place at the Tower of Babel, after which the nations were dispersed (11), descriptions of the lives of the patriarchs Abraham, Isaac, Esau, and Jacob (12–36), Joseph being betrayed and eventually reconciled with his brothers (37–45), and information on Jacob and his growing family moving to Egypt (46–50).

It is not too much to say that the book of Genesis constitutes the foundation for the rest of the Bible. Indeed, if there is a Creator, as the book of Genesis indicates, then human beings are creatures who are responsible to Him. If humans are fallen in sin, as the book of Genesis indicates, then they are guilty and are in need of redemption. God's work of redemption, as recorded throughout the rest of Scripture, would make little sense if we did not first understand these foundational truths in the book of Genesis. So, the beginnings in Genesis set the stage for the rest of the Bible.

In terms of chronology, the following timeline is based on current historical and archeological studies:

The undated past BC—The creation; Adam and Eve; Noah's Flood

2166—Abram was born

2091 — Abram entered into Canaan

2080 — Ishmael was born

2067 — Abram's name was changed to Abraham; a son was promised to Sarah

2066 — Isaac was born

2062 — Hagar and Ishmael were sent away

2031 — Terah (Abraham's father) died

2026 — Isaac married Rebekah

2006 — Jacob and Esau were born

1991 — Abraham died

1929 — Jacob fled to Paddan Aram; Esau married Ishmael's daughter

1915 — Joseph was born; Jacob's wealth increased while working for Laban

1909 — Jacob fled from Laban; Jacob sent gifts to Esau prior to their reconciliation

1898 — Joseph had dreams of exaltation; was later sold into slavery by his brothers

1887 — Joseph interpreted the dreams of the chief cupbearer and chief baker

1885 — Joseph interpreted Pharaoh's dreams, and later began ruling in Egypt

1877 — Joseph's brothers traveled to Egypt

1876 — Jacob and his family relocated to Egypt

1859 — Jacob died

1805 — Joseph died

Job lived during the same basic time frame as Abraham. Three factors lead to this conclusion: (1) Job's age at the time of his death was 140 years, a common lifespan during patriarchal days (Job 42:16). (2) Job's wealth was measured in terms of livestock ownership (1:3), just as was true among the patriarchs. (3) Job was the priest of his family, similar to Abraham, Isaac, and Jacob (1:5).

A Jewish tradition ascribes the book of Job to Moses. Other suggestions include Solomon, Elihu, Isaiah, Hezekiah, Jeremiah, and Ezra. Regardless of the author, the book is named after the principal character in the book, Job—whose name apparently derives from a Hebrew word meaning "persecuted one."

The book has become famous because it deals with a problem that many people have struggled with: *If there is a good God, and if God is just, then why do good people suffer?* In Job's case, we find an upright man who had done nothing wrong, and yet catastrophe overwhelmed him at every side. He lost his possessions as well as his family, and he found himself engulfed in heinous physical suffering.

In any event, there was quite a lot going on between the undated past and 1800 BC. It is therefore appropriate that we title this first era of our chronological journey through Scripture "Beginnings."

As a way of preparing your heart for the journey through the era Beginnings, I suggest that you spend a little time meditating on the following verses about creation:

- God existed before creation—Psalm 90:2
- In the beginning God created—Genesis 1:1
- God alone is the Creator—Isaiah 44:24
- God made the heavens and the earth—Nehemiah 9:5-6
- God spoke and it was done—Psalm 33:6,9
- Creation took place by God's great power—Jeremiah 32:17
- The creation took place in six days—Exodus 20:11
- The earth was created according to wisdom—Proverbs 3:19
- We ought to worship the Creator—Revelation 4:11

As we begin our journey together, be watching for two streams of thought in Genesis: Genesis 1–11 documents the creation of the universe and humankind, and then it broadly traces the peoples and nations as they turn away from God. In Genesis 12 – 50, God zeroes in on one family—Abraham, Isaac, Jacob, and Joseph and his brothers. This family will eventually become the nation of Israel, through which all the other nations of the earth are to be blessed.

Another thing to watch for in Genesis is the centrality of faith. Abraham's faith was especially evident when he was being obedient to God's command to sacrifice his son Isaac (Genesis 22:1-19). God stopped him just in the nick of time. Joseph, too, showed great faith, knowing that even though his brothers treated him cruelly, God was with him and was providentially working in his painful circumstances (50:20). In the end, God elevated Joseph to a supreme position in Egypt.

Preview: On Day 2, we'll examine the creation and the subsequent fall of humankind.

THE CREATION AND THE FALL

Genesis 1-3

Yesterday we introduced the era titled "Beginnings," which spans the undated past through 1800 BC. Today we turn our attention to the creation account and the tragic subsequent fall of humanity.

Key concept. God created the universe in six days. The first couple—Adam and Eve—fell into sin.

The big picture. Genesis is foundational to a proper understanding of the rest of the Bible. It not only tells us about the origins of the universe and humankind, but also human sin, suffering, and death. God's work of redemption, recorded throughout the rest of Scripture, would make little sense if we did not first understand these foundational truths. Genesis was written by Moses between 1445 and 1405 BC, though the events of Genesis took place much earlier. The earliest events recorded in Genesis—the creation, Adam and Eve, and the flood of Noah's time—took place in the undated past. That these events took place historically, however, is confirmed by Jesus in the New Testament (Matthew 24:37; Mark 10:6).

Transformational truth. Because God created us, we ought to show some creaturely respect to Him (Genesis 1:26-27). As creatures, we are responsible to obey the Creator (Psalm 100:3; 95:6-7).

A verse for meditation. "God looked over all he had made, and he saw that it was very good!" (Genesis 1:31).

A question to ponder. What does it mean to you personally that you are created in the image of God?

WICKEDNESS ESCALATES – NOAH BUILDS AN ARK

Genesis 4 – 6; 1 Chronicles 1:1-4

In the previous lesson, we explored the creation account and the tragic fall of humanity (Genesis 1–3). Today we consider how wickedness escalated among human beings, and God's command to Noah to build an ark.

Key concept. God judges human wickedness but rescues the righteous from danger.

The big picture. The time of Noah is undated, though it was very early, and preceded the time of Abraham, Isaac, and Jacob. It may have been as early as 5000 BC or before. In today's passage, we witness God's decision to destroy the world by a global flood because of human wickedness. Noah, however, found favor with God. He was a righteous man. God instructed him to build a large ark for his family and various pairs of animals. He obeyed God (Genesis 6).

Transformational truth. Genesis 5:22 tells us that "Enoch walked with God" (ESV). Noah also "walked in close fellowship with God" (6:9). You and I can enjoy a close spiritual walk with God (Proverbs 20:7). We ought to walk honestly (1 Thessalonians 4:11-12), and in a way that is worthy of the Lord (Colossians 1:10). We should walk humbly with God (Micah 6:8).

A verse for meditation. "Noah found favor with the LORD" (Genesis 6:8).

A question to ponder. How might you and I find favor with the Lord? How can we imitate Noah?

NOAH'S FLOOD

Genesis 7 – 10; 1 Chronicles 1:5-23

Yesterday we considered God's command to Noah to build an ark (Genesis 4 – 6; 1 Chronicles 1:1-4). Today we will focus on the global flood of Noah's time.

Key concept. God brings judgment upon the wicked, but shows mercy on the righteous and delivers them.

The big picture. Noah and his family entered into the ark along with many pairs of animals. The rain fell for 40 days and 40 nights. This caused a universal flood that lasted 150 days. Noah, his family, and the animals were safe the entire time (Genesis 7). The waters eventually receded. Noah, his family, and the animals exited the ark. Noah promptly worshiped the Lord (8).

Transformational truth. God is often seen rescuing His people before His judgment falls upon the rebellious (2 Peter 2:5-9). Enoch was transferred to heaven before the judgment of the flood (Genesis 5:24). Noah and his family were in the ark before the judgment of the flood (Genesis 7:1,6-7). Lot was taken out of Sodom before judgment was poured out on Sodom and Gomorrah (Genesis 19:1-22).

A verse for meditation. "The LORD said to Noah, 'Go into the boat with all your family, for among all the people of the earth, I can see that you alone are righteous'" (Genesis 7:1).

A question to ponder. How is it that righteous people still fall into sin (Genesis 9:21; Romans 7:15-20)?

ABRAM OBEYS GOD

Genesis 11 – 14; 1 Chronicles 1:24-27

Yesterday we gave consideration to Noah's flood (Genesis 7–10; 1 Chronicles 1:5-23). Today we turn our attention to Abram's obedience to God in sojourning toward Canaan.

Key concept. God called Abram to a new land, Canaan. God then made a covenant with him, promising many descendants.

The big picture. Abram was born in 2166 BC. God instructed Abram and Sarai to leave Haran and make their way to Canaan. Abraham obeyed. Lot, his nephew, accompanied them. The three arrived in Canaan in 2019 BC. God then made an unconditional covenant with Abram, promising him great blessing, a great nation, and countless descendants (Genesis 12:2-3).

Transformational truth. Abram sought harmony with Lot over a grazing land dispute (Genesis 13:1-18). Harmony and peace are always the best policies (2 Corinthians 13:11).

A verse for meditation. "The LORD had said to Abram, 'Leave your native country…and go to the land that I will show you. I will make you into a great nation. I will bless you and make you famous, and you will be a blessing to others. I will bless those who bless you and curse those who treat you with contempt. All the families on earth will be blessed through you'" (Genesis 12:1-3).

A question to ponder. Two of Abram's character traits were obedience and faith. In what ways can you express your obedience to God and your faith in Him today?

GOD REAFFIRMS THE COVENANT

Genesis 15 – 17

Yesterday we focused on Abram's obedience to God in sojourning toward Canaan (Genesis 11 – 14; 1 Chronicles 1:24-27). Today we consider God's reaffirmation of His covenant to Abram.

Key concept. God reaffirmed specific promises of a land and count-less descendants to Abram.

The big picture. God reaffirmed His covenant with Abram around 2067 BC. Because he was old, Abram had concerns about how he and Sarai could give birth to the child of promise. God reaffirmed to Abram that his descendants would be as numberless as the stars (Genesis 22:17; 26:4; Exodus 32:13). Abram believed God, and God therefore counted him as righteous (or justified) (Genesis 15:6). Sarah soon offered her handmaiden Hagar to Abram with hopes that she might bear a son to Abram on her behalf. Ishmael was born from this union, but he was not to be the child of promise (Genesis 16).

Transformational truth. We are justified by faith alone (Genesis 15:6; Romans 3:25,28,30). The word *justified* is a legal term. Negatively, the word means that one is once-for-all pronounced not guilty before God. Positively, the word means that one is once-for-all pronounced righteous. *Glorious!*

A verse for meditation. "I am changing your name. It will no longer be Abram. Instead, you will be called Abraham, for you will be the father of many nations" (Genesis 17:5).

A question to ponder. How does the doctrine of justification affect your day-to-day relationship with God?

GOD JUDGES SODOM AND GOMORRAH

Genesis 18:1 – 21:7

In the previous lesson, we took a look at God's reaffirmation of His covenant with Abraham (Genesis 15–17). Today we explore God's judgment of Sodom and Gomorrah.

Key concept. God inflicts judgment on cities that flagrantly rebel against Him.

The big picture. God had previously promised a son to Abraham. Now God tells Abraham when it will happen—"this time next year" (Genesis 18:10). God said nothing is too hard for Him (18:14). He then affirmed He will destroy Sodom and Gomorrah because of their horrendous sin. Abraham pled for the cities, but judgment was nevertheless imminent (19:1-22). The Lord rained sulfur and fire on Sodom and Gomorrah in 2056 BC (19:23-29).

Transformational truth. Even though Abraham and Sarah were too old to have a baby, the Lord said to Abraham, "Is anything too hard for the LORD?" (Genesis 18:14). God can do anything He desires: "My purpose will stand, and I will do all that I please" (Isaiah 46:10). Trust God to handle your impossible situations at just the right time.

A verse for meditation. "Is anything too hard for the LORD? I will return about this time next year, and Sarah will have a son" (Genesis 18:14 NIV).

A question to ponder. Do you ever feel like God is waiting too long to answer your prayers? What have you learned in this lesson that helps you gain perspective?

THE COVENANT SON IS BORN

Genesis 21:8 – 23:20; 11:32; 24

Yesterday we gave consideration to God's judgment of Sodom and Gomorrah (Genesis 18:1 – 21:7). Today we focus attention on the birth of the promised covenant son.

Key concept. God fulfilled His promise, just as He said. The covenant son was finally born.

The big picture. Isaac was born to Abraham and Sarah in 2066 BC. Abraham loved Isaac. In 2046 BC, God tested Abraham's faith to reveal whether he loved God more than his now-twenty-year-old child of promise. God commanded, "Sacrifice him as a burnt offering." Abraham obeyed—but God stopped the sacrifice just in time. He was satisfied with Abraham's faith and obedience (Genesis 22). Sarah later died at the age of 127, and Abraham purchased property in Canaan to bury her (23).

Transformational truth. Abraham showed unflinching faith and obeyed God's command to sacrifice his son Isaac (Genesis 22:1-19). God stopped him just in time: "Don't lay a hand on the boy!…Do not hurt him in any way, for now I know that you truly fear God. You have not withheld from me even your son, your only son" (22:12). The lesson: *Trust God no matter what!*

A verse for meditation. "Through your descendants all the nations of the earth will be blessed—all because you have obeyed me" (Genesis 22:18).

A question to ponder. What is the most difficult test of faith you've ever experienced? What did you learn in that experience?

ISAAC AND REBEKAH GIVE BIRTH

Genesis 25:1-26; 1 Chronicles 1:28-34

Yesterday we considered the birth of Isaac (Genesis 21:8–23:20; 11:32; 24). Today we turn our attention to the birth of Jacob to Isaac and Rebekah.

Key concept. The line of promise continues with the birth of Jacob to Isaac and Rebekah.

The big picture. Jacob and Esau were born to Isaac and Rebekah in 2006 BC. Rebekah suffered a difficult pregnancy. The children within her were struggling (Genesis 25:22). God revealed that two nations were in her womb (25:23). The Edomites would descend from Esau, and the Israelites from Jacob. Their struggle in the womb was a preview of things to come. God also revealed that the older son would serve the younger (25:23). While Esau was the firstborn, he would later sell his birthright to Jacob in exchange for mere food.

Transformational truth. Jacob and Esau are a classic example of sibling rivalry (Genesis 25:21-26; 27:1-46; 33:1-20). Other examples include Cain and Abel (see 4:4-9) and Joseph and his estranged brothers (37). God's desire is that there be no estrangement among brothers (see Psalm 133:1).

A verse for meditation. "The LORD told her, 'The sons in your womb will become two nations. From the very beginning, the two nations will be rivals'" (Genesis 25:23).

A question to ponder. Like Esau, do you ever struggle with physical appetites controlling you more than the things of the Spirit?

JACOB OBTAINS ESAU'S FIRSTBORN RIGHTS

Genesis 25:27–28:5

Yesterday we focused on the birth of Jacob (Genesis 25:1-26; 1 Chronicles 1:28-34). Today we take a look at Jacob's conniving to obtain Esau's firstborn rights.

Key concept. Jacob, through outright deception, obtained the firstborn rights that belonged to Esau.

The big picture. Jacob and Esau were born to Isaac and Rebekah in 2006 BC. Much later, Jacob talked a hungry and exhausted brother—Esau, Isaac's firstborn son—into giving him his firstborn rights. Esau did this in exchange for a bowl of food (Genesis 25:33). Later, a nearly blind Isaac—now 137 years old—wanted to bless Esau before passing from this life. Through Rebekah's intervention, Jacob ended up receiving Isaac's blessing, albeit through deception (27:11-27). An angry Esau vowed vengeance. Jacob fled to Paddan-Aram in 1929 BC.

Transformational truth. Rebekah was a bad parental example to Jacob (Genesis 27:11-27). Parents can also be a good influence. An example is Uzziah, who "did what was pleasing in the LORD's sight, just as his father, Amaziah, had done" (2 Chronicles 26:4).

A verse for meditation. "From that time on, Esau hated Jacob because their father had given Jacob the blessing" (Genesis 27:41).

A question to ponder. Just as God told Isaac, "I will be with you" (Genesis 26:24), so God tells us, "I will never fail you. I will never abandon you" (Hebrews 13:5). What does that mean to you personally?

JACOB HAD MANY CHILDREN

Genesis 28:6 – 30:24

In the previous lesson, we considered Jacob's conniving to obtain Esau's firstborn rights (Genesis 25:27 – 28:5). Today we focus on the many children Jacob had.

Key concept. Jacob bore many children, though not all through the same woman.

The big picture. Jacob bore many children with Leah, Zilpah, and Bilhah in the early 1900s BC. Jacob had entered an agreement with Laban to work seven years in order to marry his daughter Rachel. After the seven years, Laban slyly brought Leah to Jacob after a feast. Jacob didn't know it was Leah—it was a dark evening, she likely had a veil on, and Jacob probably drank too much. Jacob had marital relations with her. Laban then agreed to give Rachel to Jacob in exchange for *another* seven years work. Through it all, Jacob had many children through Leah, Leah's servant Zilpah, Rachel's maid Bilhah, and finally Rachel (Genesis 29:20-27). Joseph was born to Jacob and Rachel in 1915 BC.

Transformational truth. Laban was crafty with Jacob (Genesis 29:27). Jacob had earlier been crafty in obtaining Esau's birthright (25:31). Scripture instructs us to never be crafty in dealing with others (Proverbs 11:1; 20:10,23).

A verse for meditation. "God remembered Rachel's plight and answered her prayers by enabling her to have children. She became pregnant and gave birth to a son" (Genesis 30:22-23).

A question to ponder. What do you think ultimately motivates people to engage in crafty behavior?

JACOB BECOMES WEALTHY, FLEES LABAN

Genesis 30:25 – 31:55

Yesterday we considered the many children Jacob had (Genesis 28:6 – 30:24). Today we turn our attention to how Jacob became wealthy and fled from Laban.

Key concept. Jacob prospered and eventually returned to Canaan with his family.

The big picture. Jacob continued to work for Laban—but now for wages (Genesis 30:25-36). Upon learning Jacob's personal herds had greatly increased (which, in turn, made him wealthy), Laban became hostile (30:37 – 31:2). About six years later, in 1909 BC, Jacob and his wives decided to head back to Canaan (31:3-21). After Jacob and his family stealthily slipped off, Laban pursued them. God was protective of Jacob, and warned Laban in a dream not to harm him. In a heated confrontation, grievances were discussed. They agreed to an uneasy truce, and Jacob and his family continued on toward Canaan (31:22-55).

Transformational truth. Laban did not seem to be a person of his word (Genesis 31:6-7). Jesus tells us that all Christians should be truthful with no duplicity. In Matthew 5:37, Jesus instructed, "Just say a simple, 'Yes, I will,' or 'No, I won't.'"

A verse for meditation. "If the God of my father had not been on my side...you would have sent me away empty-handed. But God has seen your abuse and my hard work" (Genesis 31:42).

A question to ponder. When you are treated unfairly, do you trust in God as your Defender?

JACOB AND ESAU RECONCILE

Genesis 32:1 – 35:27

Yesterday we gave consideration to how Jacob became wealthy and then fled Laban (Genesis 30:25 – 31:55). Today we turn our attention to Jacob and Esau's reconciliation.

Key concept. Jacob took steps to assuage Esau's anger before they reconnected. They made peace.

The big picture. As Jacob drew near to Canaan, he sent a message to Esau, calling himself "your servant Jacob" and sending along some gifts (Genesis 32:4,9-21). When they reconnected, Esau welcomed him and forgave Jacob. This took place in 1909 BC. Jacob, greatly relieved, worshipped God (33:1-20). Sometime later, Jacob's daughter Dinah was raped by a Canaanite, and Jacob's sons avenged her (34:1-31). Jacob returned to Bethel and built a memorial of God's wondrous promises (35:1-15).

Transformational truth. When cheated out of his birthright, Esau could have held on to bitterness. But he let it go (Genesis 33). When we are bitter, we hurt only ourselves. When we feel cheated in life, the best thing to do is to forgive those who have wronged us (Matthew 6:12,14; 18:21-22; Luke 6:37; Ephesians 4:32) and turn the situation over to God (Philippians 4:6-7).

A verse for meditation. "Esau ran to meet him and embraced him, threw his arms around his neck, and kissed him. And they both wept" (Genesis 33:4).

A question to ponder. Do you make a conscious effort toward "living in peace with everyone" (Hebrews 12:14)?

ESAU'S DESCENDANTS

Genesis 36; 1 Chronicles 1:35 – 2:2

Yesterday we focused on Jacob and Esau's reconciliation (Genesis 32:1–35:27). Today we give consideration to Esau's descendants.

Key concept. The descendants of Esau were the Edomites, who became bitter enemies of the descendants of Jacob.

The big picture. Esau moved away from his brother, Jacob. There was simply not enough land to support all the livestock and possessions they had respectively acquired (Genesis 36:6-8). Esau permanently relocated to Edom. The descendants of Esau were the Edomites. Edom was located in a mountainous area southeast and southwest of the Dead Sea, and was largely a semi-desert that was not very conducive to agriculture (Genesis 36:8; Joshua 24:4). History reveals that the descendants of Esau became bitter enemies of the descendants of Jacob. Later in Judah's history, the Edomites invaded Judah when Jerusalem was being overrun and destroyed by the Babylonians in 587 BC.

Transformational truth. Genealogies in the Bible substantiate that God's unfolding plan of redemption among human beings was carried out in real history (Genesis 36:1-19). The genealogy of Esau was just as real history as the later genealogies of Jesus (Matthew 1:1-19; Luke 3:23-38). The Bible is a trustworthy historical document (see 1 John 1:3; 2 Peter 1:16).

A verse for meditation. "They all descended from Esau, the ancestor of the Edomites" (Genesis 36:43).

A question to ponder. What does it mean to you personally that the Bible is a historically accurate document?

JOSEPH – ENSLAVED AND IMPRISONED

Genesis 37 – 39; 1 Chronicles 2:3-6,8

In the previous lesson, we considered the descendants of Esau (Genesis 36; 1 Chronicles 1:35 – 2:2). Today we turn our attention to how Joseph was sold into slavery and later imprisoned.

Key concept. Joseph dreamed about his future exaltation under God's providence. His resentful brothers sold him into slavery. He was later imprisoned in Egypt.

The big picture. Joseph's brothers resented his dream of exaltation and sold him to slave traders in 1898 BC (Genesis 37:1-28). They brought Joseph's robe—which they stained with animal blood—to their father Jacob, implying that Joseph was dead (37:29-35). Meanwhile, the traders sold Joseph to an Egyptian official, whom Joseph faithfully served (37:36). The official's wife tried to seduce Joseph, but he resisted. She then falsely accused him, after which he was imprisoned. But God was with him through it all (Genesis 39).

Transformational truth. One sin often leads to another. Joseph's ten brothers sinned against Joseph, which then led to their ongoing deception of their father (Genesis 37 – 39). Sin, if left unchecked, grows like a cancer.

A verse for meditation. "The LORD was with Joseph, so he succeeded in everything he did as he served in the home of his Egyptian master" (Genesis 39:2). Sometime later: "The LORD was with Joseph in the prison and showed him his faithful love" (verse 21).

A question to ponder. Do you ever struggle with jealousy or resentment? How do you handle it?

GOD EXALTS JOSEPH

Genesis 40; 35:28-29; 41

Yesterday we explored how Joseph was sold into slavery and was later imprisoned (Genesis 37 – 39; 1 Chronicles 2:3-6,8). Today we zero in on God's exaltation of Joseph.

Key concept. God providentially brought about circumstances that led to Joseph's release from prison and subsequent great exaltation in Egypt.

The big picture. When Joseph was in prison, the cup-bearer and baker had dreams they could not understand. Joseph correctly interpreted both dreams (Genesis 40:1-23). Pharaoh later had two dreams. No one could interpret them. The cup-bearer—now released from prison—suddenly remembered Joseph's abilities. Joseph was released from prison and provided the correct interpretation of both of Pharaoh's dreams. Pharaoh then elevated Joseph to great authority (41). Joseph's earlier dream about future exaltation now became a reality in about 1885 BC.

Transformational truth. Joseph was a people helper (Genesis 40:1-23). We should be people helpers as well (see Hebrews 13:16; 1 John 3:17; Matthew 25:35-40). Philippians 2:4 instructs: "Don't look out only for your own interests, but take an interest in others, too."

A verse for meditation. "Pharaoh said to Joseph…'You will be in charge of my court, and all my people will take orders from you. Only I, sitting on my throne, will have a rank higher than yours'" (Genesis 41:39-40).

A question to ponder. Are you a people helper? Read Philippians 2:4 and consider how to put it into practice.

JOSEPH RECONCILES WITH HIS BROTHERS

Genesis 42:1 – 45:15

Yesterday we considered God's great exaltation of Joseph (Genesis 40; 35:28-29; 41). Today we turn our attention to Joseph's reconciliation with his estranged brothers.

Key concept. Joseph reconciled with his estranged brothers in Egypt and instructed them to go tell their father Jacob he was alive.

The big picture. Joseph's brothers had been affected by the famine. When they showed up in Egypt for food, Joseph recognized them (Genesis 42:7-8). His brothers did not recognize him because he was now thoroughly Egyptian in his clothing, hairstyle, and speech. Joseph didn't reveal himself at first. He engineered events to test their sincerity (42:9-14). He became satisfied with what he saw (44:18-34). Joseph consequently revealed himself to his brothers, and instructed them to return to Jacob and inform him that Joseph was alive (Genesis 45:1-15). This was about 1876 BC.

Transformational truth. Joseph was boastful when young. With age, he learned the importance of being clothed with humility (see Colossians 3:12; 1 Peter 1:5-6).

A verse for meditation. "It was God who sent me here, not you! And he is the one who made me an adviser to Pharaoh—the manager of his entire palace and the governor of all Egypt" (Genesis 45:8).

A question to ponder. Are you ever tempted to boast? Read 2 Corinthians 10:17 and consider how this verse may relate to Joseph. How might you make this verse a reality in your life?

JACOB AND FAMILY RELOCATE TO EGYPT

Genesis 45:16 – 47:27

Yesterday we focused on Joseph's reconciliation with his brothers (Genesis 42:1–45:15). Today we zero in on how Jacob and his family relocated to Egypt.

Key concept. With Joseph's assistance, Jacob and his family relocated to Egypt to escape the famine.

The big picture. Joseph's brothers made their way back to Jacob and informed him Joseph was yet alive and held a position of great authority in Egypt (Genesis 45:21-28). Once Jacob and his family—seventy in all—made it back to Egypt in 1876 BC, there was an emotional reunion (46:30). Jacob met Pharaoh, and was granted land to dwell upon (47:1-12). Joseph made provisions for his father and his brothers (verse 12).

Transformational truth. God used all of Joseph's painful circumstances as a means of ultimately exalting him in Egypt (Genesis 45:1–50:26). Never forget: "God causes everything to work together for the good of those who love God and are called according to his purpose for them" (Romans 8:28).

A verse for meditation. "They left Egypt and returned to their father, Jacob, in the land of Canaan. 'Joseph is still alive!' they told him. 'And he is governor of all the land of Egypt!' Jacob was stunned at the news—he couldn't believe it…Their father's spirits revived" (Genesis 45:25-27).

A question to ponder. Joseph was a man of his word. Do you ever struggle with being a person of your word?

BLESSINGS, DEATHS, AND BURIALS

Genesis 47:28 – 50:26

In the previous lesson, we explored how Jacob and his family relocated to Egypt (Genesis 45:16–47:27). Today we consider the deaths of both Jacob and Joseph.

Key concept. Following Jacob's death, his sons had a renewed fear of possible vengeance from Joseph.

The big picture. Jacob blessed Joseph's sons (Genesis 48), and then shared his last words with his own sons (49). Following his death in 1859 BC, Jacob's body was transported to Canaan for burial (50:1-14). Now that their father was gone, Joseph's brothers feared Joseph might seek revenge for their earlier crimes against him. Joseph reassured his brothers all was well (50:15-21). Joseph lived to 110 years old and died in 1805 BC.

Transformational truth. When Joseph came before Jacob, "he bowed with his face to the ground" (Genesis 48:12). As great as Joseph was in the land of Egypt, he still bowed and showed respect to his elderly father (see Job 12:12; Proverbs 16:31). As Christians, why not follow Joseph's great example and show respect to the elderly?

A verse for meditation. "You intended to harm me, but God intended it all for good. He brought me to this position so I could save the lives of many people" (Genesis 50:20).

A question to ponder. What have you learned in this lesson about the importance of walking by faith and not by sight (see Genesis 50:20)?

THE SUFFERING OF JOB

Job 1–4

Yesterday we considered Jacob's actions toward the end of his life (Genesis 47:28–50:26). Today we shift gears and focus our attention on the suffering of Job.

Key concept. God permitted Job to experience an extended time of suffering at the hands of Satan.

The big picture. The events in Job's life are thought to have occurred around the time of Abraham, Isaac, and Jacob: 2200–1800 BC. In rapid succession, Job lost his sons and daughters, his sheep and herds, his servants, and his health (Job 1–2). Yet he remained in faith (1:21). After a time, he said he wished he had never been born. That way he would have been spared all the suffering (3). Job then had to endure an extended series of incorrect accusations from his friends, who were sure he was suffering because of personal sin (4).

Transformational truth. Job was blameless and righteous (Job 2:3). Yet, God permitted him to suffer through the agency of Satan. Through it all, Job maintained strong faith in God (1:21; see also Acts 14:22). Job is a great role model for us.

A verse for meditation. "There once was a man named Job who lived in the land of Uz. He was blameless—a man of complete integrity. He feared God and stayed away from evil" (Job 1:1).

A question to ponder. What do you think it means to "fear God" as Job did?

THE MISJUDGMENT OF JOB'S FRIENDS

Job 5–7

Yesterday we considered the suffering of Job (Job 1–4). Today we zero in on the misjudgment of Job's friends.

Key concept. Job received bad advice from his friends as to why he was suffering.

The big picture. Job's friends suggested he was suffering because of personal sin (Job 5:1-7). They assured him God would heal him once he had been sufficiently punished (verses 17-27). Job defended his innocence. He knew his friends were ill-informed (6:1–7:21). He challenged them to bring proof that he had done wrong. He rebuked them for assuming his guilt (6:22-30). Though Job did not wane in his faith in God or His Word, he nevertheless expressed a desire for death, for then his suffering would be over (7:1-5). Job wondered why God was allowing all of this (verses 11-21).

Transformational truth. Friends can have good intentions and yet give very bad advice. The mentality of Job's friends is alive and well today. Someone sees a fellow believer suffering, and says: "Perhaps there is a hidden sin you need to repent of." This does more harm than good. Let's resolve to use our mouths to build up, not to tear down (see Ephesians 4:29).

A verse for meditation. "People are born for trouble as readily as sparks fly up from a fire" (Job 5:7).

A question to ponder. Have you ever been falsely accused by a friend? How did you handle it?

JOB DEBATES HIS FRIENDS

Job 8 – 11

Yesterday we witnessed the misjudgment of Job's friends (Job 5 – 7). Today we focus on Job's response to them.

Key concept. Job debates his friends Bildad and Zophar as to why he is suffering.

The big picture. Bildad said God is just and fair in all of His interactions with humans. He wondered if Job was suggesting otherwise, with God punishing an innocent man (Job 8). Job agreed in principle that God is just, but also affirmed he could only speak from his own experience. It seemed to him that God was punishing a righteous man. Job wished he had never been born (9 – 10). His friend Zophar then got personal, claiming Job had to be guilty of secret sin (11).

Transformational truth. One of the Ten Commandments states, "You must not testify falsely against your neighbor" (Exodus 20:16). We should be careful with our words. The psalmist resolved, "I will watch what I do and not sin in what I say" (Psalm 39:1). He prayed: "Take control of what I say, O LORD, and guard my lips" (Psalm 141:3; see also Proverbs 12:18; 21:23; James 1:26; 1 Peter 3:10).

A verse for meditation. "Who am I, that I should try to answer God or even reason with him?" (Job 9:14).

A question to ponder. What do you learn from Job's friends about how *not* to treat your own friends?

JOB CONTINUES DEBATING HIS FRIENDS

Job 12 – 14

In the previous lesson, we witnessed Job's response to his friends (Job 8 – 11). Today we observe Job's continued debate with them.

Key concept. Job responds to the mistaken reasoning of his friends and says he wants to take his case directly to God.

The big picture. Job was fed up with his friends. They were acting like self-righteous know-it-alls. He told them he knew just as much about God and His ways as they did. He wanted to take his case directly to God and receive a "not guilty" verdict (Job 12:1 – 14:22). Job lamented his difficulties as well as the short span of human life (14:1-2,5).

Transformational truth. Job said life is short and is full of trouble (Job 14:1-2; see also Psalm 39:5; 102:3; James 4:14). The psalmist wisely prayed: "LORD, remind me how brief my time on earth will be. Remind me that my days are numbered—how fleeting my life is... My entire lifetime is just a moment to you; at best, each of us is but a breath" (Psalm 39:4-5).

A verse for meditation. "How frail is humanity! How short is life, how full of trouble! We blossom like a flower and then wither. Like a passing shadow, we quickly disappear" (Job 14:1-2).

A question to ponder. How might it be wise to keep Job 14:1-2 (above) in mind as we live day to day?

THE DEBATE BECOMES HEATED

Job 15 – 18

Yesterday we considered Job's continued debate with his friends (Job 12 – 14). Today the debate continues.

Key concept. Things begin to heat up in Job's debate with Eliphaz and Bildad.

The big picture. Eliphaz called Job a windbag, claiming Job's words were driven by sin. He questioned Job's reverence for God (Job 15). Job lamented that his friends were "miserable comforters" who were full of "hot air" (16:3). He lamented, "My friends scorn me" (16:20). He then appealed directly to God: "You must defend my innocence, O God, since no one else will stand up for me" (17:3). Bildad then repeated the accusation that Job was suffering because of personal sin. He described the suffering of the wicked in strong terms engineered to move Job to repentance. His words rang utterly hollow to Job (18).

Transformational truth. Instead of being "miserable comforters" to our friends, let's follow the apostle Paul's advice: "Encourage each other and build each other up" (1 Thessalonians 5:11). "You already show your love for all the believers…Even so, dear brothers and sisters, we urge you to love them even more" (1 Thessalonians 4:10). "Try to build each other up" (Romans 14:19).

A verse for meditation. "What miserable comforters you are! Won't you ever stop blowing hot air? What makes you keep on talking?" (Job 16:2-3).

A question to ponder. Have you ever had "miserable comforters" speak to you? Have you yourself ever been a "miserable comforter"?

JOB SEEKS MERCY FROM HIS FRIENDS

Job 19 – 21

Yesterday we considered further details of Job's ongoing debate with his friends (Job 15 – 18). The debate continues yet today.

Key concept. Job continued to defend himself, but also sought mercy from Bildad and Zophar.

The big picture. Job said his friends should be ashamed about treating him so poorly. He appealed to them for a little mercy: "Have mercy on me, my friends, have mercy, for the hand of God has struck me" (Job 19:21). His friends were tormentors, not comforters. Zophar continued to fixate on the idea that Job must be experiencing suffering because he had acted wickedly in the past (20). Job acknowledged that the wicked do ultimately get punished. But during earthly life, it often seems like the wicked prosper and escape suffering, thus nullifying Zophar's point (21).

Transformational truth. Job drifted perilously close to despair, thinking that God perhaps viewed him as an enemy (Job 19:6). In reality, God viewed him as "the finest man in all the earth" (1:8). Sometimes we misunderstand God's purposes!

A verse for meditation. "I know that my Redeemer lives, and he will stand upon the earth at last. And after my body has decayed, yet in my body I will see God!" (Job 19:25-26).

A question to ponder. Do you think Job's eternal perspective (in Job 19:25-26) helped him to weather the storm of his personal suffering? Do you try to maintain an eternal perspective?

JOB'S CHARACTER ASSAULTED

Job 22 – 25

Yesterday we focused on yet further details of Job's debate with his friends (Job 19 – 21). More of the same today.

Key concept. Job continued to vindicate himself in the face of a character assault.

The big picture. Eliphaz assaulted Job's character by claiming, "There's no limit to your sins" (Job 22:5). He speculated that Job may have mistreated the poor, withheld water from the thirsty, and other such sins (verses 6-7). Job still desired to face God in His divine court and lay out his case. He maintained his innocence (23:11-12). Job then protested that life is unfair. He wondered why the wicked are not punished in this life (24).

Transformational truth. Job thought God might be hiding from him (Job 23:9). This reminds us of the psalmist: "O Lord, how long will you forget me? Forever? How long will you look the other way?" (Psalm 13:1). "Do not stay silent. Do not abandon me now, O Lord" (35:22). "Wake up, O Lord! Why do you sleep? Get up!" (44:23). Scripture urges us to keep our faith strong, even during times where God seems silent (Hebrews 11).

A verse for meditation. "If only I knew where to find God, I would go to his court. I would lay out my case and present my arguments" (Job 23:3-4).

A question to ponder. What do you do when God seems to be silent in the face of difficult circumstances?

JOB SPEAKS SARCASTICALLY

Job 26 – 29

In the previous lesson, we explored further details on the seemingly endless debate Job had with his friends (Job 22 – 25). The debate continues yet further today.

Key concept. Job replied to his friends with scathing sarcasm.

The big picture. Job said to Bildad: "How you have helped the powerless! How you have saved the weak! How you have enlightened my stupidity! What wise advice you have offered! Where have you gotten all these wise sayings?" (Job 26:2-4). Bildad had been making specific accusations against Job, apparently oblivious to how his own life fell far short. Job vowed before God that he would never concede his friends were right (27:5-6). He looked back to his earlier days, and compared them with his present misery. He reflected that through it all, he had unwaveringly maintained his integrity before God. He was an innocent sufferer (28 – 29).

Transformational truth. "My conscience is clear," Job affirmed (Job 27:6). The apostle Paul told young Timothy that keeping a clear conscience is critically important (1 Timothy 1:19). We can keep a clear conscience by (1) avoiding unrepentant sin; and (2) confessing to God whenever we do fall into sin (1 John 1:9).

A verse for meditation. "I will maintain my innocence without wavering. My conscience is clear for as long as I live" (Job 27:6).

A question to ponder. Have you ever struggled with a pained conscience? What did you do about it?

JOB – AN INNOCENT SUFFERER

Job 30 – 31

Yesterday we considered how Job was sarcastic to his friend Bildad (Job 26 – 29). Today we consider further details on how Job viewed himself as an innocent sufferer.

Key concept. Job was a man in great anguish. He continued to protest his innocence before his friends and before God.

The big picture. In better days, Job was honored among men and led a prosperous life. Now it was all gone (Job 30:15). Job was troubled because God was seemingly oblivious to his pain (verse 20). Instead of God coming to his rescue, he was continually mocked by other people. Job vindicated himself. He affirmed that if he had lived in wickedness, he would have deserved his present suffering. But he had lived in righteousness and integrity. Job then fell silent (31).

Transformational truth. Job took steps to avoid lust: "I made a covenant with my eyes not to look with lust at a young woman" (Job 31:1). This was a wise move in view of what Jesus later said about lust: "Anyone who even looks at a woman with lust has already committed adultery with her in his heart" (Matthew 5:28; see also 15:19).

A verse for meditation. "I cry to you, O God, but you don't answer. I stand before you, but you don't even look" (Job 30:20).

A question to ponder. Have you ever thought about making a covenant with your eyes like Job did?

ELIHU JOINS THE CONVERSATION

Job 32 – 34

Yesterday we gave attention to how Job viewed himself as an innocent sufferer (Job 30–31). Today we turn our attention to the claims of Elihu.

Key concept. Elihu had remained silent while his elders continued in the debate. Now that they had finally stopped talking, he chimed in with his assessment.

The big picture. Elihu seemed to be angry at Job and at Job's three friends (Job 32:2-3). He quoted Job's words and then questioned what he had said (32:11-12; 33:1,31; 34:5-7,35-36). He denounced Job for claiming to be innocent, and he considered Job arrogant for claiming to be righteous. He criticized Job for questioning the Creator of the universe. He suggested that Job simply could not be righteous because he was suffering, and God does not unjustly punish the righteous. Elihu's mouth was like an uncorked bottle, gushing forth pent-up feelings.

Transformational truth. Contrary to Elihu, God does sometimes allow the righteous to suffer, as was the case with the apostle Paul, who suffered a thorn in the flesh. "Three different times I begged the Lord to take it away. Each time he said, 'My grace is all you need. My power works best in weakness'" (2 Corinthians 12:8-9).

A verse for meditation. "Truly, God will not do wrong. The Almighty will not twist justice" (Job 34:12).

A question to ponder. Have you ever questioned God's justice?

ELIHU CONTINUES
HIS MONOLOGUE

Job 35–37

Yesterday we considered the initial claims of Elihu (Job 32–34). Today Elihu continues his judgmental monologue.

Key concept. Elihu continued to explain why Job was wrong in his assessment of his suffering. He suggested God may have a redemptive purpose in Job's suffering.

The big picture. Elihu suggested that God may use suffering to correct and instruct people: "God is leading you away from danger, Job, to a place free from distress" (Job 36:16). Elihu thus advised Job to be patient in the midst of suffering, recognizing that God was ultimately helping him (verses 16-21). Elihu pointed to the greatness of God. He affirmed that Job's best response was to simply revere God (37:14-24).

Transformational truth. Though not necessarily applicable in Job's case, Elihu's general principle had some merit: God *can* use suffering to keep us from evil (Job 36:21). As the psalmist put it, "I used to wander off until you disciplined me; but now I closely follow your word… My suffering was good for me, for it taught me to pay attention to your decrees" (Psalm 119:67,71).

A verse for meditation. "Be on guard! Turn back from evil, for God sent this suffering to keep you from a life of evil" (Job 36:21).

A question to ponder. Has God ever used suffering in your life to draw you to repentance and obedience?

THE LORD CHALLENGED JOB

Job 38:1–40:5

In the previous lesson, we explored Elihu's continued monologue (Job 35–37). Today we consider how the Lord Himself challenged and humbled Job.

Key concept. God finally replied to Job, demonstrating to Job how little he really knows, and why he should trust Him, despite his suffering.

The big picture. God responded to Job. And did not explain to Job the reasons for his suffering. Instead, He reminded Job that He Himself is the sovereign, omniscient, omnipotent, omnipresent God of the entire universe. God's activities in the universe are far beyond human comprehension. Humans should therefore trust God, even when they lack understanding. Job was greatly humbled in this encounter (Job 40:4-5).

Transformational truth. God instructed Job to trust Him, even though he did not understand (Job 40). A great passage for us all to keep in mind is Proverbs 3:5-6: "Trust in the LORD with all your heart; do not depend on your own understanding. Seek his will in all you do, and he will show you which path to take."

A verse for meditation. "The LORD answered Job from the whirlwind: 'Who is this that questions my wisdom with such ignorant words? Brace yourself like a man, because I have some questions for you'" (Job 38:1-3).

A question to ponder. Are you able to consistently trust in God, even though you may not know why He has allowed certain circumstances to emerge in your life?

THE LORD CONTINUES TO CHALLENGE JOB

Job 40:6 – 42:17

Yesterday we considered how the Lord challenged Job (Job 38:1 – 40:5). Today we close our study of the book of Job with the Lord's continued challenging of Job.

Key concept. The Lord continued to demonstrate Job's ignorance. Job repented, and God restored blessing to his life.

The big picture. By His questions, God reminded Job that He is the sovereign, all-powerful, omnipotent Creator of the universe. Job got the message loud and clear (Job 40 – 41). He then affirmed, "I take back everything I said, and I sit in dust and ashes to show my repentance" (42:6). God made known His anger toward Job's babble-mouthed friends and commanded them to give burnt offerings. The Lord then restored great blessing to Job's life.

Transformational truth. Job's friends were wrong in claiming he was suffering because of a hidden sin (Job 42:7-8). It is unwise to ever make personal judgments about people who are suffering.

A verse for meditation. "When Job prayed for his friends, the LORD restored his fortunes. In fact, the Lord gave him twice as much as before!...So the LORD blessed Job in the second half of his life even more than in the beginning. Job lived 140 years after that...Then he died, an old man who had lived a long, full life" (42:10,12,16,17).

A question to ponder. What is the most important spiritual lesson you have learned from the book of Job?

ERA 2:
THE BIRTH OF ISRAEL
1800 – 1406 BC

Exodus • Leviticus • Numbers • Deuteronomy
Psalm 90 • Selections from 1 Chronicles

Today we begin our survey of the second major era of biblical history, which is entitled "The Birth of Israel." While we'll primarily spend time in Exodus, Leviticus, Numbers, and Deuteronomy, the beginnings of Israel's history goes back to Abram. You will recall that in the book of Genesis, God made an amazing unconditional promise to Abram: "The LORD took Abram outside and said to him, 'Look up into the sky and count the stars if you can. That's how many descendants you will have!'" (Genesis 15:5).

God later reiterated this promise to Abram's son Isaac: "I will cause your descendants to become as numerous as the stars of the sky" (Genesis 26:4). Still later, God made a similar promise to Isaac's son Jacob: "Your descendants will be as numerous as the dust of the earth!" (28:14).

Now, fast-forward to the book of Exodus. In this book we discover that the descendants of Abraham, Isaac, and Jacob (Hebrews) were growing geometrically. When Jacob first moved to Egypt, there were relatively few people with him: "In all, Jacob had seventy descendants in Egypt, including Joseph, who was already there" (Exodus 1:5). But then they multiplied rapidly. We read that "their descendants, the Israelites, had many children and grandchildren. In fact, they multiplied so greatly that they became extremely powerful and filled the land" (1:7). It came to the point that the Israelites outnumbered the Egyptians (verse 9). For this reason, the Egyptians enslaved them, hoping to thwart their numbers. "But the more the Egyptians oppressed them, the more the Israelites multiplied and spread" (verse 12). By the time God delivered the Israelites from Egyptian bondage, "there were about

47

600,000 men, plus all the women and children" (12:37)—probably somewhere around two million people in total.

We conclude, then, that in the book of Exodus we witness God beginning to fulfill the promises He made to Abraham, Isaac, and Jacob. And the process continued. Their descendants have indeed become countless.

The book of Exodus is a continuation of the story that began in Genesis—particularly chapters 37–50. This is clear not only in the fact that the first seven verses of Exodus 1 repeat information from Genesis, but the first word of verse 1 in the Hebrew text of Exodus is the word "And." This little word connects the books of Exodus and Genesis to each other.

In the Hebrew Bible, Exodus is entitled, "And these are the names..." This title is based on the opening words of the book (Exodus 1:1). The ancients often entitled a book according to its first words.

When the Hebrew Bible was translated into the Greek language, the book was given a new title. It was called "Exodus," from the Greek word *exodos*. This is a compound word that joins two Greek words: *ek* (meaning "out of") and *odos* (meaning "a road"). Taken together, the word *exodos* means "a road out of" or "departure." This title describes the central event in the book: Israel's departure from Egypt as a result of the ten plagues God inflicted on Pharaoh and the Egyptians.

The book also deals with God's establishment of a theocratic (God-ruled) nation under Moses by means of a new "constitution" called the Sinai covenant (chapters 16–40). In this covenant, God gave instructions for the ordering of life among the Hebrew people through the commandments given to Moses at Mount Sinai.

God's covenant with Israel at Mount Sinai, following Israel's sojourn through the wilderness, constituted the formal basis of the redemptive relationship between God and the Israelites (Exodus 19:3-25). This covenant was couched in terms of ancient Hittite suzerainty treaties made between a king and his subjects. In such treaties, there would always be a preamble naming the author of the treaty, a historical introduction depicting the relationship between the respective parties, a list of stipulations explaining the responsibilities of each of the parties, a promise of either blessing or judgment invoked depending on faithfulness or unfaithfulness to the treaty, a solemn oath, and a religious ratification of the treaty. In such treaties, the motivation for obedience to the stipulations was the undeserved favor of the king making the treaty. Out of gratitude, the people were to obey the stipulations.

Such parallels between ancient treaties and God's covenant with Israel show that God communicated to His people in ways they were already familiar with. Among the parallels are that God gave stipulations to the people explaining their responsibilities (the law, Exodus 20:1-17), gave a promise of blessing for obeying the law, and then promised judgment for disobeying the law (Exodus 19:8; 24:3,7). Sadly, the rest of the Old Testament reveals that Israel was often disobedient to God's covenant (Exodus 32:1-31; Jeremiah 31:32).

The following timeline for the exodus can give you a feel for the timing of key people and events:

1885 BC—Joseph began ruling in Egypt.

1876 BC—Jacob and his family went to Egypt.

1529 BC—Aaron was born.

1526 BC—Moses was born.

1486 BC—Moses fled to Midian from Egypt.

1446 BC—Moses encountered God in the burning bush; Moses returned to Egypt; the ten plagues were unleashed on the Egyptians; the first Jewish Passover was celebrated; the Jews left Egypt; the Pharaoh and the Egyptians were defeated at the Red Sea. (1446 BC was a big year!)

1445 BC—The Ten Commandments were given; the tabernacle was built and dedicated; the priests began their work; Israel's first census was taken.

1444 BC—Israel camped at Mount Sinai.

1406 BC—Moses provided final instructions for the people before he died; Joshua was appointed; Israel finally entered into Canaan.

The books of Leviticus, Numbers, and Deuteronomy were also critically important following the birth of the nation Israel. Leviticus, written by Moses sometime after 1440 BC, contains multiple ceremonial and ritual rules and regulations designed to govern every imaginable aspect of life among the ancient Israelites. Following the exodus from Egypt, Israel was called to a new way of life involving priests, tabernacle worship, sacrifices, and the like, and hence such rules and regulations became necessary. Leviticus contains laws about offerings and sacrifices (Leviticus 1–7), laws on the appointment and conduct of priests (8–10), laws about ritual cleansing, personal hygiene, and food (11–15), instructions regarding the Day of Atonement (16), and information and laws regarding Israel's festivals (17–27).

Moses later wrote the book of Numbers between 1440 and 1405 BC (see Numbers 33:2; 36:13). The title of this book derives from the two censuses that are recorded in the book, one taken at Mount Sinai (the original Exodus generation), and one taken on the plains of Moab (the generation that grew up in the wilderness and conquered Canaan) (1; 26). The book also contains a listing of the tribes of Israel (2), regulations for the priests and the Levites (3–8), information about the Passover (9), a chronicle of Israel moving from Mount Sinai to Moab on the border of Canaan (10–21), a record of Balaam and Balak (22–32), and the Israelites' journey coming to an end (33–36). A thread that runs through much of Numbers is that Israel was purged during the wilderness sojourn as a prelude to blessing in the land.

The book of Deuteronomy, written by Moses probably about 1410–1405 BC, contains the words Moses spoke to the Israelites as they were camped on the plains of Moab and preparing to enter into the Promised Land (Deuteronomy 1:1). This was Moses's farewell address, and he was passing the mantle on to Joshua.

The word *Deuteronomy* literally means "second law," and accurately describes some of the book's contents. Indeed, the Ten Commandments recorded in Exodus 20 are repeated in Deuteronomy 5, with minor variations. Other laws recorded in Exodus are also repeated in Deuteronomy.

The book also contains a restatement and reaffirmation of the covenant God made with the Israelites at Sinai (Deuteronomy 1–30). The covenant is couched in terms of ancient Hittite suzerainty treaties made between a king and his subjects.

In what follows, we will zero in on the details of the era of "the birth of Israel." We'll focus special attention on Exodus, Leviticus, Numbers, and Deuteronomy. As we progress, be watching for the following thematic summaries:

- Exodus — God does whatever is necessary to bring deliverance and redemption to His people.

- Leviticus — God is holy. He desires His people to be holy as well.

- Numbers — God's people sometimes experience divine purging and discipline in preparation for great blessing. Unbelief is the big hindrance to watch out for.

- Deuteronomy — Each new generation of people needs to hear the Word of God with a challenge to obey it.

Preview: On Day 34, we'll turn our attention to Moses and the burning bush.

MOSES AND THE BURNING BUSH

Exodus 1:1 – 4:17; 1 Chronicles 6:1-3

Yesterday we introduced Era 2 of biblical history, "The Birth of Israel." Today we turn our attention to the Hebrews enslaved in Egypt, and how Moses was commissioned by God to be the deliverer of the Hebrews.

Key concept. Moses was God's person of choice to rescue the Hebrews from Egyptian bondage.

The big picture. The Hebrews had been enslaved in Egypt for four generations (Exodus 1:1–2:15; Genesis 15:16). Moses, having escaped to Midian in 1486 BC, encountered God in a burning bush in 1446 BC. God intended Moses to be the deliverer of the Hebrews, and commissioned him to service. While Moses had misgivings, God's assurances convinced him to go (2:16–4:31).

Transformational truth. Sometimes God's timing is not our timing. The Hebrews would have preferred not to wait four generations before being delivered (Genesis 15:16). God had purposes for the delay. His timing is always perfect (Exodus 2:23-25; Ecclesiastes 3:1; Lamentations 3:25-26; Acts 1:7; Galatians 4:4).

A verse for meditation. "I have certainly seen the oppression of my people in Egypt. I have heard their cries of distress because of their harsh slave drivers. Yes, I am aware of their suffering…Now go, for I am sending you to Pharaoh. You must lead my people Israel out of Egypt" (Exodus 3:7,10).

A question to ponder. Do you sometimes struggle with waiting on God to answer your prayers?

MOSES CONFRONTS PHARAOH

Exodus 4:18 – 7:13

In the previous lesson, we explored God's commissioning of Moses to be the deliverer of the Hebrews (Exodus 1:1–4:17). Today we consider Moses's first confrontation with the Pharaoh.

Key concept. Moses, assisted by Aaron, took his first steps as the Hebrews' deliverer.

The big picture. Moses returned to Egypt in 1446 BC to confront the Pharaoh about letting the Hebrews go. The Pharaoh responded defiantly, and vindictively forced the Hebrews to make bricks without straw. God gave assurances to the people, but they remained fearful. Aaron's rod was turned into a snake to prove God's power, but the Pharaoh was unimpressed (Exodus 4:18–7:13).

Transformational truth. The Pharaoh increased the Hebrews' hardships after Moses's demand to let them go (Exodus 5). One thing we learn from this is that hardships in life do not prove a falling from God's favor. The life of Joseph is a good case study (Genesis 39–50). The life of the apostle Paul is another (2 Corinthians 4).

A verse for meditation. "I am the LORD. I will free you from your oppression and will rescue you from your slavery in Egypt. I will redeem you with a powerful arm and great acts of judgment. I will claim you as my own people, and I will be your God" (Exodus 6:6-7).

A question to ponder. Do you ever feel like you have fallen from God's favor because of tough circumstances in life?

PLAGUES ON EGYPT – PART 1

Exodus 7:14 – 9:35

Yesterday we considered Moses's confrontation with the Pharaoh (Exodus 4:18 – 7:13). Today we focus on God's plagues against Egypt through the hand of Moses.

Key concept. Egypt's gods were no competition for the God of the Hebrews. They could not do miraculous acts. That being so, Moses said, "Let my people go."

The big picture. Ten plagues were inflicted upon the Egyptians in 1446 BC. The plagues showed the impotence of Egypt's gods. The river god Nilus could not stop the Nile from turning to blood. The goddess Heqt (shaped like a frog) could not stop the swarm of frogs. The sun god Re could not stop darkness from coming upon the land. Moses's God proved that *He alone is God.* Therefore, Moses said, "Let my people go."

Transformational truth. God is incomparably great. The Pharaoh earlier asked: "Who is the Lord? Why should I listen to him and let Israel go?" (Exodus 5:2). The Lord answered with ten unstoppable plagues. Through these plagues, God said, "I will show you that I am the Lord" (7:17).

A verse for meditation. "This is what the Lord says: 'I will show you that I am the Lord.' Look! I will strike the water of the Nile with this staff in my hand, and the river will turn to blood" (Exodus 7:17).

A question to ponder. What other evidences can you think of from Scripture that point to God's incomparable greatness?

PLAGUES ON EGYPT – PART 2

Exodus 10 – 12

Yesterday we began our investigation of God's plagues against the Egyptians through the hand of Moses (Exodus 7:14 – 9:35). Today we continue our investigation of the plagues.

Key concept. Egypt's gods were impotent in the face of God's miraculous acts. God's strong arm literally forced the Egyptians to let the Hebrews go.

The big picture. The Pharaoh's heart was still hardened against God. However, following the plagues of the locusts (Exodus 10:1-20), the darkness upon the land (10:21-29), and the death of the firstborn among the Egyptians (12:29-30), he finally relented and released the Hebrews from bondage. They departed into the desert territory east of Egypt (12:31-51).

Transformational truth. God said His deliverance of the Hebrews from Egyptian bondage should be told to "children and grandchildren" (Exodus 10:2). It's a good thing to tell our children and grandchildren what the Lord has done in our lives. This can be a great faith-booster for them.

A verse for meditation. "Pharaoh sent for Moses and Aaron during the night. 'Get out!' he ordered. 'Leave my people—and take the rest of the Israelites with you! Go and worship the Lord as you have requested.' All the Egyptians urged the people of Israel to get out of the land as quickly as possible" (Exodus 12:31,33).

A question to ponder. Why do you think it took so long for the Pharaoh to give in?

THE EXODUS AND
CROSSING OF THE RED SEA

Exodus 13 – 15

Yesterday we finished our investigation of the plagues against the
Egyptians (Exodus 10 – 12). Today we turn our attention to the
actual exodus and the crossing of the Red Sea.

Key concept. The Hebrews exited Egypt—but the journey toward
the Promised Land had only just begun.

The big picture. The Hebrews finally left Egypt and crossed the Red
Sea in 1446 BC. God led the Israelites with a cloud by day and a fire
by night (Exodus 13:21-22). Still smarting, the Pharaoh had second
thoughts and led his army in pursuit. The Lord opened a "path through
the water with a strong east wind" so the Hebrews could cross the Red
Sea on dry land (14:21). The Egyptian army, however, was promptly
swallowed up by the sea when it tried to give chase (14:1-31). This deliverance was celebrated in the "Song of Moses" (15:1-21).

Transformational truth. God guided the Hebrews with a cloud by
day and a fire by night. Today, God guides us with His Word: "Your
word is a lamp to guide my feet and a light for my path" (Psalm 119:105).

A verse for meditation. "Who is like you among the gods, O
LORD—glorious in holiness, awesome in splendor, performing great
wonders?" (Exodus 15:11).

A question to ponder. Have you, or someone you know, ever experienced a miraculous deliverance from God?

DIVINE PROVISIONS

Exodus 16 – 19

In the previous lesson, we explored the Hebrews' exodus from Egypt and their crossing of the Red Sea (Exodus 13–15). Today we consider God's miraculous provisions for the people.

Key concept. God is not only a Deliverer. He is also a Provider and a Sustainer.

The big picture. Beginning in the latter part of 1446 BC, God miraculously provided a bread-like food called manna to sustain the Hebrews in the wilderness (Exodus 16). The Lord also caused water to gush forth from a rock so they could drink (17:1-7). Moses's father-in-law Jethro soon advised an overworked Moses to delegate some of his responsibilities, which he agreed was a good idea (18). God then revealed Himself to Moses on Mount Sinai (19).

Transformational truth. The Hebrews complained whenever they encountered any inconveniences (Exodus 16:2-3; 17:2). The New Testament instructs us to "do everything without complaining" (Philippians 2:14). We are also instructed, "Enter his gates with thanksgiving" (Psalm 100:4). "Be thankful in all circumstances, for this is God's will for you who belong to Christ Jesus" (1 Thessalonians 5:18).

A verse for meditation. "If you will obey me and keep my covenant, you will be my own special treasure from among all the peoples on earth; for all the earth belongs to me" (Exodus 19:5).

A question to ponder. What have you learned in this lesson that might help you reduce any complaining in your life?

THE TEN COMMANDMENTS AND THE LAW

Exodus 20:1 – 22:15

Yesterday we considered God's provisions for His people (Exodus 16–19). Today we focus on the giving of the Ten Commandments and the law.

Key concept. God's people are called to obey all of God's commandments.

The big picture. God revealed the Ten Commandments to Moses (Exodus 20:1-17). There are two categories: The first four commandments pertain to the Israelites' relationship with God: (1) have no other gods; (2) have no graven images of God; (3) do not take the Lord's name in vain; (4) keep the Sabbath. The next six commandments deal with the Israelites' relationships with each other: (5) honor your parents; (6) do not kill; (7) do not commit adultery; (8) do not steal; (9) do not bear false witness; and (10) do not covet. God's commandments were given to Israel not to place a burden on the people, but to distinguish them from pagan nations and to make the Israelites wise, great, and pleasing to a holy God.

Transformational truth. The Ten Commandments can be summarized in two briefer commandments: (1) love God; and (2) love your neighbor (Deuteronomy 6:5; Leviticus 19:18). Jesus thus said the greatest commandment is "Love the Lord your God," while the second is "Love your neighbor as yourself" (Matthew 22:37-39).

A verse for meditation. "You must not have any other god but me" (Exodus 20:3).

A question to ponder. How would you assess your success in following the two greatest commandments?

LAWS, FESTIVALS, AND A COVENANT

Exodus 22:16 – 24:18

Yesterday we gave attention to the giving of the Ten Commandments and the law (Exodus 20:1 – 22:15). Today we turn our attention to various other laws, festivals, and God's covenant with the people.

Key concept. Detailed instructions are provided about social responsibility, Jewish festivals, and God's covenant with the people.

The big picture. Instructions were provided on various kinds of inappropriate behaviors—important for a large traveling entourage (Exodus 22:16-31). Laws related to justice and mercy were then provided (23:1-9), followed by Sabbath laws (23:10 – 13), and instructions on three annual festivals (23:14-19; compare with Leviticus 23:4-44; Numbers 28:16 – 29:40; Deuteronomy 16:1-17). God's covenant with the people was then confirmed (24:1-18).

Transformational truth. When you have wronged another person, especially as related to damaging his or her property, it is wise and good to try to make restitution when possible (Exodus 22:3-31). I see a connection with Jesus's Golden Rule: "Do to others whatever you would like them to do to you. This is the essence of all that is taught in the law and the prophets" (Matthew 7:12). Following this one rule can be life-transforming!

A verse for meditation. "You must not mistreat or oppress foreigners in any way. Remember, you yourselves were once foreigners in the land of Egypt" (Exodus 22:21).

A question to ponder. Do you ever struggle with biases against people of other countries or other races?

TABERNACLE INSTRUCTIONS

Exodus 25 – 28

Yesterday we considered various laws, festivals, and God's covenant with the people (Exodus 22:16 – 24:18). Today we consider instructions about the tabernacle.

Key concept. The tabernacle was designed to house God's presence among the people.

The big picture. The word "tabernacle" means "dwelling place." The tabernacle was the heart and center of Israelite religious life following the time of the exodus. Instructions were provided for the building of the tabernacle, as well as the various items related to it—including the Ark of the Covenant and the altar of burnt offering (Exodus 25 – 28). Of great significance is the fact that the God of glory could actually dwell in the tabernacle. In this way, the Lord could now *be among* His people.

Transformational truth. Regular sacrifices were made upon the altar of burnt offering (Exodus 27:1). Jesus, of course, made the ultimate sacrifice by shedding His own blood on our behalf. As a result, *we are forgiven of all our sins* (Hebrews 10:1-18).

A verse for meditation. "Put the atonement cover on top of the Ark. I will meet with you there and talk to you from above the atonement cover between the gold cherubim that hover over the Ark of the Covenant. From there I will give you my commands for the people of Israel" (Exodus 25:21-22).

A question to ponder. How do you think God's dwelling within the tabernacle relates to His omnipresence?

MORE TABERNACLE INSTRUCTIONS

Exodus 29 – 31

In the previous lesson, we began our discussion about the tabernacle (Exodus 25 – 28). Today we consider further details about the tabernacle.

Key concept. The tabernacle was designed to house God's presence among the people, and therefore the instructions for its construction and proper protocol were quite specific.

The big picture. Instructions on the consecration of the priests, altar, and sanctuary were provided (Exodus 29:1-46). Also provided were construction plans for the altar of incense (30:1-10), directions regarding a special tax designed to raise money for the tabernacle (30:11-16), design plans on constructing the washing basin (30:17-21), and guidelines for making the anointing oil (30:22-38). Skilled laborers were to be used in the construction of the tabernacle (31:1-11). Instructions on the Sabbath were then provided (31:12-18).

Transformational truth. The emphasis on consecration points to the holiness of God (Exodus 29:37). The word *holy* carries the idea of being set apart from sin and all that is unclean. Hebrews 12:14 instructs you and me: "Work at living a holy life, for those who are not holy will not see the Lord."

A verse for meditation. "They will know that I am the Lord their God. I am the one who brought them out of the land of Egypt so that I could live among them. I am the Lord their God" (Exodus 29:46).

A question to ponder. How do you think one can "work at living a holy life"?

IDOLATRY WITH A GOLDEN CALF

Exodus 32 – 34

Yesterday we considered tabernacle instructions (Exodus 29 – 31). Today we focus on Israel's heinous idolatry with a golden calf.

Key concept. Avoid all forms of idolatry. It will bring you down.

The big picture. Aaron and the Israelites engaged in rank idolatry during Moses's absence on Mount Sinai. They fashioned a golden calf as an object of worship (Exodus 32:1-15). Moses, as an intercessor, pled for God to forgive His sinful people. The Lord renewed His commitment to guiding and protecting them (31:1 – 34:35).

Transformational truth. Pagan nations typically believed in a plethora of gods, and these gods were often represented as statues in the form of human beings or animals. Amazingly, even Aaron fell into idolatry with the golden calf. Idolatry involves worshipping other things in place of God. Today it can take many forms—money, materialism, the pursuit of fame, sexual immorality, and more. The New Testament consistently urges Christians to beware of idolatry (1 Corinthians 5:11; 10:7,14; 2 Corinthians 6:16; Galatians 5:20).

A verse for meditation. "How quickly they have turned away from the way I commanded them to live! They have melted down gold and made a calf, and they have bowed down and sacrificed to it. They are saying, 'These are your gods, O Israel, who brought you out of the land of Egypt'" (Exodus 32:8).

A question to ponder. What forms of idolatry have you seen surface in your life?

TABERNACLE CONSTRUCTION

Exodus 35–36

Yesterday we gave attention to Israel's idolatry with a golden calf (Exodus 32–34). Today we turn our attention to the construction of the tabernacle.

Key concept. The tabernacle was designed to house God's presence among the people. It was critically important that it be built.

The big picture. At Moses's urging, the Israelites contributed the various materials that were to be used in the building of the tabernacle. This required sacrificial donations on their part—and their response was overwhelmingly positive (Exodus 35:1-35). Construction of the tabernacle then began according to the specifications provided by the Lord (36).

Transformational truth. The people cheerfully gave what they had so that the tabernacle could be constructed (Exodus 35:5-31). This reminds us of Paul's exhortation about giving. We are to freely give as we have been freely given to. And we are to give as we are able. He instructs, "Don't give reluctantly or in response to pressure. 'For God loves a person who gives cheerfully'" (2 Corinthians 9:7).

A verse for meditation. "The seventh day must be a Sabbath day of complete rest, a holy day dedicated to the Lord. Anyone who works on that day must be put to death" (Exodus 35:2).

A question to ponder. Do you think it is still important to have a "day of complete rest, a holy day dedicated to the Lord"?

TABERNACLE ITEMS CONSTRUCTED

Exodus 37:1 – 39:31

Yesterday we focused on the construction of the tabernacle (Exodus 35–36). Today we turn our attention to the construction of the various items used in relation to the tabernacle.

Key concept. The people engaged in construction "just as the LORD had commanded Moses."

The big picture. Various items related to the tabernacle were constructed, including the Ark of the Covenant (Exodus 37:1-9), the table (37:10-16), the lampstand (37:17-24), the incense altar (37:25-29), the altar of burnt offering (38:1-7), the washbasin (38:8), the tabernacle courtyard (38:9-20), and the intricate priestly clothing (39:1-31). Moses personally inspected all the work to ensure all was according to the Lord's instructions (39:32-43).

Transformational truth. In our Scripture reading, we see over and over again that all was done *just as the Lord had instructed* (Exodus 39:1,5,7,21,26,29,31). This shows an obedient attitude. A primary emphasis in the New Testament is that we show our love for Christ by our obedience to Him: "If you love me, obey my commandments... Those who accept my commandments and obey them are the ones who love me...You are my friends if you do what I command" (John 14:15,21; 15:14; see also 1 John 5:3).

A verse for meditation. "All this was done just as the LORD had commanded Moses" (Exodus 39:7).

A question to ponder. Would you say that your love for Christ consistently shows itself in your obedience to Him?

THE TABERNACLE COMPLETED

Exodus 39:32 – 40:38; Numbers 9:15-23

In the previous lesson, we considered the construction of various items used in relation to the tabernacle (Exodus 37:1 – 39:31). Today we witness the tabernacle being finally completed.

Key concept. The tabernacle was designed to house God's presence among the people. Its completion was good news for all the people.

The big picture. Once the tabernacle was completed, Moses inspected the work to ensure all was done according to the Lord's design (Exodus 39:32-43). Moses then consecrated the tabernacle for sacred use (40:1-33). The cloud that previously hovered over Mount Sinai (24:15-18) now descended upon the tabernacle and filled it with God's glory (40:34-38). *God was now among His people.* Try to imagine their joy. God was right near them—*in their immediate vicinity*—within the tabernacle!

Transformational truth. During the wilderness sojourn, God dwelt within the tabernacle (Exodus 40:38). Today, God dwells within us. The apostle Paul urged, "Don't you realize that your body is the temple of the Holy Spirit, who lives in you?" (1 Corinthians 6:19). That reality ought to affect the way we live.

A verse for meditation. "The cloud of the LORD hovered over the Tabernacle during the day, and at night fire glowed inside the cloud so the whole family of Israel could see it" (Exodus 40:38).

A question to ponder. Do you honor God with your body in light of the fact He dwells within you (1 Corinthians 6:19)?

OFFERINGS OF DEDICATION

Numbers 7

Yesterday we witnessed the tabernacle being finally completed, and God indwelling it (Exodus 39:32–40:38; Numbers 9:15-23). Today we focus on offerings of dedication generously brought by the people.

Key concept. The people expressed their joy over the tabernacle by being generous with offerings of dedication.

The big picture. Representatives of the 12 tribes of Israel brought forth offerings to support the Levites and their priestly service (Numbers 7). They provided wagons and oxen to help the Levites carry the tabernacle and the items placed within the tabernacle. Notice that the people were just as generous here as they had been earlier in providing materials for the construction of the tabernacle (Exodus 35:4-29). They were excited about God being in their midst!

Transformational truth. When Moses entered the tabernacle, he audibly heard God's voice speaking to him (Numbers 7:89). Today we "hear" the voice of God in the pages of Scripture (see Revelation 2:7,11,17,29; 3:6). God calls us not just to *hear* His Word but to *obey* it (James 1:22). Jesus said, "Blessed are all who hear the word of God and put it into practice" (Luke 11:28).

A verse for meditation. "Whenever Moses went into the Tabernacle to speak with the LORD, he heard the voice speaking to him from between the two cherubim above the Ark's cover" (Numbers 7:89).

A question to ponder. Are you committed to being both a *hearer* and a *doer* of God's Word (James 1:22)?

THE LEVITES AND VARIOUS OFFERINGS

Numbers 8:1 – 9:23; Leviticus 1 – 3

Yesterday we considered dedication offerings (Numbers 7). Today we examine the dedication of the Levites and instructions on offerings.

Key concept. Rightly relating to God for the Jews included dedications, festivals, and offerings.

The big picture. The Levites were purified and dedicated so they could serve under the direction of Aaron and the priests in the tabernacle (Numbers 8:5-26). The Passover, which celebrates the escape of the Jews from Egypt under Moses's leadership, was to be observed annually (9:1-14). God assured the Israelites He would be with them and guide them (9:15-23). Instructions were provided for the burnt offering (Leviticus 1), the grain offering (2), and the peace offering (3).

Transformational truth. Animals used for sacrifices were to be without defect (Leviticus 1:3-4). Jesus, the Lamb of God, was also without defects, for He was sinless. Jesus "did not sin" (Hebrews 4:15). He was "holy and blameless, unstained by sin" (Hebrews 7:26). "There is no sin in him" (1 John 3:5), for He was "the sinless, spotless Lamb of God" (1 Peter 1:19). He was thus a perfect sacrifice for our sins.

A verse for meditation. "Lay your hand on the animal's head, and the LORD will accept its death in your place to purify you, making you right with him" (Leviticus 1:4).

A question to ponder. What does it mean to you personally that Jesus's one-time perfect sacrifice has brought you salvation?

VARIOUS OFFERINGS

Leviticus 4 – 6

Yesterday we focused on the dedication of the Levites and instructions on offerings (Numbers 8:1–9:23; Leviticus 1–3). Today we continue our study of offerings.

Key concept. For the Israelites, rightly relating to God included dealing with sin and engaging in various offerings.

The big picture. Detailed instructions were provided for the sin offering—including the offerings for priests, the whole Israelite community, tribal leaders, and other members of the community (Leviticus 4:1–5:13). Guidelines were then provided for the guilt offering (5:14–6:7). Such offerings were at the very heart of the Hebrews' rightly relating to God.

Transformational truth. Among the Israelites, confession of sin was required for a right relationship with God (Leviticus 5:5). When you and I sin, we too need to confess to God, for "if we confess our sins to him, he is faithful and just to forgive us our sins and to cleanse us from all wickedness" (1 John 1:9). The Greek word translated "confess" literally means "to say the same thing." When we confess, we're saying the same thing about our sin that God says about it. *No excuses!*

A verse for meditation. "When you become aware of your guilt in any of these ways, you must confess your sin" (Leviticus 5:5).

A question to ponder. When you become aware of personal sin, do you immediately confess to God, as instructed in the New Testament (1 John 1:9)?

ORDINATION FOR THE PRIESTS

Leviticus 7–8

I n the previous lesson, we explored sin and guilt offerings (Leviticus 4–6). Today we examine priestly ordination.

Key concept. For Old Testament Israelites, there was a proper protocol necessary for worshipping God. The priest played a central role.

The big picture. Aaron and his sons participated in an ordination service (Leviticus 8:1-4). Aaron was decked out in his priestly garments (8:5-9). The tabernacle altar, utensils, and other items were consecrated with anointing oil, and sacrifices were offered (8:10-13,14-29). Aaron and his sons were then anointed with oil and blood. They were required to stay in the tabernacle court for the next seven days (8:30-36). This ceremony pointed to their important role in proper worship among the Israelites.

Transformational truth. Aaron was anointed as the high priest among the Hebrews (see Leviticus 8:12). Jesus is our eternal High Priest who shed His own blood on our behalf (Hebrews 7:27). He also prays on our behalf (Hebrews 7:25). And He helps us in our weaknesses: "This High Priest of ours understands our weaknesses, for he faced all of the same testings we do, yet he did not sin" (Hebrews 4:15).

A verse for meditation. "Everything we have done today was commanded by the LORD in order to purify you, making you right with him" (Leviticus 8:34).

A question to ponder. Have you ever thought about what Jesus—as your High Priest—might be praying on your behalf (Hebrews 7:25)?

PRIESTLY WORK AND CONDUCT

Leviticus 9 – 11

Yesterday we considered priestly ordination (Leviticus 7 – 8). Today we focus on priestly work and conduct.

Key concept. There is a right way and a wrong way for priests to do their work. For the people's sake, they had to get it right!

The big picture. Having just been ordained, the priests began their ministry. They first made the sin offering and then the voluntary offerings (Leviticus 9:1-21). Following this, Aaron blessed the people (22). When Nadab and Abihu, two of Aaron's sons, offered incense that had not been kindled from the altar, they were consumed by supernatural fire. Tragically, they were careless with God's instructions and paid the ultimate penalty (10:1-5). Guidelines were then provided on proper priestly conduct (8-20). Instructions were also given on ritual cleanness and uncleanness (11).

Transformational truth. The Hebrews had to become clean through rituals (Leviticus 11). But you and I are made clean by the blood of Jesus Christ: "If we are living in the light, as God is in the light, then we have fellowship with each other, and the blood of Jesus, his Son, cleanses us from all sin" (1 John 1:7).

A verse for meditation. "You must distinguish between what is sacred and what is common, between what is ceremonially unclean and what is clean" (Leviticus 10:10).

A question to ponder. Why do you think God responded so severely to Aaron's sons' act of disobedience?

RITUAL LAWS

Leviticus 12:1 – 14:32

Yesterday we gave attention to priestly work and conduct (Leviticus 9–11). Today we turn our attention to various ritual laws related to purification.

Key concept. An "unclean" person must undergo a purification ritual.

The big picture. The ancient Jews believed there were a number of things that could render a person unclean. A woman was rendered ceremonially unclean during menstruation and following childbirth (Leviticus 12:2-5). A person with a skin infection was considered unclean (Leviticus 13:3). An unclean person had to go through the purification rituals prescribed by the Mosaic law. For example, one could go through a purification ritual for skin diseases (Leviticus 13–14).

Transformational truth. Jesus taught that the true "unclean" part of a human being is the human heart within: "It's not what goes into your body that defiles you; you are defiled by what comes from your heart" (Mark 7:15). The only possible cleansing for this condition comes through being born again and then experiencing the transformative ministry of the Holy Spirit (1 Corinthians 6:19; 2 Corinthians 5:17; Galatians 5:16-23; Titus 3:5).

A verse for meditation. "Those who suffer from a serious skin disease must tear their clothing and leave their hair uncombed. They must cover their mouth and call out, 'Unclean! Unclean!'" (Leviticus 13:45).

A question to ponder. Are you ever surprised at the wickedness that still remains in your "unclean" heart as a Christian? (See Romans 7:15-25 for more on this.)

THE DAY OF ATONEMENT

Leviticus 14:33 – 16:34

Yesterday we focused on various ritual laws related to purification (Leviticus 12:1–14:32). Today we'll give consideration to the Day of Atonement.

Key concept. Only blood can atone for sin.

The big picture. On the Day of Atonement, Aaron, the high priest, had to first secure forgiveness for his own sins. He did this by sacrificing a bull as a sin offering for himself. Only then could he go on to offer sacrifices on behalf of the people of Israel. He would first kill a goat for the sins of the people. Then a second goat was laid hands on, and the high priest would symbolically transfer the guilt of the people to it, after which it was driven into the desert, thereby signifying that their sins had been taken away (Leviticus 14:33–16:34).

Transformational truth. Just as the people's sins were taken away by the scapegoat, so Jesus as the Lamb of God "takes away the sin of the world" (John 1:29). "Jesus came to take away our sins, and there is no sin in him" (1 John 3:5).

A verse for meditation. "As the goat goes into the wilderness, it will carry all the people's sins upon itself into a desolate land" (Leviticus 16:22).

A question to ponder. Does an understanding of the Old Testament sacrificial system increase your appreciation for what Jesus, the Lamb of God, accomplished at the cross on your behalf?

LAWS ON LIVING RIGHT

Leviticus 17 – 19

In the previous lesson, we focused on the Day of Atonement (Leviticus 14:33 – 16:34). Today we zero in on laws for living right.

Key concept. Do the right thing in your personal relationships.

The big picture. Today's Scripture reading focuses on rules for holy living, particularly as related to personal relationships. Moses zeroed in on sexual relationships that defile the individual and pollute the land. Individuals who engaged in deviant practices were to be cut off from the land (Leviticus 18:1-28). Chapter 19 contains a powerful list of dos and don'ts in relating to other people.

Transformational truth. Today's passage stipulates that people should show no partiality or favoritism (Leviticus 19:15). The New Testament affirms that "God does not show favoritism" (Romans 2:11). God carries out His righteous standards justly and with equity (Zephaniah 3:5; Romans 3:26). We, too, must avoid showing partiality (James 2:4). After all, the wisdom from above "shows no favoritism and is always sincere" (James 3:17). We must remember that we all "have the same Master in heaven, and he has no favorites" (Ephesians 6:9; Colossians 3:25). Indeed, "the heavenly Father to whom you pray has no favorites" (1 Peter 1:17).

A verse for meditation. "Do not twist justice in legal matters by favoring the poor or being partial to the rich and powerful. Always judge people fairly" (Leviticus 19:15).

A question to ponder. Are you ever tempted to show partiality in your dealings with people?

AVOIDING SIN—
RULES FOR PRIESTS

Leviticus 20–22

Yesterday we considered laws relating to personal relationships (Leviticus 17–19). Today we focus on avoiding certain kinds of sin. We also touch on some rules for priests.

Key concept. Live God's way.

The big picture. Moses in Leviticus 20 spelled out two categories of sins—those against true religion (verses 2-6,27) and those against the family (verses 9-21). Such sins, if left unchecked, could injure or even destroy the community. The people—individually and as a community—ought to consistently seek holy living (verses 7-8,22-26). Moses then laid out the moral and ritual regulations for priests. Obviously, they were held to a higher standard because they were in service to the Lord (verses 21-22).

Transformational truth. Moses listed specific commands against sexual sins, and punishments for violating them (Leviticus 20:10-21). In the New Testament, Paul said, "Run from sexual sin! No other sin so clearly affects the body as this one does. For sexual immorality is a sin against your own body...God bought you with a high price. So you must honor God with your body" (1 Corinthians 6:18-20).

A verse for meditation. "Set yourselves apart to be holy, for I am the LORD your God. Keep all my decrees by putting them into practice, for I am the LORD who makes you holy" (Leviticus 20:7-8).

A question to ponder. What do you think it means to "set yourselves apart to be holy"? What does that look like in everyday life?

SPECIAL DAYS AND YEARS

Leviticus 23:1–25:23

Yesterday we gave attention to avoiding certain kinds of sin, as well as rules for priests (Leviticus 20–22). Today we turn our attention to various festivals, the Sabbath year, and the year of Jubilee.

Key concept. Notable events in Israel's past are remembered and celebrated on special days and festivals.

The big picture. God called the Israelites to celebrate certain special days and festivals as a way of remembering and celebrating notable events of Israel's past. Moses also instructed that farmland was to be given a one-year rest every seventh year (Leviticus 25:1-7). He directed that every fiftieth year was to be a liberating year called Jubilee (25:8-55). Debts were to be cancelled, people who had sold themselves into slavery were to be set free, and land that had been sold because of hard times was to be returned to its original owners.

Transformational truth. Though Christians don't celebrate special days or festivals, we can nevertheless worshipfully celebrate what the Lord has done—*and is continuing to do*—in our lives. "Worship the LORD with gladness. Come before him, singing with joy…We are his people, the sheep of his pasture. Enter his gates with thanksgiving" (Psalm 100:2-4).

A verse for meditation. "The seventh day is a Sabbath day of complete rest" (Leviticus 23:3).

A question to ponder. Do you think one day a week of "complete rest" is workable in your life?

BLESSINGS AND PUNISHMENTS

Leviticus 25:24 – 26:46

Yesterday we focused on various festivals, the Sabbath year, and the year of Jubilee (Leviticus 23:1 – 25:23). Today we consider blessings for obedience and punishments for disobedience.

Key concept. Choices have consequences.

The big picture. God's covenant with Israel was conditional. (Don't confuse this with the unconditional Abrahamic covenant.) God's covenant said that if the people obeyed the covenant's stipulations, they would enjoy great blessing, thrive in the land, and God would be with them (Leviticus 26:1-13). If, however, the people disobeyed the stipulations, God would withdraw His presence and the people would experience the punishments enumerated in the covenant (26:14-46). Old Testament history reveals that the Israelites disobeyed God often, and consequently suffered the consequences.

Transformational truth. In the New Testament, our lives as Christians are centered on the new covenant — an unconditional covenant God made with humankind in which He promised to provide for the total forgiveness of sin based entirely on the sacrificial death and resurrection of Jesus Christ (Jeremiah 31:31-34; 1 Corinthians 11:25).

A verse for meditation. "Do not make idols or set up carved images, or sacred pillars, or sculptured stones in your land so you may worship them. I am the LORD your God" (Leviticus 26:1).

A question to ponder. Does it strike you, as it does me, that Christians have a much better covenant than the ancient Hebrews did?

THE FIRST CENSUS

Leviticus 27; Numbers 1

In the previous lesson, we explored blessings for obedience and punishments for disobedience (Leviticus 25:24–26:46). Today we turn our attention to Israel's first census.

Key concept. The census enabled Israel's leaders to determine Israel's military strength, as well as figure out proper land allotments in the Promised Land.

The big picture. God instructed Moses to take a census of all able-bodied Israelite men who were 20 years old or older and able to go to war (Numbers 1:2-3). The census would determine Israel's military strength—information that was vital in view of Israel's upcoming conquest of the Promised Land. Representatives from the various tribes assisted with the counting (1:4-17), and the Levites were exempted (1:47-54). The total number came to 603,550—an impressive force.

Transformational truth. The census was taken for planning purposes. Preparing for the future is wise. Joseph planned ahead so that people could survive the famine (Genesis 41). Planning ahead financially leads to prosperity (Proverbs 21:5). Planning ahead for heaven involves building up treasures there (Matthew 6:19-20).

A verse for meditation. "From the whole community of Israel, record the names of all the warriors by their clans and families. List all the men twenty years old or older who are able to go to war" (Numbers 1:2-3).

A question to ponder. Do your plans make you focus solely on your earthly life, or are some of your plans motivated by your future in heaven?

CAMP ORGANIZATION AND THE CONSECRATION OF THE LEVITES

Numbers 2–3

Yesterday we considered Israel's first census (Leviticus 27; Numbers 1). Today we turn our attention to the organization of Israel's camp and the consecration of the Levites.

Key concept. The Lord was to be the center of Jewish life.

The big picture. Numbers 2 addresses the layout of the various tribes of Israel. Notice that the tabernacle—where God personally dwelt—was located at the very center of the camp, with the various tribes being placed around the tabernacle. We can infer from this placement that God was intended to be at the heart and center of the Jewish community. In chapter 3, the Levites were consecrated for their religious duties on behalf of the other tribes of Israel.

Transformational truth. Jesus is the heart and center of Christianity. To know Jesus is to know God. To see Jesus is to see God. To believe in Jesus is to believe in God. To receive Jesus is to receive God. To worship Jesus is to worship God (Luke 24:27; John 5:39-40; Hebrews 12:2). No wonder Jesus said the Scriptures were "concerning himself" (Luke 24:27), were "written about me" (verse 44), were "written of me" (Hebrews 10:7), and "point to me" (John 5:39).

A verse for meditation. "The people of Israel did everything as the Lord had commanded Moses" (Numbers 2:34).

A question to ponder. What do you think it looks like for Jesus to be at the heart of a Christian's spiritual experience?

CLAN DUTIES AND MAINTAINING PURITY

Numbers 4 – 5

Yesterday we considered the organization of Israel's camp and the consecration of the Levites (Numbers 2 – 3). Today we turn our attention to the duties of the various clans in the tribe of Levi, and the importance of maintaining purity.

Key concept. The care of the tabernacle by the Levites was of utmost importance, for it housed God's presence.

The big picture. Moses detailed the tabernacle duties of the three branches of the Levites — the Kohathites, Gershonites, and Merarites (Leviticus 4:1-49). The Levites were servants of all the tribes of Israel, for they cared for the tabernacle, which represented the heart of spiritual life among the Israelites. Instructions were then provided regarding people who had infectious skin diseases and those caught in adultery (5).

Transformational truth. When the family unit erodes, society erodes. That's one reason it's important to take a strong stand against adultery (Leviticus 5:11-31). Jesus pronounced adultery wrong even in its basic motives (Matthew 5:27-28). Paul called adultery an evil work of the flesh (Galatians 5:19). Job followed a helpful policy: "I made a covenant with my eyes not to look with lust at a young woman" (Job 31:1).

A verse for meditation. "If any of the people — men or women — betray the LORD by doing wrong to another person, they are guilty" (Numbers 5:6).

A question to ponder. Do you think following Job's lead might be one way to help avoid sexual sin (Job 31:1)?

NAZIRITE VOWS

Numbers 6; 10

Yesterday we focused on the duties of the various clans, and the importance of maintaining purity (Numbers 4–5). Today we turn our attention to Nazirite vows.

Key concept. It is good to set an example to others of what it means to live a holy life.

The big picture. Israelites who took a Nazirite vow set themselves apart to the Lord in a special way (Numbers 6:1-21). Such vows were generally taken for a short time. Individuals who took such vows served as a reminder to all Israelites to live holy lives. Later, in Numbers 10, Moses made two trumpets to alert the Israelites when to assemble for battle, and when it was time to move the camp.

Transformational truth. Just as those who took a Nazirite vow set examples for others, so leaders in New Testament times were to live exemplary lives (1 Peter 5:3). Each of us as Christians can also be good examples to others. Paul told the Thessalonians believers, "You have become an example to all the believers in Greece—throughout both Macedonia and Achaia" (1 Thessalonians 1:7).

A verse for meditation. "May the LORD bless you and protect you. May the Lord smile on you and be gracious to you. May the LORD show you his favor and give you his peace" (Numbers 6:24-26).

A question to ponder. How would you evaluate the kind of example you've been over the past year?

COMPLAINTS – SCOUTING CANAAN

Numbers 11–13

In the previous lesson, we explored the Nazirite vow (Numbers 6; 10). Today we consider the grumbling complaints of the people, as well as the scouting of Canaan.

Key concept. Don't complain. Be thankful.

The big picture. God had provided the Israelites everything they needed, and yet they complained (Numbers 11:1-35). Even Miriam and Aaron complained about Moses (12:1-16). Such grumbling was like a slap in the face to God, telling Him, "You haven't done good enough for us." God was angered. Moses then sent 12 scouts to spy on Canaan (13:1-16). They reported that the land was nice, but it was too well defended (13:17-33). Caleb and Joshua disagreed, and thought the Israelites could conquer the land.

Transformational truth. Instead of complaining, how much better it is to be thankful. The psalmist had the right idea: "Enter his gates with thanksgiving; go into his courts with praise. Give thanks to him and praise his name" (Psalm 100:4). "O Lord my God, I will give you thanks forever" (Psalm 30:12). "I will praise God's name with singing, and I will honor him with thanksgiving" (Psalm 69:30).

A verse for meditation. "The people began to complain about their hardship, and the Lord heard everything they said. Then the Lord's anger blazed against them" (Numbers 11:1).

A question to ponder. Can you think of ten things you can offer thanksgiving to God for in your life? Why not do it now?

THE PEOPLE REBEL –
MOSES INTERCEDES

Numbers 14–15

Yesterday we considered the complaints of the people, as well as the scouting of Canaan (Numbers 11–13). Today we turn our attention to the rebellion of the Israelites and Moses's intercession for them.

Key concept. Grumbling and rebellion reveal a lack of faith in God.

The big picture. The people rebelled after hearing the pessimistic report of the Jewish spies. Moses interceded for the people, begging God not to destroy them. God honored Moses's request, but the entire generation of Israelites was now doomed to wander in the wilderness for 40 years, until every person over 20 years of age had died. *Choices have consequences* (Numbers 14)!

Transformational truth. Moses interceded for the people before God (Numbers 14:13-25). You and I ought to intercede for other people as well. We are to "pray for each other" (James 5:16). Paul urged, "Be persistent in your prayers for all believers everywhere" (Ephesians 6:18). He also said, "Pray for all people. Ask God to help them; intercede on their behalf" (1 Timothy 2:1).

A verse for meditation. "They have all seen my glorious presence and the miraculous signs I performed both in Egypt and in the wilderness, but again and again they have tested me by refusing to listen to my voice" (Numbers 14:22).

A question to ponder. Do you know someone who is hurting and who needs your intercessory prayers?

PRIESTLY REBELLION

Numbers 16 – 18

Yesterday we considered the Israelite rebellion and Moses's intercession for them (Numbers 14–15). Today we focus on some rebellious priests.

Key concept. Willful sin brings severe consequences.

The big picture. A family of Levites challenged Moses's leadership, and charged that priestly duties should be given to others in the camp (Numbers 16:1-15). God's support of Moses and Aaron was more than obvious to all when the earth suddenly opened up and swallowed the rebellious Levites (16:16-34). Fire from the Lord then consumed those who were pretentiously acting as priests (16:35-40). The following day, some in the camp accused Moses of killing God's people. Moses again interceded, and Aaron quickly sought purification for the sinning Israelites, but 14,700 of them forfeited their lives as a result of God's judgment on them (16:41-50).

Transformational truth. God, in His covenant with the people, had informed them that if they obeyed Him, He would bless them. If they disobeyed Him, they would suffer heavy consequences (Exodus 15:26; 19:5; 23:22; Leviticus 26:3-4; Deuteronomy 4:40; 7:12; 12:28; 15:5; 28:1). Our God is a God of love (Jeremiah 31:3; 1 John 4:8), but He is also a God of holiness and judgment (Isaiah 6:3; Revelation 20:11-15).

A verse for meditation. "The LORD is the one you and your followers are really revolting against!" (Numbers 16:11).

A question to ponder. Why is it important to view God in accordance with *all* His attributes, and not just our favorite (like love)?

MOSES AND AARON OFFEND GOD

Numbers 19 – 21

Yesterday we focused on some rebellious priests (Numbers 16–18). Today we turn our attention to how Moses and Aaron offended God.

Key concept. Don't swerve off the path of obedience. Remembering God's past faithfulness will strengthen your resolve for the future.

The big picture. The 40-year wilderness wandering was now nearly over. God instructed Moses to speak to a rock, from which water would flow. Moses instead struck the rock twice with his staff. For this, Moses and Aaron forfeited the opportunity to enter into the Promised Land (Numbers 20:1-13). They would die before entering it. Deuteronomy 34:4 tells us that God allowed Moses to see the Promised Land from a distance before he died.

Transformational truth. God's treatment of Moses and Aaron (Numbers 20:12) reveals that He truly shows no partiality. No one gets special treatment from God (Deuteronomy 10:17; Ephesians 6:9; 1 Peter 1:17). God calls us to imitate Him in this (James 2:4-5; 3:17).

A verse for meditation. "The LORD said to Moses and Aaron, 'Because you did not trust me enough to demonstrate my holiness to the people of Israel, you will not lead them into the land I am giving them!'" (Numbers 20:12).

A question to ponder. How does it strike you that Moses and Aaron were prohibited from entering the Promised Land?

BALAAM'S MESSAGES AND GOD'S PROVIDENCE

Numbers 22–24

In the previous lesson, we explored how Moses and Aaron offended God (Numbers 19–21). Today we consider the messages of the seer Balaam, as guided by God's providence.

Key concept. There is no need to consult God about an issue when He has already made His will clear on that matter.

The big picture. In view of Israel's military successes, King Balak and the Midianites hired the seer Balaam to curse Israel (Numbers 22:1-7). Balak wasn't counting on God's sovereign intervention. Though Balaam initially sought to call upon God to curse Israel, he was instructed by God instead to bless Israel (23:1-10). This angered Balak. Now Israel was even stronger. Balaam ended up speaking yet another blessing on Israel (24:1-9). Balak was beside himself and ordered Balaam to leave (24:10-14).

Transformational truth. Proverbs 16:9 instructs, "We can make our plans, but the LORD determines our steps." Proverbs 19:21 says, "You can make many plans, but the LORD's purpose will prevail." Proverbs 21:30 affirms: "No human wisdom or understanding or plan can stand against the LORD." God Himself says, "Everything I plan will come to pass, for I do whatever I wish" (Isaiah 46:10 ESV).

A verse for meditation. "God is not a man, so he does not lie. He is not human, so he does not change his mind" (Numbers 23:19).

A question to ponder. What have you learned about God and His sovereign plans in today's lesson?

MOAB SEDUCES ISRAEL – THE SECOND CENSUS

Numbers 25 – 26

Yesterday we considered the messages of the seer Balaam (Numbers 22 – 24). Today we turn our attention to Moab's seduction of Israel, and Israel's second census.

Key concept. God's people always remain vulnerable to sins of the flesh.

The big picture. Balaam had failed in cursing Israel (Numbers 23 – 24). Balaam advised Balak that if he were able to cause the Israelites to corrupt themselves, God might curse them. Balak therefore sent young women to seduce the Israelites into idolatry (25:1-3). Many Israelites feasted with the women and worshipped false gods. At God's command, apostate Israelites were executed (25:4-5). Before it was all over, 24,000 were dead (25:6-9). A second census revealed that all the original Exodus generation had died except Caleb and Joshua (26).

Transformational truth. The desires of the sinful nature include sexual immorality, impurity, lustful pleasures, and idolatry (Galatians 5:19-20). The sinful nature is always with us on this side of eternity. *The only remedy:* "Walk by the Spirit, and you will not gratify the desires of the flesh…The fruit of the Spirit is love, joy, peace, patience, kindness, goodness, faithfulness, gentleness, self-control" (Galatians 5:16,22,23).

A verse for meditation. "Moses ordered Israel's judges, 'Each of you must put to death the men under your authority who have joined in worshiping Baal of Peor' " (Numbers 25:5).

A question to ponder. What do you think it means to "walk by the Spirit" (Galatians 5:16)?

JOSHUA APPOINTED
TO LEADERSHIP

Numbers 27–29

Yesterday we considered Moab's seduction of Israel (Numbers 25–26). Today we consider Joshua's appointment to leadership over Israel.

Key concept. In view of our mortality, we should make responsible preparations for the future.

The big picture. God informed Moses that he would soon die. Moses asked God to appoint a new man to take his place. God chose Joshua as the future leader. God instructed Moses to present Joshua to Eleazar the priest before the community and publicly commission him to leadership. Moses obeyed (Numbers 27:12-23). This ensured there would not be a power struggle after Moses's death. For the short time Moses continued to live, he delegated work to Joshua so the people could see for themselves the transition in leadership.

Transformational truth. The time of our death is in God's hands: "Every day of my life was recorded in your book. Every moment was laid out before a single day had passed" (Psalm 139:16). "You have decided the length of our lives" (Job 14:5).

A verse for meditation. "O LORD…Please appoint a new man as leader for the community. Give them someone who will guide them wherever they go and will lead them into battle, so the community of the LORD will not be like sheep without a shepherd" (Numbers 27:15-17).

A question to ponder. Does it comfort you to know that the time of your death is in God's sovereign hands?

CONQUEST OF THE MIDIANITES

Numbers 30 – 31

Yesterday we focused on Joshua's appointment to leadership over Israel (Numbers 27 – 29). Today we turn our attention to Israel's conquest of the Midianites.

Key concept. God blesses those whom He calls to service.

The big picture. Israel's time of wandering in the wilderness was almost over. God sent a small force of 12,000 Israelite men to attack the much larger Midianite forces, and they were successful. Among the casualties were the seer Balaam and the Midianite women who earlier seduced the Israelites. Not a single Israelite died in battle. This demonstrated that God was on the side of His people (Numbers 30 – 31).

Transformational truth. It is said that "one plus God is a majority." The Israelites who attacked the Midianites were much smaller in number, but because God was with them, they succeeded. The shepherd David also learned that one plus God is a majority in his bout with the much larger and stronger Goliath (1 Samuel 17). This is a truth to remember when you're facing a problem bigger than your capabilities to handle it.

A verse for meditation. "A man who makes a vow to the LORD or makes a pledge under oath must never break it. He must do exactly what he said he would do" (Numbers 30:2).

A question to ponder. Does it strike you as severe that Moses commanded that the Midianite women be executed (Numbers 31:15-17)? Why do you think that was necessary?

THREE TRIBES SETTLE

Numbers 32–33

I n the previous lesson, we explored Israel's conquest of the Midianites (Numbers 30–31). Today we consider the settling of three of Israel's tribes.

Key concept. Finish the job. Oust *all* of the Canaanites and possess the land.

The big picture. The tribes of Reuben, Gad, and half the tribe of Manasseh requested Moses to grant them the fertile pasturelands east of the Jordan River. Moses said that so long as they continued helping the other tribes oust the Canaanites, the land was theirs (Numbers 32). Meanwhile, Moses kept a record of Israel's route toward the Promised Land. God reaffirmed His promise to give Israel the land of Canaan—but all the Canaanites were to be driven out (33).

Transformational truth. Like the three tribes, we ought to follow the maxim "Finish the job" (in their case, ousting all of the Canaanites). A great attitude to maintain as we finish what we start is to *do all things as unto the Lord*: "Whatever you do, work heartily, as for the Lord and not for men" (Colossians 3:23 ESV; see also 4:17).

A verse for meditation. "If you fail to drive out the people who live in the land, those who remain will be like splinters in your eyes and thorns in your sides. They will harass you in the land where you live" (Numbers 33:55).

A question to ponder. Have you ever fallen short of completing a task, only to later suffer consequences for it?

DIVIDING UP THE LAND

Numbers 34 – 36

Yesterday we considered the settling of three of Israel's tribes (Numbers 32–33). Today we will focus on Israel's dividing of the land.

Key concept. Land allotments were accomplished in an orderly and equitable fashion.

The big picture. God established the territorial boundaries where Israel's tribes were to settle (Numbers 34:1-15). Representatives from the various tribes were chosen to serve with Joshua and Eleazer in dividing up the land (34:16-29). The tribe of Levi (the priestly tribe) was not to receive a specific territory, but rather was to live among the other tribes (35). The tribal allotments were to remain intact in the future (36).

Transformational truth. God is a relentless promise keeper. He had promised Israel a wonderful land. Now Israel was finally settling into that land, even as the conquest of the land continued (Numbers 33). Joshua would later affirm, "Every promise of the LORD your God has come true. Not a single one has failed" (Joshua 23:14). "The LORD always keeps his promises" (Psalm 145:13). "God can be trusted to keep his promise" (Hebrews 10:23).

A verse for meditation. "The LORD said to Moses, 'Give these instructions to the Israelites: When you come into the land of Canaan, which I am giving you as your special possession, these will be the boundaries'" (Numbers 34:1-2).

A question to ponder. Do you anchor yourself on God's promises in Scripture?

ENTERING THE PROMISED LAND

Deuteronomy 1:1–3:20

Yesterday we considered Israel's dividing of the land (Numbers 34–36). Today we consider Deuteronomy, which contains another account of Israel entering the Promised Land.

Key concept. Moses provided final instructions as the people prepared to enter the Promised Land.

The big picture. Deuteronomy contains the words Moses spoke to the Israelites as they were preparing to enter the Promised Land in 1405 BC (Deuteronomy 1:1). This was Moses's farewell address. He was passing the mantle on to Joshua. Moses provided a historical review of the wilderness sojourn. He reviewed the sending out of the spies (1:19-25), the murmuring of the Israelites (1:26-46), and the conquest of Transjordan (2:26–3:20).

Transformational truth. We make life more difficult for ourselves when we disobey God. An example is how God sentenced the grumbling and rebellious Israelites to wander for 40 years before entering the Promised Land (Deuteronomy 2:15-16). We can forfeit God's mercies when we sin: "Those who worship false gods *turn their backs* on all God's mercies" (Jonah 2:8).

A verse for meditation. "The LORD your God has blessed you in everything you have done. He has watched your every step through this great wilderness. During these forty years, the LORD your God has been with you, and you have lacked nothing" (Deuteronomy 2:7).

A question to ponder. Do you think it possible that you may have—at some point in the past—forfeited some of God's mercies in your life because of sin?

MOSES ADDRESSES THE PEOPLE

Deuteronomy 3:21–5:33

Yesterday we witnessed Moses beginning his farewell address to the Jewish people (Deuteronomy 1:1–3:20). Today we continue our focus on Moses's address.

Key concept. Learn a lesson from those who went before you: *Obedience to God is the wisest course.*

The big picture. Moses addressed the people in 1405 BC. In contrast to the disobedience and rebellion of the previous generation, Moses now called all the people to obedience to Yahweh (Deuteronomy 4:1-43). This obedience centered on the Ten Commandments, which Moses now recounted (5:6-21). This was necessary because Israel's present generation had been mere children when the Ten Commandments were given to their parents some 40 years earlier.

Transformational truth. We should learn from the mistakes of others. Moses urged, "You saw for yourself...the LORD your God destroyed everyone who had worshiped Baal, the god of Peor. But all of you who were faithful to the LORD your God are still alive today—every one of you" (Deuteronomy 4:3-4).

A verse for meditation. "Do not add to or subtract from these commands I am giving you. Just obey the commands of the LORD your God that I am giving you" (Deuteronomy 4:2).

A question to ponder. What do you think motivated Moses to instruct the people not to add to or subtract from God's commandments? Do you think there was a danger of this happening?

LOVE THE LORD, BE HOLY, OBEY

Deuteronomy 6 – 9

In the previous lesson, we further considered Moses's final address to the people (Deuteronomy 3:21–5:33). Today we explore additional details of that address.

Key concept. We show our love for God by personal holiness and obedience.

The big picture. Parents are responsible to teach God's commandments to their children (Deuteronomy 6). God reiterated He would give His people victory over the pagans in Canaan and would prosper them in the land (7). Once His people experienced the good life, however, they must be cautious not to neglect Him (8). They must avoid ignoring Him and falling into the worship of false gods (9).

Transformational truth. Moses urged, "You must commit yourselves wholeheartedly to these commands that I am giving you today. Repeat them again and again to your children" (Deuteronomy 6:6-7). The original Hebrew text of Deuteronomy 6 indicates that parents are called to *whet their children's appetites* for the things of God. They should make the things of God palatable to their children so they'll grow in their desire for them.

A verse for meditation. "Listen, O Israel! The LORD is our God, the LORD alone. And you must love the LORD your God with all your heart, all your soul, and all your strength" (Deuteronomy 6:4-5).

A question to ponder. What do you think it means to love God "with all your heart, all your soul, and all your strength"?

OBEDIENCE AND BLESSING

Deuteronomy 10 – 12

Yesterday we considered additional details of Moses's farewell address to the people (Deuteronomy 6–9). Today we consider Moses's words on love and obedience to God.

Key concept. Two choices lie before people: (1) Be faithful and be blessed; or (2) be unfaithful and be cursed.

The big picture. Moses reminded the new generation in 1405 BC about how God had provided the Ten Commandments a second time on stone (Deuteronomy 10:1-5), and how He performed mighty miracles on behalf of His people (10:6-22). God then instructed the people regarding two possible choices they could make: (1) Be faithful to God and experience His tremendous blessings; or (2) turn to false gods and suffer God's disfavor (11:1-32).

Transformational truth. Moses told the people, "Commit yourselves wholeheartedly to these words of mine. Tie them to your hands and wear them on your forehead as reminders" (Deuteronomy 11:18). Wholehearted devotion to God is a common theme in Scripture. The psalmist reflected: "You have charged us to keep your commandments *carefully.* Oh, that my actions would *consistently* reflect your decrees" (Psalm 119:4-5).

A verse for meditation. "Now, Israel, what does the LORD your God require of you? He requires only that you fear the LORD your God, and live in a way that pleases him, and love him and serve him with all your heart and soul" (Deuteronomy 10:12).

A question to ponder. What do you think it means to "fear the LORD"?

MORE INSTRUCTIONS
FROM MOSES

Deuteronomy 13:1–16:17

Yesterday we gave attention to Moses's words on obedience to God and subsequent blessing (Deuteronomy 10–12). Today we consider further instructions from Moses.

Key concept. Follow all of God's instructions.

The big picture. Various instructions were provided by Moses. False prophets were to be executed (Deuteronomy 13:1-18). The Lord reiterated which animals were suitable for food and which were not (14:1-21). The Israelites were to be faithful in tithing (14:22-29). The poor must be treated fairly (15:1-18). Firstborn animals were to be presented as offerings to God (15:19-23). Instructions on celebrating festivals were also provided (16:1-17).

Transformational truth. Regarding the poor, Moses instructed, "Do not be hard-hearted or tightfisted toward them. Instead, be generous and lend them whatever they need" (Deuteronomy 15:7-8). Proverbs 14:31 affirms that the person who is generous to the needy honors the Lord. Proverbs 19:17 tells us: "If you help the poor, you are lending to the LORD—and he will repay you." By contrast, "those who shut their ears to the cries of the poor will be ignored in their own time of need" (21:13).

A verse for meditation. "You have been set apart as holy to the LORD your God, and he has chosen you from all the nations of the earth to be his own special treasure" (Deuteronomy 14:2).

A question to ponder. In what way do you think the Israelites are God's "own special treasure"?

LAWS FOR RULING THE NATION

Deuteronomy 16:18 – 21:9

Yesterday we focused on various instructions from Moses (Deuteronomy 13:1–16:17). Today we turn our attention to laws for ruling the nation.

Key concept. Laws regarding secular and religious leadership are critical to the survival of the nation.

The big picture. Instructions were provided in 1405 BC regarding Israel's judicial system (Deuteronomy 16:18–17:13). The laws regarding secular leadership (the king) were enumerated, the most important being the duty of learning God's law (17:14-20). Laws regarding religious leadership were then provided—including provisions for the support of priests and Levites, prohibitions against idolatry, and the marks of a true prophet (18:1-22). Also provided were various laws regarding cities of refuge and property boundaries (19:1-21), instructions on engaging in warfare (20:1-20), and details about dealing with unsolved murders (21:1-9).

Transformational truth. The underlying theme of Deuteronomy 19 is the pursuit of justice. This is a common theme in Scripture. God's people are warned not to pervert justice (Leviticus 19:15), for God loves it (Psalm 99:4). The Lord Himself works justice for the oppressed (Psalm 103:6), and affirms that those who seek justice are blessed (Psalm 106:3). Good comes to those who seek justice (Psalm 112:5).

A verse for meditation. "Your rule should be life for life, eye for eye, tooth for tooth, hand for hand, foot for foot" (Deuteronomy 19:21).

A question to ponder. How do you respond to this rule of justice: "life for life, eye for eye"?

LAWS REGARDING HUMAN RELATIONSHIPS

Deuteronomy 21:10 – 25:19

In the previous lesson, we explored laws for ruling the nation (Deuteronomy 16:18 – 21:9). Today we consider laws regarding human relationships.

Key concept. There are dos and don'ts when it comes to human relationships.

The big picture. Moses set forth laws concerning captive women (Deuteronomy 21:10-14), the rights of a firstborn in the family (21:15-17), and how to deal with a rebellious son (21:18-21). He also set forth laws on personal property (22:1-12) and on sexual immorality (22:13-30). Some of the laws may seem severe to us, but they were intended to protect the community at large. Regulations on a variety of other issues were provided, including ritual purity, justice and fairness, and the levirate marriage (23:1 – 25:19).

Transformational truth. Moses provided a number of laws on sexual immorality (Deuteronomy 22:13-30). He made a big deal about all this because sexual sin can damage and even destroy personal relationships (see Colossians 3:5-9). This was an important matter, given that three million people were about to enter the Promised Land.

A verse for meditation. "When you make a vow to the LORD your God, be prompt in fulfilling whatever you promised him. For the LORD your God demands that you promptly fulfill all your vows, or you will be guilty of sin" (Deuteronomy 23:21).

A question to ponder. Why do you think God's laws were so strict for the Israelites? What might be God's motive?

OBEDIENCE VERSUS DISOBEDIENCE

Deuteronomy 26:1–29:1

Yesterday we considered laws regarding human relationships (Deuteronomy 21:10-25:19). Today we take yet another look at the results of obedience versus disobedience.

Key concept. Obedience to God brings blessing, while disobedience brings cursing.

The big picture. Once the Israelites occupied the Promised Land in 1405 BC, there were two rituals of thanksgiving that were to be performed (Deuteronomy 26:1-15). A call to obey the Lord's commands was issued (26:6-19). Moses then said that upon entering Canaan, the people were to build an altar on Mount Ebal with the words of God's law written on its stones (27:1-10). Through a somewhat unique ceremony, the clear message was communicated that obedience would bring blessing from the Lord, but disobedience would bring terrible curses (27:11–29:1). All this was part and parcel of God's covenant with the people.

Transformational truth. Our Scripture reading today reminds us that *choices have consequences* (Deuteronomy 28). Bible commentator Matthew Henry (1662–1714) remarked, "No marvel that our sorrows are multiplied when our sins are." The Israelites often learned this truth the hard way.

A verse for meditation. "Today the LORD your God has commanded you to obey all these decrees and regulations. So be careful to obey them wholeheartedly" (Deuteronomy 26:16).

A question to ponder. Have you ever personally experienced the truth that "our sorrows are multiplied when our sins are"?

A CALL TO COMMITMENT

Deuteronomy 29:2 – 31:29

Yesterday we considered the results of obedience versus disobedience (Deuteronomy 26:1–29:1). Today we consider Moses's call to commitment.

Key concept. Make the right choice. Obey God and live.

The big picture. Moses again emphasized that obedience to God brings blessing while disobedience brings pain and disaster (Deuteronomy 29:2–30:29). Moses called upon the Israelites to be brave and courageous in facing the Canaanites in battle (31:1-13). The Lord then informed Moses that His people would, in fact, be unfaithful and suffer the consequences (31:14-29).

Transformational truth. Deuteronomy 29:29 affirms, "The secret things belong to the LORD our God" (ESV). This reminds us of Isaiah 55:8-9: " 'My thoughts are nothing like your thoughts,' says the LORD. 'And my ways are far beyond anything you could imagine. For just as the heavens are higher than the earth, so my ways are higher than your ways and my thoughts higher than your thoughts.' " Don't be disappointed if you don't always get all the answers you want on this side of eternity.

A verse for meditation. "Today I have given you the choice between life and death, between blessings and curses. Now I call on heaven and earth to witness the choice you make. Oh, that you would choose life, so that you and your descendants might live!" (Deuteronomy 30:19).

A question to ponder. Despite our natural curiosity about God's "secret things," how might it be in our best interest *not* to know them?

THE SONG OF MOSES

Deuteronomy 31:30 – 32:52; Psalm 90

Yesterday we focused on Moses's call to commitment (Deuteronomy 29:2 – 31:29). Today we turn our attention to the Song of Moses.

Key concept. God chose Israel. Israel sinned. Yet God still has a future for Israel.

The Big Picture. The Song of Moses, recited by Moses in 1405 BC, spans Israel's past and future. In poetic style, the song speaks of Israel as Yahweh's own chosen people. And yet Israel idolatrously betrayed God. God still has a future planned for Israel (Deuteronomy 32:1-43; see Romans 9–11). Psalm 90 is a prayer of Moses that acknowledges human frailty (90:3-6), human sinfulness (90:7-8), and the brevity of human life (90:9-12). Moses prayed for God's grace upon His people (90:13-17).

Transformational truth. The psalmist asked God, "Teach us to realize the brevity of life, so that we may grow in wisdom" (Psalm 90:12). This reminds us of Psalm 39:4: "Lord, remind me how brief my time on earth will be. Remind me that my days are numbered—how fleeting my life is." It is wise to be cognizant of one's mortality.

A verse for meditation. "There is no other god but me! I am the one who kills and gives life; I am the one who wounds and heals; no one can be rescued from my powerful hand!" (Deuteronomy 32:39).

A question to ponder. Why do you think God described Himself in this way to the Israelites (Deuteronomy 32:39)?

MOSES BLESSES
THE PEOPLE AND DIES

Deuteronomy 33 – 34

In the previous lesson, we explored the Song of Moses (Deuteronomy 31:30 – 32:52; Psalm 90). Today we consider Moses's final blessing upon the people and his subsequent death.

Key concept. Moses blessed the people, then died.

The Big Picture. Moses bade his people farewell, and wished God's very best for them (Deuteronomy 33:1-29). He then died on Mount Nebo in 1405 BC, but not before seeing the Promised Land from a distance (34:1-12). Though Moses authored Deuteronomy, another person—probably Joshua—penned this last chapter about Moses's death, appending it to what Moses had already written. Of course, this was done under the superintendence of the Holy Spirit, who inspired all of Scripture (2 Timothy 3:16).

Transformational truth. Death has been called the great equalizer. It afflicts the young and the old, the weak and the strong, the king and the commoner, the rich and the poor, the educated and the ignorant, both male and female, and people of all colors. Death has no favorites. All are equally victims of the grim reaper. In this world of uncertainty, death is something you can really count on. It is therefore wise to maintain an eternal perspective throughout life (Colossians 3:1-2).

A verse for meditation. "The eternal God is your refuge, and his everlasting arms are under you" (Deuteronomy 33:27).

A question to ponder. Does God's role as "your refuge" give you a sense of security in day-to-day life?

ERA 3: POSSESSING THE PROMISED LAND 1406 – 1050 BC

Joshua • Judges • Ruth
Selections from 1 Samuel • 1 Chronicles

As we survey this era, titled "Possessing the Promised Land," we will get an overview of what happened with Israel in 1406–1050 BC. The Bible books that report on this era include Joshua, Judges, and Ruth, along with portions of 1 Samuel and 1 Chronicles. Our focus will be on Israel's possession of the land of Canaan, in fulfillment of God's promise to Abraham (Genesis 12:1).

The backdrop is that God delivered the Hebrews from Egyptian bondage, after which they wandered in the wilderness for 40 years while en route to the Promised Land. Now they were on the edge of that land, and the conquest of it was about to begin under Joshua's able leadership.

The book of Joshua was written by Joshua between 1405 and 1385 BC. Joshua was Moses's assistant leader during the exodus and the desert wanderings (Joshua 17:9). He was an extremely effective military commander and leader, and for this reason, he was a natural successor to Moses (see Deuteronomy 34; Joshua 1:1-18). This would have been when Joshua was about 90 years old.

Joshua was one of only two Israelites who had left Egypt and would enter into the Promised Land because he had the faith and courage to trust God (Caleb was the other—Numbers 14:38). Joshua would certainly need this kind of faith and courage while leading the Israelites in conquering Canaan. His name is a shortened form of *Yehoshua*, which literally means "the Lord is salvation." The Lord's "salvation" would be evident in bringing victory over the inhabitants of Canaan.

The book of Joshua has a simple outline. The book focuses on Israel's entering the land of Canaan (Joshua 1:1–5:15), Israel's conquering of the land (6:1–12:24), and the dividing of the land among the 12 tribes of Israel (13:1–24:33), all under the effective leadership of Joshua. This was to be the initial fulfillment of the land promises given to Abraham and his descendants (Genesis 15:7; 26:2).

A key theme of Joshua is the necessity of faith in God and obedience to Him. At the end of the book, an aged Joshua reminded the people of God's covenant promises and urged them to continue obeying Him. Without such faith and obedience, God's blessing could not remain on the people. The Israelites should have learned this lesson well, for they witnessed time and time again that when they were obedient, God gave them military victory over their enemies, even though their enemies were more powerful than them (see Joshua 6–8).

The book of Judges was later written by an unidentified author between 1043 and 1000 BC. Jewish tradition, in the Talmud, says the author was the prophet Samuel. The book covers the time beginning with Joshua's death and ending with the rise of the prophet Samuel (Judges 2:6-9).

Primary attention is placed on the judges of Israel at that time. While the book is called Judges, the Hebrew term for the title (*Shophet*) can mean "Deliverers" or "Saviors." This points to the intended role of these judges. As Judges 2:16 puts it, "Then the Lord raised up judges to rescue the Israelites from their attackers."

The backdrop is that Joshua's conquest, while effective, still left pockets of resistance that continued to cause trouble for the Israelites. The judges were raised up specifically as military champions to lead the tribes of Israel against these culprits and to bring about final and complete conquest. These judges were needed, for at that time the 12 tribes of Israel had no central leadership. Four of the judges are listed in the faith Hall of Fame in Hebrews 11 — Gideon, Barak, Sampson, and Jephthah (see Judges 6:1–4:1-11; 8:32; 10:6–12:7; 13:1–16:31).

Unfortunately, Israel was unfaithful to God during this time, even giving allegiance to some of the false local gods of paganism. Despite the fact that God had repeatedly blessed them, they always seemed to revert to going their own way instead of God's way (Judges 3:7; 6:1; 10:6; 13:1).

The book of Ruth was likely written during the time of the judges in about 1000 BC. Some scholars believe the book was written by the prophet Samuel, but there is no hard proof of this. The word *Ruth* is probably a derivative of the Hebrew term *reuit*, which means "friendship." The word is appropriate, for it describes Ruth's character. We will see that God pulled off a rather amazing providential miracle in enabling Ruth to settle in the land.

The book of 1 Samuel was written by a prophet of the same name sometime after 931 BC. Samuel was the last and greatest of the judges of Israel, and was a wonderful prophet in his own right. He ruled Israel his entire life, and is noted for bringing the people back to God's laws. The two books of Samuel chronicle the transition in Israelite leadership from judges to kings. (We'll talk more about the kings in the biblical era, "The United Monarchy," which dates 1050–930 BC.)

First and 2 Chronicles were written by an unidentified author between 450 and 425 BC. These books draw most of their information from the books of Samuel and the books of Kings. As was true in the previous books, 1 and 2 Chronicles emphasize that the nation was blessed by God when it was obedient to Him, but it was punished by Him when it was disobedient.

In the coming chapters, we will learn many interesting details about this era. The following dates provide a helpful chronological orientation:

1446 — The first Jewish Passover was celebrated; the Jews left Egypt.

1444 — Israel encamped at Mount Sinai.

1443 — The spies checked out Canaan.

1406 — Moses died; Joshua was appointed as the new leader; Israel entered into Canaan.

1405–1385 — Joshua wrote the book of Joshua.

1375 — Judges began ruling in Israel.

1367 — Othniel began judging.

1209 — Deborah began judging.

1162 — Gideon began judging.

1105 — Samuel the prophet was born.

1100 – 1000 — The events recorded in the book of Ruth transpired.

1075 — Samson began judging.

1043 – 1000 — The book of Judges was written.

1000 — The book of Ruth was written.

931 — The book of 1 Samuel was written.

Preview: In Day 85, we'll zero in on Israel's conquest of Canaan.

ENTERING CANAAN

Joshua 1-6

Yesterday we introduced Era 3, titled "Possessing the Promised Land." Today we begin our study of Israel's conquest of Canaan.

Key concept. Joshua obeyed God in initiating the conquest of the Promised Land.

The big picture. Moses died in 1406 BC. God commissioned Joshua for service (Joshua 1:1-9), after which Joshua instructed the people regarding the conquest of the land (1:10-18). Two spies were sent out to reconnoiter the land. The prostitute Rahab rescued them from the pursuit of town officials (2:1-24). The Jordan was then crossed (3:1-17), followed by Joshua's setting up of a stone memorial of this event (4:1-24). Joshua renewed circumcision—a sign of the covenant—for the people of this new generation (5:1-12). Jericho fell (6).

Transformational truth. Regular meditation on the Word of God brings success in life (Joshua 1:8). Biblical meditation involves deeply pondering God's Word and His faithfulness (Psalm 119:148).

A verse for meditation. "Study this Book of Instruction continually. Meditate on it day and night so you will be sure to obey everything written in it. Only then will you prosper and succeed in all you do" (Joshua 1:8).

A question to ponder. Why is it good to make a regular habit of meditating on Scripture?

OBEDIENCE AND VICTORY

Joshua 7–9; 1 Chronicles 2:7

In the previous lesson, we witnessed Israel beginning to enter Canaan (Joshua 1–6). Today we consider how obedience to God is necessary for victory.

Key concept. Overconfidence and sin lead to quick defeat.

The big picture. Joshua's army attacked Ai and was defeated. This was due to both overconfidence and sin in the camp (Joshua 7:3,15,24). Achan, a soldier in Joshua's army, sinned by stealing treasure from Jericho and hiding it in his family's tent. This sin was purged at the execution of Achan and his family. Joshua's subsequent attack on Ai was successful (8).

Transformational truth. Beware of overconfidence. Joshua and his army had just won a major victory over Jericho (Joshua 6). Basking in glory, they now needed to face Ai, a much smaller city. They sent a much smaller army, confident of success (Joshua 7:1-5). They were defeated. Our confidence must be rooted not in ourselves, but in the Lord (Proverbs 3:26).

A verse for meditation. "There's no need for all of us to go up there; it won't take more than two or three thousand men to attack Ai. Since there are so few of them, don't make all our people struggle to go up there" (Joshua 7:3).

A question to ponder. Do you tend more toward self-confidence or God-confidence?

SUCCESSFUL CONQUESTS

Joshua 10:1 – 12:6

Yesterday we considered how obedience to God is necessary for victory (Joshua 7–9; 1 Chronicles 2:7). Today we focus on successful conquests.

Key concept. A summary of conquests is presented.

The big picture. Israel defeated the southern armies (Joshua 10:1-15), killed five southern kings who escaped and hid in caves (10:16-27), and destroyed the southern towns (10:28-43). Israel then defeated the northern armies (11) and kings east of the Jordan (12:1-6). These were successful conquests under God's providence.

Transformational truth. Our successes come from the Lord. "'Do not be afraid of them,' the LORD said to Joshua, 'for I have given you victory over them. Not a single one of them will be able to stand up to you'" (Joshua 10:8). Always involve the Lord in the battles you must face in life.

A verse for meditation. "So Joshua took control of the entire land, just as the LORD had instructed Moses. He gave it to the people of Israel as their special possession, dividing the land among the tribes. So the land finally had rest from war" (Joshua 11:23).

A question to ponder. Can you see the close connection between success in life and doing things *just as the Lord has instructed*?

LAND ALLOTMENTS

Joshua 12:7 – 15:19

Yesterday we gave attention to successful conquests (Joshua 10:1–12:6). Today we turn our attention to specific land allotments.

Key concept. Specific land allotments are made to some of the tribes.

The big picture. The kings and territories that were captured west of the Jordan River under Joshua's leadership are listed (Joshua 12:7-24). God reminded an aging Joshua of the significant remaining territories yet to be conquered (13:1-7). The territories east of the Jordan River that had already been designated to the tribes of Reuben and Gad and one-half of the tribe of Manasseh are listed (13:8-31). There's also an account of the land given to the tribe of Judah (15:1-12), as well as a special allotment of land to Caleb (15:13-19).

Transformational truth. Scripture often speaks of following the Lord wholeheartedly, as Caleb had (Joshua 14:8). This reminds us of the psalmist, who affirms, "Joyful are those who obey his laws and search for him *with all their hearts*" (119:2). He says, "I will obey your instructions; I will put them into practice *with all my heart*" (verse 34). He prays, "*May I be blameless* in keeping your decrees" (verse 80).

A verse for meditation. "For my part, I wholeheartedly followed the LORD my God" (Joshua 14:8).

A question to ponder. Why is wholehearted devotion to the Lord so important?

MORE LAND ALLOTMENTS

Joshua 15:20 – 17:18

Yesterday we focused on land allotments (Joshua 12:7 – 15:19). More of the same today.

Key concept. More land allotments are made among the tribes.

The big picture. Specific towns were allocated to Judah (Joshua 15:20-63), and land was given to Ephraim and West Manasseh (16:1 – 17:13). The tribes of Manasseh and Ephraim requested additional land because of their numerous people, and Joshua granted their request (17:14-18).

Transformational truth. Joshua's life-goal was to do *as the Lord commanded* (Joshua 17:4; 8:18,27; 10:40; 11:13,15). In the New Testament, obeying God's commands is necessary for maintaining fellowship with God (1 John 3:24). Those who obey also demonstrate their true love for Christ: "If you love me, obey my commandments" (John 14:15). Remember that our being saved by grace alone (Ephesians 2:8-9) is not incompatible with God's desire that we continue to walk in obedience to Him.

A verse for meditation. "Joshua gave them a grant of land…as the LORD had commanded" (Joshua 17:4).

A question to ponder. Have you ever been tempted to misuse the marvelous grace of God as a license for disobedience to some of God's commands?

MORE LAND ALLOTMENTS

Joshua 18:1 – 19:48

In the previous lesson, we continued our study of land allotments (Joshua 15:20 – 17:18). More of the same today.

Key concept. Land allotments among the tribes continues.

The big picture. Joshua sent out representatives from each tribe to survey the remaining land so it could then be divided among the tribes who had not yet received their allotments (Joshua 18:1-10). Land was then given to the tribes of Benjamin (18:11-28), Simeon (19:1-9), Zebulun (19:10-16), Issachar (19:17-23), Asher (24-31), Naphtali (19:32-39), and Dan (19:40-48).

Transformational truth. Some of the tribes put off the task of fully possessing the land (Joshua 18:3). It's human nature to put things off that seem difficult. We prefer to stay in our comfort zones. But Joshua urged the people to move on and take full possession. Lesson: Let's not procrastinate on what we know needs to be done (Matthew 8:21-22).

A verse for meditation. "Joshua asked them, 'How long are you going to wait before taking possession of the remaining land the LORD, the God of your ancestors, has given to you?'" (Joshua 18:3).

A question to ponder. What happened the last time God moved you outside your comfort zone?

SPECIAL LAND USES

Joshua 19:49 – 21:45; 1 Chronicles 6:54-81

Yesterday we continued our study of land allotments (Joshua 18:1 – 19:48). Today we focus on Joshua's land allotment, cities of refuge, and living arrangements for the Levites.

Key concept. Special land allotments were made for Joshua and cities of refuge.

The big picture. Joshua was granted his own city in recognition of his faithful leadership (Joshua 19:49-51). Six cities scattered throughout the tribes were designated as cities of refuge (20:1-9). If a person committed involuntary manslaughter, he had the right to flee to a city of refuge, where he would have to stay to remain safe from retribution from, say, the family members or friends of the slain. Because the Levites were given no land inheritance, they were assigned 48 cities throughout the territory of the tribes (21:1-45).

Transformational truth. The ancient Israelites weren't the only recipients of God's promises (Joshua 21:45). He makes promises to us too: "He has given us great and precious promises" (2 Peter 1:4).

A verse for meditation. "Not a single one of all the good promises the LORD had given to the family of Israel was left unfulfilled; everything he had spoken came true" (Joshua 21:45).

A question to ponder. Do you avail yourself of the promises of God in Scripture?

A CALL TO FAITHFULNESS

Joshua 22 – 24

Yesterday we gave attention to Joshua's land allotment, cities of refuge, and living arrangements for the Levites (Joshua 19:49 – 21:45; 1 Chronicles 6:54-81). Today we turn our attention to Joshua's call for the people to remain faithful to God.

Key concept. Joshua called the people to be loving and faithful to the divine Deliverer.

The big picture. Joshua, now an old man, reminded the people that God had fulfilled His promise to them of a land to dwell in. Joshua thus urged the people to keep obeying God (23:1-16). Joshua reviewed the love and faithfulness God had shown to Israel, which prompted him to urge love and faithfulness shown back to God (24:1-28).

Transformational truth. Joshua challenged the people to live according to this life plan: "Love the LORD your God, walk in all his ways, obey his commands, hold firmly to him, and serve him with all your heart and all your soul" (Joshua 22:5). This sounds similar to Jesus's suggested life plan: "You must love the LORD your God with all your heart, all your soul, and all your mind" (Matthew 22:37).

A verse for meditation. "Choose today whom you will serve...As for me and my family, we will serve the LORD" (Joshua 24:15).

A question to ponder. Have you driven the stake into the ground as to whom you will serve throughout life?

JOSHUA DIED – JUDGES AROSE

Judges 1:1 – 3:30

Yesterday we focused on Joshua's call to remain faithful to God (Joshua 22–24). Today we consider Joshua's death and the rise of judges.

Key concept. God raised up judges to continue the conquest of the land.

The big picture. Joshua's conquest, while effective, still left pockets of resistance that continued to cause trouble for the Israelites. The judges were raised up specifically as military champions to lead the tribes of Israel against these culprits and to bring about complete conquest. These judges were needed, for at that time, the 12 tribes had no central leadership. They began their work in 1375 BC.

Transformational truth. Tears over sin is not enough. Judges 2:3-4 informs us that when the Lord confronted the people about their sin, they wept. But their sorrow was short-lived. The people remained unfaithful to God (2:11-23). Their tears did not lead to ongoing repentance. They felt bad for a while, then plummeted right back into sin. *That's a bad policy!*

A verse for meditation. "When the people of Israel cried out to the Lord for help, the Lord raised up a rescuer to save them" (Judges 3:9).

A question to ponder. Why is it that we are sometimes fickle about obeying God?

THE ROLES OF SPECIFIC JUDGES

Judges 3:31 – 6:40

In the previous lesson, we explored Joshua's death and the rise of the judges (Judges 1:1–3:30). Today we consider the roles of specific judges.

Key concept. Specific judges carried out their roles as God-appointed deliverers.

The big picture. The judge Shamgar led the Israelites in victory over the Philistines (Judges 3:31). Deborah delivered the Israelites from oppression by the Canaanites (4:1-24). The Song of Deborah constitutes a celebration of this deliverance (5). But then the Israelites sinned, and the Lord handed them over to the Midianites for seven years. The Israelites cried out to God. God raised up the judge Gideon to deliver them. But Gideon requested a sign of assurance from God (6).

Transformational truth. Gideon thought he was about to die, but the Lord granted him immediate peace (Judges 6:23). God promises His followers today a supernatural peace. As Jesus put it, "I am leaving you with a gift—peace of mind and heart. And the peace I give is a gift the world cannot give. So don't be troubled or afraid" (John 14:27).

A verse for meditation. "Peace be to you. Do not fear; you shall not die" (Judges 6:23 ESV).

A question to ponder. What kinds of circumstances tend to rob you of your peace?

GIDEON'S VICTORY OVER THE MIDIANITES

Judges 7:1 – 9:21

Yesterday we considered the roles of specific judges (Judges 3:31–6:40). Today we focus on Gideon's victory over the Midianites.

Key concept. Through God's providence, Gideon and his small army attained victory over the Midianites.

The big picture. The Lord trimmed the size of Gideon's army from 32,000 to 22,000 to 10,000, and finally to just 300. He did this to demonstrate that Israel's victory over the Midianites would be dependent on Him alone (Judges 7:1-8). Gideon's surprise attack against the Midianites that night was successful (7:16-25). Following Gideon's death, the Israelites fell into Baal worship (8:28-35). Gideon's son Abimelech took over leadership. He killed 70 of Gideon's remaining sons—Jotham alone was spared—to eliminate potential challengers to the throne (9:1-6). Jotham cursed him.

Transformational truth. Corrupt leaders have a corrupting influence. The judges Gideon (Judges 8:24-27), Jephthah (11:30-31,34-40), and Samson (14–16) all fell into sin, thereby contributing to the ails of the Israelites. The only judge who was a consistent bright light among the Israelites was Deborah (4:6,14; 5:7).

A verse for meditation. "The LORD told Gideon, 'With these 300 men I will rescue you and give you victory over the Midianites. Send all the others home'" (Judges 7:7).

A question to ponder. Does your sufficiency lie in God alone?

GOD JUDGES SIN

Judges 9:22 – 11:28

Yesterday we gave attention to Gideon's victory over the Midianites (Judges 7:1 – 9:21). Today we turn our attention to how God judged the wicked Abimelech and the idolatrous Israelites.

Key concept. God providentially brought judgment against Abimelech and the Israelites.

The big picture. God arranged for the people of Shechem to turn against Abimelech for his sin of murdering 70 of Gideon's sons. He was killed when a woman dropped a millstone on his head (Judges 9:22-57). Israel again turned to idol worship. God responded by raising up the Philistines and Ammonites as their oppressors (10:6-18). Eventually, the judge Jephthah led Israel to victory over the Ammonites (11).

Transformational truth. God's timing is not our timing. Abimelech was a terrible judge, but God waited three years before judging him (Judges 9:22-24). God often does not render immediate judgment, but allows time for repentance (Revelation 2:21). Not until the time is right does God bring judgment.

A verse for meditation. "You have abandoned me and served other gods. So I will not rescue you anymore. Go and cry out to the gods you have chosen! Let them rescue you in your hour of distress!" (Judges 10:13-14).

A question to ponder. Can you think of reasons why God might delay in bringing judgment against obvious evil?

JEPHTHAH AND SAMSON

Judges 11:29 – 15:20

Yesterday we focused on how God judged Abimelech and the idol-atrous Israelites (Judges 9:22 – 11:28). Today we turn our attention to how God used two flawed human beings—Jephthah and Samson—to battle the adversaries of Israel.

Key concept. God led Jephthah to victory over the Ammonites. God used Samson in battling the Philistines.

The big picture. Jephthah, apparently doing what was right in his own eyes (but not God's eyes—see Judges 21:25), sacrificed his daughter following victory over the Ammonites. Samson, though a flawed human being, was then used by God to do battle against the Philistines (13:1–15:20).

Transformational truth. Samson was not entirely committed to God. His lustful lifestyle showed he was self-focused (Judges 14:3-4). Samson had no intention of battling the Philistines out of a spiritual commitment to God. God therefore used Samson's self-interests to incite his anger against the Philistines, which ultimately resulted in Israel's deliverance. God brought good out of evil (Romans 8:28).

A verse for meditation. " 'Oh, my daughter!' he cried out. 'You have completely destroyed me! You've brought disaster on me! For I have made a vow to the LORD, and I cannot take it back' " (Judges 11:35).

A question to ponder. Have you ever encountered a person who seemed sure he was doing God's will, but he quite obviously was not?

SAMSON KILLS MANY PHILISTINES

Judges 16 – 18

In the previous lesson, we explored how God used Jephthah and Samson in battles against Israel's adversaries (Judges 11:29 – 15:20). Today we continue this study and consider how Samson went about killing many Philistines.

Key concept. Samson gave up his own life to kill many Philistines.

The big picture. Samson kept feeding Delilah bogus information on how to make him weak (Judges 16). Each time he did this, an attempt was made to weaken him. It was therefore the height of folly for Samson to reveal the true means of weakening him — cutting his hair. Contextually, Samson's long hair was a sign of the Nazirite vow he had taken before God. The cutting of his hair therefore amounted to breaking that vow before God.

Transformational truth. Samson sacrificed his life for a greater cause (Judges 16). Recall what Jesus Himself taught: "There is no greater love than to lay down one's life for one's friends" (John 15:13). This is precisely what Samson did.

A verse for meditation. "In those days Israel had no king; all the people did whatever seemed right in their own eyes" (Judges 17:6).

A question to ponder. Have you ever been tempted to do what is "right in your own eyes" as opposed to what you know Scripture teaches?

A CRIME OF PASSION

Judges 19 – 21

Yesterday we considered how Samson went about killing many Philistines (Judges 16 – 18). Today we focus on a crime of passion in the city of Gibeah.

Key concept. There were great consequences to a morally reprehensible sexual crime.

The big picture. A Levite's concubine was sexually violated and killed by some of the perverted residents of Gibeah in the territory of the tribe of Benjamin. This Levite promptly informed the other Israelite tribes, who then took action against the city of Gibeah and the Benjaminites (Judges 19). The various tribes attacked the Benjaminites at Gibeah, destroying most of the tribe (20). To prevent the utter extinction of the Benjaminites, however, wives were provided for the remaining men of the tribe (21).

Transformational truth. Contrary to the moral relativism that reigned supreme during this time in Israel's history, absolute morals are grounded in the absolutely moral God of the Bible (Matthew 5:48). Moral law flows from the moral Lawgiver of the universe—God. God stands against the moral relativist (Deuteronomy 12:8; Judges 17:6; 21:2).

A verse for meditation. "In those days Israel had no king; all the people did whatever seemed right in their own eyes" (Judges 21:25, *repeated from 17:6, and therefore important*).

A question to ponder. Why is it vital to make a daily habit of grounding yourself in God's absolute truth?

NAOMI, RUTH, AND BOAZ

Ruth 1:1 – 4:12

Yesterday we considered a crime of passion in Gibeah (Judges 19 – 21). Today we consider how Boaz rescued Ruth and Naomi as a "kinsmen redeemer."

Key concept. God's provisions can far exceed human expectations.

The big picture. Naomi's husband and sons died in Moab. This left Naomi in a predicament. In Bible times, women were dependent upon husbands and sons for provisions in life. Naomi returned to Bethlehem, and her Moabite daughter-in-law, Ruth, accompanied her (Ruth 1:6-18). Upon arriving, they found themselves in poverty (1:19-22). In God's providence, however, Ruth met a distant relative of her first husband's family—a man named Boaz (2:1-7). He fulfilled his family duty as "kinsman redeemer" and married Ruth (4:1-12). These events transpired 1100 – 1000 BC.

Transformational truth. Kindness is a thread that runs through the book of Ruth. Ruth was kind to Naomi (Ruth 1:16-17; 2:11,18,23). Boaz was kind to Ruth (2:20; 4:9-10,13). God was kind to Ruth, Naomi, and Boaz by bringing them all together (4:1-17).

A verse for meditation. "Wherever you go, I will go; wherever you live, I will live. Your people will be my people, and your God will be my God" (Ruth 1:16).

A question to ponder. Why do you think kindness is contagious?

HANNAH LAMENTS CHILDLESSNESS

1 Samuel 1:1-8; Ruth 4:13-22;
1 Chronicles 2:9-55; 4:1-23

Yesterday we focused on how Boaz rescued Ruth and Naomi as a "kinsmen redeemer" (Ruth 1:1–4:12). Today we turn our attention to Hannah's sorrow over being childless.

Key concept. Hannah yearned to give birth to a child.

The big picture. Boaz married Ruth, and the couple soon gave birth to a son named Obed. Obed would later become the father of Jesse, who gave birth to King David (Ruth 4:13-22). Unlike Ruth, Hannah lamented that she had not yet conceived a child (1 Samuel 1:1-8).

Transformational truth. When speaking to a downhearted person, it's great to provide an encouraging word, as Elkanah did to Hannah (1 Samuel 1:8). Bible expositor William Barclay said: "One of the highest human duties is the duty of encouragement…It is easy to discourage others. The world is full of discouragers. We have a Christian duty to encourage one another" (see 1 Thessalonians 4:18; 5:11).

A verse for meditation. " 'Why are you crying, Hannah?' Elkanah would ask. 'Why aren't you eating? Why be downhearted just because you have no children? You have me—isn't that better than having ten sons?' " (1 Samuel 1:8).

A question to ponder. Do you know of someone who needs an encouraging word? What can you say?

HANNAH GIVES BIRTH TO A SON

1 Samuel 1:9 – 4:11

In the previous lesson, we considered Hannah's sorrow over being childless (1 Samuel 1:1-8; Ruth 4:13-22; 1 Chronicles 2:9-55; 4:1-23). Today we consider how God answered Hannah's prayer and enabled her to give birth to a son.

Key concept. God answered Hannah's prayer.

The big picture. Hannah asked the Lord for a son and promised to devote him to the Lord if her prayer were answered (1 Samuel 1:9-18). Samuel was soon born, and Hannah devoted him by presenting him to Eli the priest (1:19-28). Hannah sang a song of thanksgiving (2:1-10). As Samuel grew, he helped Eli with religious duties (2:11-21). Meanwhile, Eli's sons committed sexual sin (2:22-36). The Lord revealed to Samuel that he would soon bring judgment (3:10 – 4:11).

Transformational truth. Eli's sons were priests, and yet sexually sinned (1 Samuel 2:22). God judged them. Such sin should never occur among spiritual leaders of God's people.

A verse for meditation. "If you will look upon my sorrow and answer my prayer and give me a son, then I will give him back to you. He will be yours for his entire lifetime" (1 Samuel 1:11).

A question to ponder. What do you think about making vows to the Lord?

THE PHILISTINES RETURN THE ARK

1 Samuel 4:12 – 7:17

Yesterday we considered how God answered Hannah's prayer and gave her a son (1 Samuel 1:9 – 4:11). Today we focus on what happened with the Ark of the Covenant.

Key concept. The Philistines returned the Ark of the Covenant to Israel.

The big picture. Eli died upon hearing that his two sons had been killed and that the Ark of the Covenant had been captured by the Philistines (1 Samuel 4:1-11). God sent plagues upon the Philistines for capturing the Ark (5:1-12). The Philistines then returned it to Israel (6:1-21). Samuel called his people to repentance (7:3-17).

Transformational truth. The Philistines did not return the Ark of the Covenant until tumors broke out on their bodies (1 Samuel 5:6-7). Tragically, many of God's people do not respond to God until they experience pain: "My suffering was good for me, for it taught me to pay attention to your decrees" (Psalm 119:71).

A verse for meditation. "If you want to return to the LORD with all your hearts, get rid of your foreign gods…Turn your hearts to the LORD and obey him alone; then he will rescue you from the Philistines" (1 Samuel 7:3).

A question to ponder. Has personal suffering ever led you to recommit your life to the Lord?

ERA 4: THE UNITED MONARCHY 1050 – 930 BC

Books in whole or in part: 1 Samuel
2 Samuel • 1 Kings • 1 Chronicles • 2 Chronicles
Psalms • Proverbs • Ecclesiastes • Song of Solomon

Today we begin our study of a new biblical era, titled "The United Monarchy," which took place during 1050–930 BC. Bible books pertinent to our study—in whole or in part—include 1 Samuel, 2 Samuel, 1 Kings, 1 Chronicles, 2 Chronicles, Psalms, Proverbs, Ecclesiastes, and the Song of Solomon.

Israel had been a theocracy—a God-ruled nation. God had taken care of the Israelites ever since He delivered them from Egyptian bondage. But there came a time when they wanted a human king, like the nations around them.

The prophet Samuel tried to explain the downsides of a human king (1 Samuel 8:10-18), but the people would not listen. All they saw were positive benefits. Ultimately, this desire for a human king stemmed from a lack of faith in God. The people sought to trade a God who loved them for a human king who would end up exploiting them.

Israel's first king was appointed by the prophet Samuel (1 Samuel 10–11). His name was Saul, and he was said to be "the most handsome man in Israel," and "head and shoulders taller than anyone else in the land" (9:2). He looked great—just the kind of person the people would want to be king. The kingdom united under him.

A problem soon surfaced. After Saul became king, he was not fully obedient to the Lord. God had commanded Saul, "Go and completely destroy the entire Amalekite nation—men, women, children, babies, cattle, sheep, goats, camels, and donkeys" (1 Samuel 15:3). Saul, however, obeyed only part of God's instructions: "Saul and his men spared Agag's life and kept the best of the sheep and goats, the cattle, the fat calves, and the lambs—everything, in fact, that appealed to them.

They destroyed only what was worthless or of poor quality" (verse 9). Saul did *part* of what God commanded, but not *all*.

As a result, God lamented, "I am sorry that I ever made Saul king, for he has not been loyal to me and has refused to obey my command" (1 Samuel 15:11). Our text then tells us: "Samuel was so deeply moved when he heard this that he cried out to the LORD all night" (verse 12). *Partial obedience amounts to disobedience.*

Meanwhile, because of David's growing fame in the land, King Saul became increasingly jealous of him, and even sought to kill him. This resulted in David having to live as an outlaw for a number of years. It is to David's credit that he did not respond in like manner, and seek to take Saul's life. How ironic that during this same time David developed a close friendship with Saul's son, Jonathan (1 Samuel 20).

When it came time for David to be selected as Israel's new king, God reminded Samuel of an important factor: "Don't judge by his appearance or height...The LORD doesn't see things the way you see them. People judge by outward appearance, but the LORD looks at the heart" (1 Samuel 16:7). "The LORD has sought out a man after his own heart" (13:14), and that man was David.

From a human vantage point, David probably would not have been selected as the person most likely to achieve great stature. After all, David, as Jesse's youngest son, was just a humble shepherd boy, and shepherding was considered a lowly job. However, under God's sovereign plan, David was to become Israel's second king.

David had earlier become instantly famous for killing Goliath, the giant Philistine warrior (1 Samuel 17). The fact that David as a young boy would go up against such a gargantuan warrior showed the tremendous trust David had in God. Of course, during his years as a shepherd boy, David had become increasingly proficient in using a slingshot, which he was able to use, with God's blessing, in defeating Goliath. Even in his younger years, then, God was preparing David for his future role.

David finally became king of Israel at 30 years of age (2 Samuel 2:1-7). He assumed leadership following Saul's death. He was a good king, and united the kingdom. He made Jerusalem his capital, and ruled for 40 years. In his old age, David summoned his son Solomon and anointed him king. He then died at 71 years of age in his own bed.

Solomon became king in 970 BC, at about 20 years of age (1 Kings 11:42). He inherited a peaceful kingdom from his father David, and he worked hard to maintain that peace via military strength. It is significant that Solomon's name literally means "peaceful." Israel enjoyed a golden age under Solomon's reign. He built Israel into a powerful industrial and trading nation (see 1 Kings 1 – 8). However, not all was perfect. Heavy taxes were inflicted upon the people as a means of paying for Israel's impressive building projects (12:4). Those who could not afford to pay such taxes found themselves doing hard labor.

One thing that seems obvious during this biblical era is that God is the true King. So long as the human king—whether Saul, David, or Solomon—obeyed the divine King's orders, they prospered and succeeded. However, if the human kings departed from the will of God, they were judged. We learn from this that earthly kings, no matter how powerful they may seem, are nothing next to the power of the divine King.

In the coming chapters, we will journey through portions of 1 Samuel, 2 Samuel, 1 Kings, 1 Chronicles, 2 Chronicles, Psalms, Proverbs, Ecclesiastes, and the Song of Solomon. In case you're wondering, some of the psalms date to the era of the united monarchy because they were written by David, one of the kings of this era. Likewise, Ecclesiastes, the Song of Solomon, and most of Proverbs also belong to this era because they were written by Solomon, another king of that time span.

The following dates provide a helpful chronological orientation:

1105 BC — Samuel was born.

1080 BC — Saul was born.

1050 BC — Saul was anointed as king, and the kingdom united under his leadership.

1040 BC — David was born.

1025 BC — David slew Goliath.

1010 BC — Saul died; David became king of Judah.

1003 BC—David became king of all Israel.

1000 BC—David captured Jerusalem; the Lord made a covenant with David.

997 BC—David sinned with Bathsheba.

991 BC—Solomon was born.

970 BC—Solomon became king.

931 BC—The books of 1 and 2 Samuel were written.

Preview: In Day 105, we will witness Saul being anointed as the king.

SAUL IS ANOINTED KING

1 Samuel 8 – 12

Yesterday we introduced Era 4, titled "The United Monarchy," encompassing 1050 – 930 BC. Today we turn specifically to Saul being anointed as king.

Key concept. Saul is anointed as Israel's first king.

The big picture. Israel was a theocracy—a nation ruled by God. But eventually the people clamored for a human king—they wanted to be like all the nations around them (1 Samuel 8). Samuel tried to talk them out of this, but they would not listen. Saul was anointed as king in 1050 BC.

Transformational truth. The true King of the universe is God Himself. God as King is sovereign over all earthly kings. This is why the prophet Samuel warned that the people *and* the king must obey God (1 Samuel 12:14; see also Psalm 102:12).

A verse for meditation. " 'Do everything they say to you,' the LORD replied, 'for they are rejecting me, not you. They don't want me to be their king any longer' " (1 Samuel 8:7).

A question to ponder. What does it mean to you personally that God is your King?

SAUL'S SUCCESSES AND FAILURES

1 Samuel 13–14; 1 Chronicles 9:35-39

Yesterday we focused on Saul being anointed as king (1 Samuel 8–12). Today we turn our attention to Saul's successes and failures.

Key concept. While Saul was an effective military leader, he disobeyed the Lord.

The big picture. Saul was militarily successful in battling against the Ammonites (1 Samuel 11:11), the Philistines (13:3; 14:20-23), and others (14:47-48). But more importantly, he disobeyed the Lord: "You have not kept the command the LORD your God gave you" (13:13). Because of his unfaithfulness, the Lord ultimately removed him as king (13:13-14; 15:26). God would soon choose a new king—"a man after his own heart" (13:14).

Transformational truth. Saul took credit for destroying a Philistine outpost, even though it was Jonathan who did it (1 Samuel 13:3-4). Saul was prideful. Let us not forget: "Pride goes before destruction, and haughtiness before a fall" (Proverbs 16:18). James 4:4 urges, "Humble yourselves before the Lord, and he will lift you up in honor."

A verse for meditation. "The LORD has sought out a man after his own heart. The LORD has already appointed him to be the leader of his people" (1 Samuel 13:14).

A question to ponder. What characteristics in Saul's life would you like to avoid in your own?

THE PARTIAL OBEDIENCE OF SAUL

1 Samuel 15:1 – 17:31

In the previous lesson, we explored Saul's successes and failures (1 Samuel 13 – 14; 1 Chronicles 9:35-39). Today we consider the partial obedience of King Saul.

Key concept. God regretted making Saul king in view of his partial obedience.

The big picture. Saul and his army only *partially* destroyed the Amalekites (1 Samuel 15). He spared the king and the best of the animals. Samuel thus urged, "Obedience is better than sacrifice" (15:22). While the people looked only at Saul's outer appearance, the Lord looks at the heart, and that is why He would soon choose David—a shepherd—as the one who would become the new king (16:7). David's victory over Goliath brought him great acclaim (17).

Transformational truth. Partial obedience won't cut it with God (1 Samuel 15:3,9). God lamented, "I am sorry that I ever made Saul king, for he has not been loyal to me and has refused to obey my command" (11). God desires total obedience.

A verse for meditation. "The LORD said to Samuel...'The LORD doesn't see things the way you see them. People judge by outward appearance, but the LORD looks at the heart'" (1 Samuel 16:7).

A question to ponder. What characteristics in David's life would you like to see in yours?

DAVID SLAYS GOLIATH

1 Samuel 17:32 – 19:24; Psalm 59

Yesterday we considered the partial obedience of King Saul (1 Samuel 15:1–17:31). Today we focus on how David slayed Goliath.

Key concept. David, by faith in God, brought Goliath down.

The big picture. As a shepherd boy, David had grown proficient at using a slingshot, which he used to defeat Goliath (1 Samuel 17). While Jonathan, Saul's son, was heir to the throne, he recognized David as God's choice (18). Saul resented all the attention given to David and sought to kill him (19).

Transformational truth. It's not the size of the obstacle that is important; rather, it's the power and blessing of God. Just as David, by faith in God, overcame Goliath (1 Samuel 17), so you and I can overcome giant obstacles by faith in God (Ephesians 3:20).

A verse for meditation. "David replied to the Philistine, 'You come to me with sword, spear, and javelin, but I come to you in the name of the LORD of Heaven's Armies—the God of the armies of Israel, whom you have defied'" (1 Samuel 17:45).

A question to ponder. Are there any "Goliaths" in your life for which you need to turn to God for help?

DAVID FLEES FOR HIS LIFE

1 Samuel 20 – 21; Psalm 34

Yesterday we gave attention to how David slayed Goliath (1 Samuel 17:32–19:24). Today we see what happened when David fled for his life.

Key concept. Jonathan warned David to flee for his life from Saul.

The big picture. Jonathan—Saul's son and David's friend—warned David that Saul sought to kill him, and that David should flee for his life. This meant parting ways for a time, which was difficult for both of them (1 Samuel 20). David obtained food and Goliath's sword upon visiting the priest Ahimelech at Nob (21:1-9). David then pretended to be insane—"scratching on doors and drooling down his beard" (21:13)—in order to find sanctuary with King Achish of Gath in Philistine territory.

Transformational truth. Jonathan and David were close friends. Jonathan asked David to be sure to treat his children kindly in the future. David made sure he fulfilled this promise. He later invited Jonathan's son Mephibosheth to live in David's place (1 Samuel 20:15; 2 Samuel 9). The lesson: Like David, *be a person of your word.*

A verse for meditation. "Saul has killed his thousands, and David his ten thousands" (1 Samuel 21:11).

A question to ponder. What insights do you learn about true friendship from Jonathan and David?

DAVID HUNTED BY SAUL

*1 Samuel 22:1 – 23:12; 1 Chronicles
12:8-18; Psalms 52; 57; 142*

Yesterday we focused on David fleeing for his life (1 Samuel 20 – 21; Psalm 34). Today we continue along the same line, as David is hunted by Saul.

Key concept. David continues to elude an angry Saul.

The big picture. David hid in a cave in Adullam, protected by a 400-man group of outcasts (1 Samuel 22:1-5). He arranged for his parents to live securely in Moab. Meanwhile, Saul killed 85 priests of Nob for assisting David (22:6-23). While being hunted by Saul, David and his band of outcasts defeated a Philistine force to save the city of Keilah (23:1-5). David continued eluding Saul in the wilderness (23:6-29).

Transformational truth. Bad things sometimes happen to good people, as happened with the 85 innocent priests (1 Samuel 22:18-19). While evil exists in our world, no one is getting away with anything. The wicked will one day face God at the great white throne judgment (Revelation 20:11-15). Justice will prevail in the end.

A verse for meditation. "Doeg the Edomite turned on them and killed them that day, eighty-five priests in all, still wearing their priestly garments" (1 Samuel 22:18).

A question to ponder. In what ways does the existence of evil challenge your faith?

DAVID CONFRONTS SAUL

1 Samuel 23:13 – 25:44; Psalm 54

In the previous lesson, we considered how David was hunted by Saul (1 Samuel 22:1 – 23:12). Today we consider David's confrontation of Saul from a distance.

Key concept. David confronted Saul.

The big picture. In a dark cave, David got close enough to Saul to cut off a piece of his robe. He had the chance to kill Saul, but chose not to. He felt he would be violating God's will by doing so. From a distance, David shouted to Saul that his restraint proved he had no intention of harming Saul (1 Samuel 24:1-15). Saul conceded that David was righteous, and that he would no doubt become the next king of Israel (16 – 22).

Transformational truth. Abigail affirmed to David, "Even when you are chased by those who seek to kill you, your life is safe in the care of the LORD your God, secure in his treasure pouch!" (1 Samuel 25:29). God is our shield (Psalm 3:3; 7:10; 18:2,30; 28:7).

A verse for meditation. "Jonathan went to find David and encouraged him to stay strong in his faith in God" (1 Samuel 23.16).

A question to ponder. Is there someone you know who may need encouragement to stay strong in his or her faith in God?

SAUL CONSULTS A MEDIUM

1 Samuel 26 – 29; 1 Chronicles 12:1-7,19; Psalm 56

Yesterday we considered David's confrontation of Saul (1 Samuel 23:13 – 25:44; Psalm 54). Today we focus on Saul's consultation with a medium.

Key concept. Saul consulted with a medium and learned of impending defeat at the hands of the Philistines.

The big picture. David again had opportunity to kill Saul in close proximity, but chose not to. David confronted him from a distance, and Saul again conceded he had been wrong (1 Samuel 26). David and his men then sought sanctuary in Philistine territory. Extreme circumstances called for extreme solutions (27). The Philistines assembled against Saul, and Saul sought direction from the Lord but received none. He therefore hired a medium to conjure up the spirit of Samuel. God sovereignly allowed Samuel to appear to inform Saul that he would be defeated by the Philistines (28).

Transformational truth. David chose not to kill Saul because he feared the Lord (1 Samuel 26:9-11). Fear of the Lord is part and parcel of a healthy spirituality (Deuteronomy 5:29; 6:13).

A verse for meditation. "[Saul] asked the LORD what he should do, but the LORD refused to answer him, either by dreams or by sacred lots or by the prophets" (1 Samuel 28:6).

A question to ponder. What does a healthy fear of the Lord look like?

THE PHILISTINES DEFEAT SAUL

1 Samuel 30 – 31; 1 Chronicles 9:40-44;
10:1-14; 12:20-22; 2 Samuel 1; 4:4

Yesterday we read about Saul's consultation with a medium (1 Samuel 26 – 29). Today we see Saul's defeat at the hands of the Philistines.

Key concept. The Philistines defeated Saul and his army.

The big picture. David and his band of men defeated the Amalekites (1 Samuel 30:1-21). He showed his generosity by sharing the spoils of war with his wounded warriors and his fellow Israelites in several select cities (30:22-31). Meanwhile, the Philistines defeated Saul and his army at Mount Gilboa. Among the dead were Saul and his three sons (31:1-13).

Transformational truth. Life and death are in God's sovereign hands. First Samuel 31:4-5 says Saul took his own life. And yet, this was within God's sovereign will. We know this because 1 Chronicles 10:13-14 says Saul "died because he was unfaithful to the Lord." Indeed, "the Lord killed him and turned the kingdom over to David son of Jesse" (Deuteronomy 32:39; Psalm 139:16).

A verse for meditation. "David was now in great danger…But David found strength in the Lord his God" (1 Samuel 30.6).

A question to ponder. Reflecting back on the entire book of 1 Samuel, what insights can you glean about God's sovereignty?

DAVID BECOMES KING OF JUDAH

2 Samuel 2:1 – 3:5; 23:8-39; 1 Chronicles 3:1-4; 11:10-47

Yesterday we considered Saul's defeat by the Philistines (1 Samuel 30 – 31). Today we read about David becoming king of Judah.

Key concept. David is anointed as king of Judah and honors the Lord in his behavior.

The big picture. David was anointed king of Judah in 1010 BC (2 Samuel 2:1-7), while Saul's son Ishbosheth became king over the other tribes of Israel (2:8-11). The two factions battled, and David's forces overcame those of Ishbosheth's (2:12-32). David's dynasty grew in strength; Ishbosheth's declined (3:1-5).

Transformational truth. David already knew he would one day become king. But he still depended on God in day-to-day life. That's why he asked God, "Should I move back to one of the towns of Judah?" (2 Samuel 2:1). This reminds us of the psalmist, who acknowledged, "My future is in your hands" (Psalm 31:15).

A verse for meditation. "That was the beginning of a long war between those who were loyal to Saul and those loyal to David. As time passed David became stronger and stronger, while Saul's dynasty became weaker and weaker" (2 Samuel 3:1).

A question to ponder. How do you think Saul and David illustrate the teachings in Psalm 1?

AN ALLIANCE AND A MURDER

2 Samuel 3:6 – 4:12

In the previous lesson, we witnessed David becoming king of Judah (2 Samuel 2:1–3:5). Today we consider Abner's alliance with David and his subsequent murder by Joab.

Key concept. Abner joined forces with David, but was then murdered by Joab.

The big picture. The powerful leader Abner offered his support to David, seeking to "establish the throne of David over Israel as well as Judah" (2 Samuel 3:10). However, he was soon assassinated by Joab. David made sure everyone knew he was not responsible (3:22-39). Ishbosheth was then murdered and his decapitated head was presented to David (4:1-8). David executed Ishbosheth's assassins (4:9-12).

Transformational truth. Abner knew God had promised David the throne (2 Samuel 3:9-10,17-18), and yet early on he engaged in armed resistance to David. There's a big difference between *knowing* God's truth and *embracing* God's truth for oneself. That's a trap any of us could fall into.

A verse for meditation. "Now is the time! For the LORD has said, 'I have chosen David to save my people Israel from the hands of the Philistines and from all their other enemies'" (2 Samuel 3:18).

A question to ponder. Can you remember a time in your life when you may have known the truth from Scripture but failed to embrace it and follow it?

DAVID BECOMES
KING OF ALL ISRAEL

*2 Samuel 5:1-13,17-25; 6:1-11; 1 Chronicles
3:4; 11:1-9; 12:23 – 14:2,8-17*

Yesterday we considered Abner's alliance with David and his subsequent murder by Joab (2 Samuel 3:6–4:12). Today we focus on
David becoming king of all Israel.

Key concept. After David became king of all Israel, he captured
Jerusalem.

The big picture. With King Ishbosheth now dead, David was recognized as the king of all Israel in 1003 BC (2 Samuel 5:1-5). David
captured Jerusalem from the Jebusites and made it his headquarters
(5:6-10). He battled the Philistines and defeated them (5:17-25). He
then moved the Ark of the Covenant from Abinadab's house to Obed-
edom's house. While the ark was in transport, Uzzah touched it inap-
propriately and died (6:1-11).

Transformational truth. After Uzzah died for touching the ark,
"David was afraid of the Lord that day" (2 Samuel 6:6-9). Perhaps
David didn't have sufficient fear of the Lord prior to this time. But he
certainly learned to fear the Lord quickly (Deuteronomy 13:4).

A verse for meditation. "David became more and more powerful,
because the Lord God of Heaven's Armies was with him" (2 Samuel
5.10).

A question to ponder. Why is it so essential to "fear the Lord"? (See
Deuteronomy 6:2; 13:4; Ecclesiastes 12:13.)

MICHAL'S CONTEMPT FOR DAVID

2 Samuel 6:12-23; 1 Chronicles 15 – 16

Yesterday we gave attention to David becoming king of all Israel (2 Samuel 5:1-13,17-25; 6:1-11; 1 Chronicles 3:4; 11:1-9; 12:23 – 14:2,8-17). Today we turn our attention to Michal's contempt for David.

Key concept. David's wife Michal had contempt for David after seeing him dance festively.

The big picture. When the Ark of the Covenant was moved from Obed-edom's house to Jerusalem, David danced to music in a celebratory fashion (2 Samuel 6:12-19). Michal, David's wife, witnessed the spectacle and was put off by it. David said his dance was an act of worship before the Lord (6:20-23). David then presented offerings to the Lord before the ark (16:1-6) and offered a prayer of praise and thanksgiving to God (16:7-36).

Transformational truth. Michal was put off by David's dancing around in a celebratory procession (2 Samuel 6:20-22). She was focused on external appearances, whereas David was expressing his inner spiritual state before God. He didn't care about looking foolish. He wanted to openly worship God.

A verse for meditation. "David danced before the LORD with all his might, wearing a priestly garment" (2 Samuel 6:14).

A question to ponder. Do you feel comfortable publicly worshipping the Lord?

THE DAVIDIC COVENANT

2 Samuel 7:1 – 8:14; 1 Chronicles 17:1 – 18:13; Psalm 60

Yesterday we focused on Michal's contempt for David (2 Samuel 6:12-23). Today we consider God's unconditional covenant with David.

Key concept. God made an unconditional covenant with David.

The big picture. God promised David that one of his descendants would rule forever (2 Samuel 7:12-13; 22:51). This was an unconditional covenant. It did not depend on David in any way for its fulfillment. David realized this when he received the promise from God, and responded with an attitude of humility and a recognition of God's sovereignty over the affairs of men.

Transformational truth. God's messianic promise in the Davidic covenant is just one of more than 100 messianic prophecies in the Old Testament. The Bible is a Jesus book—even in the Old Testament. Jesus Himself affirmed that "the writings of Moses and all the prophets" spoke of "things concerning himself" (Luke 24:27,44). *Don't ignore the Old Testament!*

A verse for meditation. "How great you are, O Sovereign LORD! There is no one like you. We have never even heard of another God like you!" (2 Samuel 7:22).

A question to ponder. Can you think of any other messianic prophecies that appear in the Old Testament?

DAVID'S KINDNESS TO MEPHIBOSHETH

2 Samuel 8:15 – 10:19; 1 Chronicles 6:16-53; 18:14 – 19:19

In the previous lesson, we explored God's unconditional covenant with David (2 Samuel 7:1 – 8:14; 1 Chronicles 17:1 – 18:13; Psalm 60). Today we consider David's kindness to Mephibosheth.

Key concept. David showed kindness to Mephibosheth, the son of his deceased friend Jonathan.

The big picture. David's beloved friend Jonathan once said to him, "The LORD is the witness of a bond between us and our children forever" (1 Samuel 20:42). Jonathan was now dead. David sought out Jonathan's son so he could show him kindness. This son was Mephibosheth.

Transformational truth. David was an effective leader. He "reigned over all Israel and did what was just and right for all his people" (2 Samuel 8:15), took the initiative in showing kindness (9:1,3,7), and openly displayed loyalty (10:2). Good leaders are characterized by justice, equity, kindness, and loyalty.

A verse for meditation. "I intend to show kindness to you because of my promise to your father, Jonathan. I will give you all the property that once belonged to your grandfather Saul, and you will eat here with me at the king's table!" (2 Samuel 9:7).

A question to ponder. What does 2 Samuel 9:7 tell you about David's commitment to his friends?

DAVID PLUMMETS INTO SIN

*1 Chronicles 3:5-9; 14:3-7; 20:1; 2 Samuel
5:14-16; 11:1–12:25; Psalm 51*

Yesterday we considered David's kindness to Mephibosheth (2 Samuel 8:15–10:19). Today we look at David's fall into sin.

Key concept. David fell into serious sexual sin.

The big picture. While David was a man after God's own heart (Acts 13:22), he was still vulnerable to sin. One day he saw Bathsheba bathing on a rooftop. He sent for her, slept with her, and got her pregnant (2 Samuel 11:1-5). Before his deceit came to an end, David broke four of the Ten Commandments: "You must not murder" (Exodus 20:13); "You must not commit adultery" (verse 14); "You must not steal" (verse 15); "You must not covet your neighbor's wife" (verse 17). David grievously sinned against God.

Transformational truth. David got "Nathanized" (2 Samuel 12:1-7). Nathan described a particular man's horrible crime, and David's anger was kindled against the man. "You are the man," Nathan told him. *How ugly our sins look when we behold them in other people!*

A verse for meditation. "Why...have you despised the word of the LORD and done this horrible deed? For you have murdered Uriah the Hittite with the sword of the Ammonites and stolen his wife" (2 Samuel 12:9).

A question to ponder. How does today's passage illustrate the "domino effect" regarding human sin?

CONFLICT BETWEEN AMNON AND ABSALOM

2 Samuel 12:26 – 14:33; 1 Chronicles 20:2-3

Yesterday we gave attention to David's fall into sin (1 Chronicles 3:5-9; 14:3-7; 20:1; 2 Samuel 5:14-16; 11:1–12:25; Psalm 51). Today we turn our attention to how conflict emerged between two sons of David—Amnon and Absalom.

Key concept. Lethal conflict had emerged between two sons of David—Amnon and Absalom.

The big picture. Amon, a son of David, raped Tamar, his half-sister (2 Samuel 13:1-19). Absalom—David's son, Tamar's full brother, and Amnon's half-brother—avenged Tamar and killed Amnon (13:20-33). Fearful, Absalom went into hiding (13:34-39). David and Absalom were now estranged. Years later, they reconciled (14:29-33).

Transformational truth. Absalom, David's son, was a murderer (2 Samuel 13:20-33), was vain and arrogant (14:25-28), and eventually tried to usurp David's throne (16–17). He would eventually end up losing his life (18). We are reminded of Galatians 6:7: "Whatever one sows, that will he also reap" (ESV).

A verse for meditation. "All of us must die eventually. Our lives are like water spilled out on the ground, which cannot be gathered up again" (2 Samuel 14:14).

A question to ponder. Does the scriptural teaching that "whatever one sows, that will he also reap" motivate any changes in your life?

ABSALOM'S CONSPIRACY AGAINST DAVID

2 Samuel 15:1 – 17:14

Yesterday we focused on how conflict emerged between two sons of David—Amnon and Absalom (2 Samuel 12:26–14:33). Today we consider how David's son Absalom conspired against him.

Key concept. David's son Absalom treacherously conspired against him, seeking his throne.

The big picture. Absalom connived to turn the people of Israel against his father David and cultivate loyalty to himself. He amassed a force in Hebron to stand against David's kingship (2 Samuel 15:1-12). David and those with him fled Jerusalem to hide in the wilderness (15:13-23). Absalom wanted the kingship for himself. But he was advised to first gather a large army before seeking to attack David (17:1-14).

Transformational truth. David acted strategically. He could have easily and rapidly squashed Absalom's rebellion against him (2 Samuel 15:14). But he did not want Jerusalem to become a war zone and get destroyed, nor did he want his son Absalom to die. He felt that if he handled things right, both Jerusalem and Absalom could be spared. Contrary to his wishes, Absalom died.

A verse for meditation. "A messenger soon arrived in Jerusalem to tell David, 'All Israel has joined Absalom in a conspiracy against you!'" (2 Samuel 15:13).

A question to ponder. What evidences for God's sovereignty do you see in today's Scripture reading?

ABSALOM DIES, DAVID GRIEVES

2 Samuel 17:15 – 19:30; Psalms 3; 63

In the previous lesson, we explored how David's son Absalom conspired against him (2 Samuel 15:1 – 17:14). Today we consider Absalom's death and David's subsequent grief.

Key concept. Absalom died, thereby causing David inconsolable grief.

The big picture. David's army was led by three military leaders — Joab, Abishai, and Ittai. They launched an attack against Absalom and his army, but were instructed by David not to harm Absalom (2 Samuel 18:1-8). Joab disobeyed David's order and found easy opportunity to kill Absalom when his hair got tangled in a tree branch (18:9-18). David was full of grief upon discovering Absalom's fate (18:19-33).

Transformational truth. David experienced inconsolable grief upon the death of his son Absalom (2 Samuel 18:33). God's people are not immune to the pain of grief, but we do not "grieve like people who have no hope" (1 Thessalonians 4:13). Christians will enjoy a grand reunion in heaven (4:14-18; see also 1 Corinthians 15:55).

A verse for meditation. "He (David) cried, 'O my son Absalom! My son, my son Absalom! If only I had died instead of you! O Absalom, my son, my son'" (2 Samuel 18:33).

A question to ponder. Do you know anyone presently suffering grief to whom you might be a comfort?

AVENGING THE GIBEONITES

2 Samuel 19:31 – 21:22; 1 Chronicles 20:4-8; Psalm 7

Yesterday we considered Absalom's death and David's grief (2 Samuel 17:15 – 19:30). Today we focus on David's goal of making things right with the Gibeonites.

Key concept. David wanted to restore right relations with the Gibeonites.

The big picture. Joshua, 400 years previous to David's time, had made a treaty with the Gibeonites, guaranteeing their safety (Joshua 9:3-27). Saul, however, killed some Gibeonites, thereby breaking the treaty. David wanted to make things right. He did this by allowing the Gibeonites to execute seven of Saul's surviving descendants (2 Samuel 21:1-9).

Transformational truth. No one on this earth will get away with sin. It seemed like Joab was getting away with murder in knifing Amasa (2 Samuel 20:7-10; see also 3:26-27), but lethal justice came soon enough (1 Kings 2:28-35). Justice also awaits people in the afterlife. The wicked will face Christ at the great white throne judgment (Revelation 20:11-15).

A verse for meditation. "David asked them, 'What can I do for you? How can I make amends so that you will bless the LORD's people again?'" (2 Samuel 21:3).

A question to ponder. Are you aware of anyone you've wronged in the past with whom it would be appropriate to make amends?

DAVID'S SONG OF PRAISE

2 Samuel 22; Psalm 18

Yesterday we gave attention to David's goal of making things right with the Gibeonites (2 Samuel 19:31–21:22; 1 Chronicles 20:4-8; Psalm 7). Today we turn our attention to David's song of praise to the Lord.

Key concept. David sang a heartfelt song of praise to the Lord for providing various victories.

The big picture. David sang a song of praise and thanksgiving to God for granting him victory over his many enemies (2 Samuel 22). This song of praise also appears in Psalm 18. David referred to God with such descriptive titles as "my rock," "my fortress," "my savior," "my shield," and "my refuge." God was portrayed as One who answers prayer and rescues His people from trouble.

Transformational truth. David's song of praise is a great Old Testament example of praise (2 Samuel 22). Praise is seen in the New Testament as well. Ephesians 5:19-20 says we should address "one another in psalms and hymns and spiritual songs, singing and making melody to the Lord with your heart."

A verse for meditation. "The LORD rewarded me for doing right; he restored me because of my innocence" (2 Samuel 22:21).

A question to ponder. What are the most important ideas you learn about God from David's song of praise in 2 Samuel 22?

DAVID'S CENSUS

2 Samuel 24; 1 Chronicles 21:1 – 22:19

Yesterday we focused on David's song of praise to the Lord (2 Samuel 22; Psalm 18). Today we turn our attention to David's census of the people.

Key concept. David took a census of his fighting men, and angered God in the process.

The big picture. David instructed Joab to count all the fighting men throughout the tribes of Israel. David sinned in ordering this census. The purpose of taking this census was apparently not for God's glory, but his own. David seemed more concerned with his kingdom rather than God's (2 Samuel 24).

Transformational truth. David apparently measured his army in a prideful way. He wanted to glory in the size of his fighting forces. This resulted in God's chastisement. As Scripture says, "Pride goes before destruction, and haughtiness before a fall" (Proverbs 16:18).

A verse for meditation. "Will you choose three years of famine throughout your land, three months of fleeing from your enemies, or three days of severe plague throughout your land? Think this over and decide what answer I should give the LORD who sent me" (2 Samuel 24.13).

A question to ponder. Why does pride get us into trouble? Conversely, why is humility more desirable?

DUTIES OF THE LEVITES, PRIESTS, AND MUSICIANS

1 Chronicles 23 – 25

In the previous lesson, we explored David's census of the people (2 Samuel 24; 1 Chronicles 21:1 – 22:19). Today we consider the duties of the Levites, priests, and musicians.

Key concept. Specific groupings and duties of the Levites, priests, and musicians are delineated.

The big picture. The Levites were organized by David into several different groups that had specific duties, such as doorkeeper and assistants to priests (1 Chronicles 23:2-32). He then organized the priests into 24 groups that served on a rotating basis (24:1-19). Musicians also took turns serving (25:1-31).

Transformational truth. In the Old Testament, there is a very close relationship between praise and music. Music accompanied praise among Moses and the Israelites (Exodus 15:1-21) as well as Deborah and Barak (Judges 5:1-12). Many of the Psalms were originally accompanied by music. Believers are exhorted to sing new songs of praise (see Psalm 33:3; 40:3; Revelation 5:9; 14:3).

A verse for meditation. "All these men were under the direction of their fathers as they made music at the house of the LORD. Their responsibilities included the playing of cymbals, harps, and lyres at the house of God" (1 Chronicles 25:6).

A question to ponder. What blesses you more — contemporary worship songs or traditional hymns? Or both?

DAVID INSTRUCTS SOLOMON

1 Chronicles 26 – 28

Yesterday we considered the duties of the Levites, priests, and musicians (1 Chronicles 23 – 25). Today we look at the various personnel listings and David's instructions to Solomon.

Key concept. David instructs Solomon and encourages complete commitment to God.

The big picture. Today's Scripture reading provides various listings — including Levites who served as gatekeepers to the temple (26:1-19), Levites who oversaw storing offerings (26:20-32), David's military forces (27:1-15), tribal leaders (27:16-24), and advisors (27:25-34). David informs everyone that Solomon will be assuming leadership (28:1-8). David encourages Solomon to remain faithful to God (28:9-21).

Transformational truth. David exhorted: "Be strong and courageous, and do the work. Don't be afraid or discouraged, for the LORD God, my God, is with you. He will not fail you or forsake you" (1 Chronicles 28:20). These are good words for all of us.

A verse for meditation. "Solomon, my son, learn to know the God of your ancestors intimately. Worship and serve him with your whole heart and a willing mind…If you seek him, you will find him. But if you forsake him, he will reject you forever" (1 Chronicles 28:9).

A question to ponder. What lessons can you apply to your own life from David's advice to Solomon?

GIFTS FOR THE BUILDING OF THE TEMPLE

1 Chronicles 29; 1 Kings 1

Yesterday we read about various personnel listings and David's instructions to Solomon (1 Chronicles 26–28). Today we consider gifts donated for temple construction.

Key concept. Gifts were donated for the building of the temple.

The big picture. David encouraged the leaders of Israel to contribute gold and silver beyond what he had already donated for the temple's construction (1 Chronicles 29:1-9). He offered a prayer of thanksgiving to God (29:10-19), the leaders offered sacrifices to God, and Solomon was accepted as Israel's new king (29:10-25).

Transformational truth. David and Israel's leaders provided material gifts for temple construction (1 Chronicles 29:1-9). In the New Testament, emphasis is placed on giving freely to the church—what we might call "grace giving." We are to freely give as we have been freely given to. We are to give as we are able (2 Corinthians 8:12).

A verse for meditation. "Wealth and honor come from you alone, for you rule over everything. Power and might are in your hand, and at your discretion people are made great and given strength" (1 Chronicles 29:12).

A question to ponder. Are you a cheerful giver at your church? (See 2 Corinthians 9:7.)

DAVID'S LAST WORDS TO SOLOMON

1 Kings 2:1-12; 2 Samuel 23:1-7; 1 Chronicles 29:26-30; Psalms 4 – 6; 8 – 9; 11

Yesterday we focused on gifts donated for temple construction (1 Chronicles 29; 1 Kings 1). Today we turn our attention to David's last words to Solomon.

Key concept. David spoke his final words to Solomon, urging him to honor and obey the Lord.

The big picture. When David gave his final advice to Solomon, obedience to God was at the top of the list (1 Kings 2:1-12). That would dictate the success or failure of Solomon's kingship. David had learned this by hard experience. He died in 970 BC.

Transformational truth. David spoke of death as "going where everyone on earth must someday go" (1 Kings 2:2). Everyone dies. But Christians have an eternal hope. The apostle Paul urged Christians, "Set your sights on the realities of heaven" (Colossians 3:1-2).

A verse for meditation. "Observe the requirements of the LORD your God, and follow all his ways. Keep the decrees, commands, regulations, and laws written in the Law of Moses so that you will be successful in all you do and wherever you go" (1 Kings 2:3).

A question to ponder. Does the fact of your mortality change the way you live as a Christian?

TRUSTING GOD

Psalms 12 – 17; 19 – 21

In the previous lesson, we listened to David's last words to Solomon (1 Kings 2:1-12). Today we consider the trustworthiness of God and His Word.

Key concept. God's Word can be trusted because God Himself is trustworthy.

The big picture. This psalm and those that follow were written between 1050 and 930 BC, which places them squarely in the era of the united monarchy. These psalms are rich in meaning. God's Word and His promises are trustworthy (Psalm 12). We should not despair, but turn to God in faith (13). It's foolish to deny God exists (14). We should not do anything that could thwart our worship of God (15). The one true God is our only Master (16). Pray to God when in need; He will answer (17). God's creation is a clear evidence He exists (19). Turn to God in times of trouble (20 – 21).

Transformational truth. The psalmist said to God, "O LORD, how long will you forget me? Forever?" (Psalm 13:1). We often find the psalmist urging God to "awake," "be not silent," "rouse yourself," and "make haste" to deliver him (35:22-23; 40:13; 44:23).

A verse for meditation. "May the words of my mouth and the meditation of my heart be pleasing to you, O LORD, my rock and my redeemer" (Psalm 19:14).

A question to ponder. Why do you think it might be wise to daily pray, "Keep your servant from deliberate sins! Don't let them control me" (Psalm 19:13)?

THE LORD IS OUR SHEPHERD

Psalms 22 – 26

Yesterday we considered the trustworthiness of God and His Word (Psalm 12 – 17; 19 – 21). Today we focus on God as shepherd of our lives.

Key concept. God is your divine shepherd, who is near your side day in and day out.

The big picture. God can be trusted, even if He may seem silent at the moment (Psalm 22). He is our shepherd and is always nearby. He watches over us (23). God — the Creator of the world — is worthy of praise (24). We can turn to the Lord for protection, guidance, and pardon (25). The Lord can deliver us from the fate of the wicked (26).

Transformational truth. The psalmist said, "Even when I walk through the darkest valley, I will not be afraid, for you are close beside me" (Psalm 23:4). Christians need not fear, even in the midst of bad circumstances, for God is always close by (Psalm 145:18). He is also all-powerful (Psalm 147:5; Isaiah 14:27; 43:13; Ephesians 1:19-21).

A verse for meditation. "The LORD is my shepherd; I have all that I need. He lets me rest in green meadows; he leads me beside peaceful streams" (Psalm 23:1-2).

A question to ponder. How is the Lord's role as shepherd of your life a comfort to you?

CONFESS YOUR SINS

Psalms 27–32

Yesterday we considered God as shepherd of our lives (Psalms 22–26). Today we read about the importance of confessing our sins to God.

Key concept. Confess your sins, or God's hand of discipline may fall upon you.

The big picture. Be confident in the Lord, and wait upon Him. He will act (Psalm 27). The wicked will suffer just judgment (28). God controls and reveals Himself in the world of nature (29). He is our great deliverer and is worthy of praise (30). When in physical distress or danger, turn to the Lord for deliverance (31). Confess your sins to Him, or He may discipline you (32).

Transformational truth. The psalmist affirmed, "When I refused to confess my sin, my body wasted away, and I groaned all day long. Day and night your hand of discipline was heavy on me...Finally, I confessed all my sins to you...You forgave me!" (Psalm 32:3-5). It is always best to be a consistent confessor.

A verse for meditation. "Oh, what joy for those whose disobedience is forgiven, whose sin is put out of sight! Yes, what joy for those whose record the Lord has cleared of guilt, whose lives are lived in complete honesty!" (Psalm 32:1-2).

A question to ponder. Why should you make it a habit to consistently confess sins to God?

BETTER TO BE GODLY

Psalms 35 – 38

Yesterday we focused on the importance of confessing our sins to God (Psalms 27 – 32). Today we turn our attention to the importance of godliness.

Key concept. Commit everything you do to the Lord, and He will come to your aid.

The big picture. Psalm 35 was written during the time David was being hunted by Saul. David thus petitioned the Lord for deliverance and for the destruction of his enemies. The psalmist prayed for continued protection and the defeat of his enemies (36). The righteous are exhorted to trust in the Lord and not fret the wicked (37). David again affirmed the distress that comes from sin, and how God's chastisement causes that distress (38).

Transformational truth. The psalmist said, "It is better to be godly and have little than to be evil and rich" (Psalm 37:16). This reminds us of 1 Timothy 6:6: "Godliness with contentment is itself great wealth." Be careful not to fall in love with money (1 Timothy 6:10).

A verse for meditation. "Take delight in the Lord, and he will give you your heart's desires. Commit everything you do to the Lord. Trust him, and he will help you" (Psalm 37:4-5).

A question to ponder. What do you think it means to "take delight in the Lord"?

our hearts find peace & fulfilment in Him
Delight in the eternal things of God, our
desires will begin to parallel His
and we will never go unfulfilled

Matthew 6:33 "But seek first His Kingdom
and his righteousness ..... and all
these things (the necessities of life) will be
given to you as well

THE BREVITY OF HUMAN LIFE

Psalms 39 – 41; 55; 58

In the previous lesson, we explored the importance of godliness (Psalms 35 – 38). Today we consider the brevity of human life.

Key concept. Life is short. We grow old so quickly. And then we die.

The big picture. David asked God to help him have a right perspective on the brevity of human life (Psalm 39). He then recalled past deliverances from the Lord and brought a new need for deliverance to Him (40). He affirmed it is the merciful who receive mercy in return (41). He did the right thing when he felt overwhelmed—he prayed to the Lord (55). He then called for the destruction of the wicked so the righteous can rejoice (58).

Transformational truth. The psalmist said, "LORD, remind me how brief my time on earth will be. Remind me that my days are numbered—how fleeting my life is" (Psalm 39:4). Scripture often speaks of the brevity of life (Job 7:7; 14:1; Psalm 102:3; James 4:14). This fact motivates us to think about heaven.

A verse for meditation. "You have made my life no longer than the width of my hand. My entire lifetime is just a moment to you; at best, each of us is but a breath" (Psalm 39:5).

A question to ponder. What is your attitude toward your own mortality?

CONFESSED SIN AND ANSWERED PRAYER

Psalms 61 – 62; 64 – 67

Yesterday we considered the brevity of human life (Psalms 39 – 41; 55; 58). Today we focus on the importance of confessing sin to God as a precondition to answered prayers.

Key concept. Unconfessed sin can be a potent prayer-block.

The big picture. David prayed for strength and security based on the confidence that comes from God's awesome faithfulness (Psalm 61). He waited on God to act in his present circumstances and urged others to trust in Him (62). He continued to appeal to God for protection from His enemies (64). He then praised God for His favor and His greatness (65). People worldwide were exhorted to praise the Lord in view of His awesome deeds (66). Thanksgiving to God was invoked (67).

Transformational truth. The psalmist affirmed, "If I had not confessed the sin in my heart, the LORD would not have listened" (Psalm 66:18). This reminds us of 1 John 3:21, which tells us, "If we don't feel guilty, we can come to God with bold confidence." If you want your prayers answered, spend the first part of your prayer confessing known sins to God.

A verse for meditation. "You faithfully answer our prayers with awesome deeds, O God our savior" (Psalm 65:5).

A question to ponder. Are you satisfied with your prayer life? Why or why not?

LIVING IN PURITY

Psalms 68 – 70; 86; 101

Yesterday we considered the importance of confessing sin to God as a precondition to answered prayers (Psalm 61–62; 64–67). Today we read about living in purity.

Key concept. Choose to live in purity.

The big picture. Psalm 68 was written for David's procession with the Ark of the Covenant from the house of Obed-edom to Jerusalem (see 2 Samuel 6:12). It calls for God to scatter Israel's enemies. We then read of David's despair in being persecuted and his desire for his enemies to be punished (Psalm 69). Psalm 70 contains a prayer for deliverance. David then prayed for deliverance, protection, mercy, and happiness (86). David committed to living in integrity (101).

Transformational truth. The psalmist declared, "I will refuse to look at anything vile and vulgar" (Psalm 101:3). This is a commitment every Christian needs to make, especially as related to Internet pornography (see Acts 15:20; 1 Corinthians 6:18; Colossians 3:5; 2 Timothy 2:22).

A verse for meditation. "Teach me your ways, O Lord, that I may live according to your truth! Grant me purity of heart, so that I may honor you" (Psalm 86:11).

A question to ponder. Why might it be wise to pray daily, "Grant me purity of heart, so that I may honor you"?

THE FORGIVENESS OF SINS

Psalms 103; 108 – 110; 122; 124

Yesterday we considered living in purity (Psalm 68 – 70; 86; 101). Today we look at the forgiveness of sins.

Key concept. Complete forgiveness of sins is an awesome blessing.

The big picture. God is praised for His incredible blessings, His love, and especially His unconditional forgiveness (Psalm 103). David offered praise and thanksgiving for God's unfailing love (108). He cried out for God's judgment on his false accusers and petitions God for deliverance (109). The divine Messiah is pictured as a King, a Priest, and a mighty Warrior (110). The psalmist called for the peace and prosperity of Jerusalem, the spiritual center of Israel (122). He then offered thanksgiving for how God had been Israel's deliverer (124).

Transformational truth. The psalmist proclaimed, "He has removed our sins as far from us as the east is from the west" (Psalm 103:12). To remove sins "as far from us as the east is from the west" is, by definition, to put them where no one can ever find them (see also Isaiah 43:25; Hebrews 10:17).

A verse for meditation. "Let all that I am praise the LORD; may I never forget the good things he does for me" (Psalm 103:2).

A question to ponder. Why should praising the Lord be a regular part of your worship experience?

PRAYER AND TRUSTING GOD

Psalms 131; 133; 138 – 141; 143

In the previous lesson, we explored the forgiveness of sins (Psalm 103). Today we consider prayer and trusting God with everything in our lives.

Key concept. Trust God with everything, and pray a lot.

The big picture. David expressed childlike trust in God (Psalm 131). Unity among brothers is precious (133). The psalmist praised God for answered prayer (138). He portrayed God as all-knowing, everywhere-present, all-powerful, and holy (139). He prayed for rescue from evil people (140). He wisely asked God to keep him from ill-considered speech and actions (141). He prayed for deliverance from his enemies and for relief from depression (143).

Transformational truth. The psalmist prayed, "Search me, O God, and know my heart; test me and know my anxious thoughts. Point out anything in me that offends you, and lead me along the path of everlasting life" (Psalm 139:23-24). Getting rid of all that offends God draws us closer to God!

A verse for meditation. "Every day of my life was recorded in your book. Every moment was laid out before a single day had passed" (Psalm 139:16).

A question to ponder. How does it make you feel that God's intimate knowledge of you encompasses your entire life?

OUR AWESOME GOD

Psalms 144 – 145; 88 – 89

Yesterday we considered prayer and trusting God with everything in our lives (Psalms 131; 133; 138 – 141; 143). Today we will focus on how awesome God is.

Key concept. God is awesome and is worthy to be praised.

The big picture. Psalm 144 contains praise to God for past victories, requests for present deliverance, and an anticipation of future blessings. The psalmist then praised God for His awesome greatness, His attributes, His everlasting kingdom, His ongoing mercies, and His righteousness (145). The psalmist lamented the difficulties facing him and was emotionally distraught over what was happening to him (88). He expressed praise for God's unfailing love, His faithfulness, His covenant, His great wonders, His sovereign rule, and His glorious strength (89).

Transformational truth. The psalmist was acutely aware of his mortality: "Remember how short my life is, how empty and futile this human existence! No one can live forever; all will die. No one can escape the power of the grave" (Psalm 89:47-48). Awareness of mortality helps us to keep an eternal perspective.

A verse for meditation. "Let each generation tell its children of your mighty acts; let them proclaim your power" (Psalm 145:4).

A question to ponder. What long-term benefit might come to children as their parents speak about God's miraculous acts?

BEING THANKFUL

Psalms 50; 73–74

Yesterday we considered how awesome God is (Psalms 144–145; 88–89). Today we look at the importance of thankfulness.

Key concept. Thankfulness is a better sacrifice than insincere animal offerings.

The big picture. God indicted the people for their insincere animal sacrifices. Thankfulness is a better kind of sacrifice. God also indicted His people for unethical practices. He instructed them to correct all this (Psalm 50). The psalmist noticed that the wicked seem to prosper on earth, but acknowledges that their ultimate end is destruction. The righteous, by contrast, have a glorious destiny ahead (73). The psalmist asked God to punish the enemies of Israel, who had destroyed Jerusalem's temple (74).

Transformational truth. The Lord said, "Make thankfulness your sacrifice to God" (Psalm 50:14). This is a common theme in the psalms: "Let us come to him with thanksgiving" (95:2). "Enter his gates with thanksgiving" (100:4). It is also a common New Testament theme (Matthew 11:25; Ephesians 5:20; Philippians 4:6; Colossians 2:7).

A verse for meditation. "Whom have I in heaven but you? I desire you more than anything on earth. My health may fail, and my spirit may grow weak, but God remains the strength of my heart; he is mine forever" (Psalm 73:25-26).

A question to ponder. Do you have a supreme desire for God, as the psalmist did?

REMAINING LOYAL TO GOD

Psalms 75 – 78

Yesterday we focused on the importance of thankfulness (Psalms 50; 73 – 74). Today we turn our attention to the importance of remaining loyal to God.

Key concept. God has been consistently loyal to His people. They, in turn, ought to remain faithful to Him.

The big picture. In Psalm 75, Asaph praised God, who will judge the whole earth, and the wicked are warned of this judgment. Psalm 76 celebrates God's deliverance of Israel from her enemies. Psalm 77 rehearses many of the wondrous acts of the Lord on behalf of Israel. Psalm 78 urges that in view of Israel's fickle past, future generations would be wise to remain loyal to God and His commands.

Transformational truth. Speaking of the Israelites in the wilderness sojourn, the psalmist lamented, "All they gave him was lip service; they lied to him with their tongues. Their hearts were not loyal to him. They did not keep his covenant" (Psalm 78:36-37). God seeks authenticity instead of lip service.

A verse for meditation. "Each generation should set its hope anew on God, not forgetting his glorious miracles and obeying his commands" (Psalm 78:7).

A question to ponder. Have there been times in your Christian life that you have been characterized more by lip service than by authenticity?

DELIVERANCE AND RESTORATION

Psalms 79 – 82

I n the previous lesson, we explored the importance of remaining loyal to God (Psalms 75–78). Today we consider Israel's desire for deliverance and restoration.

Key concept. An appeal is made to God to act on behalf of His people.

The big picture. Psalm 79 describes a time of national disaster for Israel, and an appeal is made to God for deliverance from shame. Psalm 80 says that while Israel was once a healthy vine, it has now been cut down. The psalmist asked God for a restoration of Israel to its former glory. Psalm 81 contrasts God's faithfulness with Israel's fickleness. Psalm 82 speaks of how God will judge leaders who abuse their authority by oppressing others.

Transformational truth. "Oh, that my people would listen to me! Oh, that Israel would follow me, walking in my paths! How quickly I would then subdue their enemies! How soon my hands would be upon their foes!" (Psalm 81:13-14). Choices have consequences. Choosing to disobey God thwarts His blessing.

A verse for meditation. "Turn us again to yourself, O LORD God of Heaven's Armies. Make your face shine down upon us. Only then will we be saved" (Psalm 80:19).

A question to ponder. Have you ever wondered whether you might be presently forfeiting blessing because of unrepentant disobedience in your life?

SOLOMON ASKS GOD FOR WISDOM

1 Chronicles 29:23-25; 2 Chronicles 1;
1 Kings 2:13 – 3:15; Psalm 83

Yesterday we considered Israel's desire for deliverance and restoration (Psalms 79–82). Today we focus on Solomon's famous prayer.

Key concept. Solomon asked God for wisdom.

The big picture. Solomon became king in 970 BC. He asked God for wisdom so he might be a wise and just king over Israel. God was pleased with this request. He gave Solomon not only wisdom, but also riches and fame (1 Kings 3:3-15; 2 Chronicles 1:1-13).

Transformational truth. Solomon prayed to God, "Give me an understanding heart so that I can govern your people well and know the difference between right and wrong. For who by himself is able to govern this great people of yours?" (1 Kings 3:9). We too can ask God for wisdom: "If you need wisdom, ask our generous God, and he will give it to you" (James 1:5).

A verse for meditation. "I will give you a wise and understanding heart such as no one else has had or ever will have! And I will also give you what you did not ask for—riches and fame!" (1 Kings 3:12-13).

A question to ponder. Are you presently facing any circumstances in which you could use God's wisdom?

SOLOMON CONSTRUCTS THE TEMPLE

1 Kings 3:16-28; 5 – 6; 2 Chronicles 2:1 – 3:14

Yesterday we considered Solomon's request for wisdom from God (1 Chronicles 29:23-25). Today we read about Solomon's construction of the temple.

Key concept. Solomon built a magnificent temple for God.

The big picture. Construction of the temple began in 966 BC. Solomon entered into a trade agreement with King Hyram of Tyre so that materials could be obtained for the building project (1 Kings 5). Hyram also provided skilled craftsmen to help out (2 Chronicles 2). Solomon's temple was completed in seven years, by 959 BC (1 Kings 6).

Transformational truth. God gives wisdom so it can be used in practical situations. In 1 Kings 3:16-28—where two women each claimed a living baby was theirs—Solomon used the wisdom God had given him to resolve their dispute. Like Solomon, you and I must put into action the wisdom God gives us (see James 1:5).

A verse for meditation. "This must be a magnificent Temple because our God is greater than all other gods. But who can really build him a worthy home? Not even the highest heavens can contain him!" (2 Chronicles 2:5).

A question to ponder. Did you know that today, Christians themselves are the temple of the Holy Spirit (1 Corinthians 6:19)?

SOLOMON BUILDS
THE ROYAL PALACE

1 Kings 7; 2 Chronicles 3:15 – 4:22

Yesterday we reviewed Solomon's construction of the temple (1 Kings 3:16-28; 5–6). Today we consider Solomon's construction of the royal palace.

Key concept. Solomon's royal palace was built, and various temple items were constructed.

The big picture. It took about 13 years for Solomon to complete building his royal palace and various administrative buildings (1 Kings 7:1-12). Solomon hired a skilled metal worker to construct various items for the temple (7:23-51). Temple furnishings included a central altar, a huge water basin, smaller basins, tables, candlesticks, and utensils (2 Chronicles 4).

Transformational truth. Too many people begin a big task or project but then either fall behind or stagnate in finishing it. Like King Solomon, who "finished all his work on the Temple," we ought to finish what we begin (1 Kings 7:51; see also 2 Timothy 4:7; 2 Corinthians 8:10-12).

A verse for meditation. "King Solomon finished all his work on the Temple of the LORD. Then he brought all the gifts his father, David, had dedicated—the silver, the gold, and the various articles—and he stored them in the treasuries of the LORD's Temple" (1 Kings 7:51).

A question to ponder. Are you a *completer* or a *stagnater* when it comes to major tasks or projects?

GOD'S GLORY ENTERS THE TEMPLE

1 Kings 8; 2 Chronicles 5 – 6

In the previous lesson, we read about Solomon's construction of the royal palace (1 Kings 7). Today we consider how God's glory entered the temple.

Key concept. God's glory indwelt the completed temple.

The big picture. The Ark of the Covenant was placed within the most holy place in the inner court of the temple. Following this, the Lord's presence filled the temple in a cloud of glory (1 Kings 8:1-11). Solomon then led the people in a temple dedication ceremony, during which sacrificial offerings were made, which pointed to their commitment to obey the Lord (8:12-66). Solomon prayed the people would remain faithful to God (2 Chronicles 5 – 6).

Transformational truth. Solomon said, "Will God really live on earth? Why, even the highest heavens cannot contain you. How much less this Temple I have built" (1 Kings 8:27). The truth is that God is everywhere-present (Psalm 139:2-12; Isaiah 66:1).

A verse for meditation. "Praise the LORD who has given rest to his people Israel, just as he promised. Not one word has failed of all the wonderful promises he gave through his servant Moses" (1 Kings 8:56).

A question to ponder. Do you make a habit of claiming the promises God has given in the Bible?

171

GOD AND THE TEMPLE

1 Kings 9:1-14; 2 Chronicles 7

Yesterday we read about God's glory entering the temple (1 Kings 8). Today we consider God's commitment to dwell in the temple so long as His people honor Him.

Key concept. Dishonoring God will cause Him to withdraw His presence.

The big picture. The temple was dear to God's heart. He said that if the people honored Him, He would dwell within it. If the people dishonored and disobeyed Him, He would withdraw and allow the temple to be destroyed and Israel uprooted (1 Kings 9:1-14; 2 Chronicles 7).

Transformational truth. "If my people who are called by my name will humble themselves and pray and seek my face and turn from their wicked ways, I will hear from heaven and will forgive their sins and restore their land" (2 Chronicles 7:14). This was written to Israel. But God universally blesses humility, prayer, and seeking His face.

A verse for meditation. "I have set this Temple apart to be holy—this place you have built where my name will be honored forever. I will always watch over it, for it is dear to my heart" (1 Kings 9:3).

A question to ponder. Do you think 2 Chronicles 7:14 might be a good guideline for America?

SOLOMON'S FAME GROWS

2 Chronicles 1:14-17; 8; 9:1-28; 1 Kings 9:15 – 10:29

Yesterday we considered God's commitment to indwell the temple so long as His people honored Him (1 Kings 9:1-14). Today we look at how Solomon became famous for his great wisdom.

Key concept. Solomon's wisdom brought him great notoriety.

The big picture. Solomon was honored by the leaders of other nations because of his incredible wealth and wisdom (1 Kings 9:15-28). The queen of Sheba is an example (10:1-13). Solomon's riches continued to grow because of his relationships with other nations (10:14-29).

Transformational truth. Solomon's kingship and great wisdom were rooted in God alone. The queen of Sheba spoke of Solomon's fame, "which brought honor to the name of the LORD" (1 Kings 10:1). It was "the LORD your God" who made Solomon king (10:9). People from all around came to "hear the wisdom God had given him" (10:24).

A verse for meditation. "King Solomon became richer and wiser than any other king on earth. People from every nation came to consult him and to hear the wisdom God had given him" (1 Kings 10:23-24).

A question to ponder. Would you like to pray for wisdom today (James 1:5), given that it can affect the entire course of your life?

SOLOMON'S INCREDIBLE PRODUCTIVITY

1 Kings 4; Psalms 72; 127

Yesterday we considered how Solomon became famous for his great wisdom (2 Chronicles 8). Today we turn our attention to Solomon's incredible productivity.

Key concept. Solomon was unparalleled in his productivity.

The big picture. The various officials in Solomon's administration are listed (1 King 4:1-10). The extent of Solomon's wealth and reign are described (4:21-28). Solomon—well known for his great wisdom—wrote thousands of songs and proverbs (4:29-34). In Psalm 72, Solomon prayed that his reign would be characterized by righteousness (verses 1-4), peace (verses 5-7), power (verses 8-11), compassion (verses 12-14), and prosperity (verses 15-17). Psalm 127 stresses that life should be lived in dependence on the Lord, as did Solomon during these early years.

Transformational truth. In Psalm 72, Solomon prayed, "Give your love of justice to the king, O God, and righteousness to the king's son. Help him judge your people in the right way; let the poor always be treated fairly" (Psalm 72:1-2). Solomon's abilities as a king were clearly from God.

A verse for meditation. "May the king's rule be refreshing like spring rain on freshly cut grass, like the showers that water the earth" (Psalm 72:6).

A question to ponder. What unique gifts has God given you to use for serving Him?

THE BENEFIT OF WISDOM

Proverbs 1–4

In the previous lesson, we explored Solomon's incredible productivity (1 Kings 4). Today we consider how wisdom can keep a person on the right path in life.

Key concept. Wisdom can guide a person's every step.

The big picture. Solomon composed his proverbs between 971 and 931 BC, which places them squarely in the era of the united monarchy. King Hezekiah's scribes later compiled additional proverbs written by Solomon between 729 and 686 BC. Proverbs is a "wisdom book"—it contains maxims of moral wisdom, mostly written by Solomon. The maxims were engineered to help the young acquire mental skills that promote wise living. In the first four chapters of Proverbs, Solomon emphasized wisdom's value: Wisdom rebukes sin (Proverbs 1:8-33), it rewards those who seek it (2–3), and it keeps one from dangerous paths (4).

Transformational truth. Living according to biblical wisdom yields peace (Proverbs 3:2), success (3:4), long life and honor (3:16,35; 4:8), pleasantness (3:17), stability (3:23; 4:12), security (3:24), health (4:22), and a straight path to follow throughout life (4:25-27). The more biblical wisdom one gains, the better.

A verse for meditation. "Trust in the Lord with all your heart; do not depend on your own understanding" (Proverbs 3:5).

A question to ponder. Why do we sometimes depend too much on our own understanding of things rather than trust the Lord?

AVOIDING DANGER THROUGH WISDOM

Proverbs 5 – 7

Yesterday we considered how wisdom can keep a person on the right path in life (Proverbs 1–4). Today we focus on how wisdom can keep a person from straying onto dangerous paths.

Key concept. Wisdom can keep a person on a safe path throughout life.

The big picture. Solomon urged that wisdom warns against the danger of sensuality (Proverbs 5), motivates the slothful (6:1-19), represses lustful desires (6:20-35), and warns against seductive women who seek to entrap men (7).

Transformational truth. Solomon warned that an immoral woman might try to use seductive words to lure a man into a sexual encounter (Proverbs 5:3; 7:21). If he gives in to the temptation, he will pay an enormous price (7:22-23). It is better to "drink water from your own well" — that is, limit sexual activities to your spouse alone (5:15).

A verse for meditation. "Can a man scoop a flame into his lap and not have his clothes catch on fire? Can he walk on hot coals and not blister his feet? So it is with the man who sleeps with another man's wife. He who embraces her will not go unpunished" (Proverbs 6:27-29).

A question to ponder. How does our culture make it easier than ever to stray from a life of purity?

LIVING ACCORDING TO WISDOM

Proverbs 8 – 10

Yesterday we considered how wisdom can keep a person from straying onto dangerous paths (Proverbs 5 – 7). Today we examine how living wisely brings positive consequences.

Key concept. Because choices have consequences, it is best to live according to wisdom and not folly.

The big picture. Wisdom rejoices in God (Proverbs 8) and is in notable contrast to the ways of folly (9). Solomon contrasted wise living with wicked or foolish living in many different ways. He noted there are definite consequences to one's choices in life. For this reason, we are exhorted to choose wisely (10).

Transformational truth. Proverbs 9:10 tells us, "Fear of the LORD is the foundation of wisdom." All goes well for those who fear God (1 Samuel 12:14). God's mercy goes out to those who fear Him (Luke 1:50), and He fulfills their desires (Psalm 145:19). He blesses them (Psalm 115:13), and a fear of the Lord can lengthen one's life (Proverbs 10:27).

A verse for meditation. "Wisdom will multiply your days and add years to your life. If you become wise, you will be the one to benefit. If you scorn wisdom, you will be the one to suffer" (Proverbs 9:11-12).

A question to ponder. What changes do you want to make in your life so that you show a proper fear of the Lord?

BE CAREFUL WHAT YOU SAY

Proverbs 11 – 13

Yesterday we focused on how living wisely brings positive conse-quences (Proverbs 8 – 10). Today we turn our attention to the importance of being careful about what you say.

Key concept. Choose your words wisely.

The big picture. Solomon continued to contrast the wise and the foolish, the righteous and the unrighteous, the godly and the wicked (Proverbs 10 – 12): "The words of the godly are a life-giving fountain; the words of the wicked conceal violent intentions" (10:11). "The wise don't make a show of their knowledge, but fools broadcast their fool-ishness" (12:23). "The godly give good advice to their friends; the wicked lead them astray" (12:26).

Transformational truth. Words can either build people up or tear them down. "Some people make cutting remarks, but the words of the wise bring healing" (Proverbs 12:18). "A gentle answer deflects anger, but harsh words make tempers flare" (15:1). "Gentle words are a tree of life; a deceitful tongue crushes the spirit" (15:4; see also 16:24; 25:11).

A verse for meditation. "Those who control their tongue will have a long life; opening your mouth can ruin everything" (Proverbs 13:3).

A question to ponder. Did you know Solomon made almost 150 ref-erences to the tongue, mouth, and lips in Proverbs, thereby indicating that proper speech was one of his top priorities?

WALK WISELY, AVOID FOLLY

Proverbs 14 – 16

In the previous lesson, we explored the importance of being careful about what you say (Proverbs 11–13). Today we consider how we should consistently walk in wisdom and avoid folly.

Key concept. Walk always in wisdom. You won't be sorry!

The big picture. Solomon continued to contrast the wise and the foolish, the righteous and the unrighteous, the godly and the wicked (Proverbs 14–15). For example: "Those who follow the right path fear the LORD; those who take the wrong path despise him" (14:2). "Sensible children bring joy to their father; foolish children despise their mother" (15:20). Solomon then gave moral and ethical advice on a variety of subjects (16).

Transformational truth. Solomon said that "the LORD...delights in the prayers of the upright" (Proverbs 15:8). He affirmed, "The LORD is far from the wicked, but he hears the prayers of the righteous" (15:29). *Cause and effect!* Righteous living opens God's ears to your prayers. As Psalm 66:18 puts it, "If I had not confessed the sin in my heart, the LORD would not have listened."

A verse for meditation. "There is a path before each person that seems right, but it ends in death" (Proverbs 14:12).

A question to ponder. What important lesson can we learn by combining Proverbs 14:12 with Proverbs 3:5-6?

THE BENEFITS OF LIVING MORALLY

Proverbs 17–19

Yesterday we considered how we ought always to walk in wisdom and avoid folly (Proverbs 14–16). Today we will focus on how a moral lifestyle brings many benefits.

Key concept. Living morally pays rich dividends in life.

The big picture. Solomon wrote many proverbs rich with moral and ethical advice (Proverbs 17–19). For example, "The crooked heart will not prosper; the lying tongue tumbles into trouble" (17:20). "Haughtiness goes before destruction; humility precedes honor" (18:12). "Keep the commandments and keep your life; despising them leads to death" (19:16).

Transformational truth. It is wise to choose your friends carefully. Look for a friend who will stay closer to you than a brother (Proverbs 18:24). Beware of superficial friends who buddy up to you because you have money (19:4). Those aren't true friends. Try to avoid making friends with an angry person (19:11). Also, avoid those who are not trustworthy with private matters you share with them (17:9). A true friend loves you at all times—and treats you lovingly—no matter what (17:17).

A verse for meditation. "There are 'friends' who destroy each other, but a real friend sticks closer than a brother" (Proverbs 18:24).

A question to ponder. Which of your friends meet Solomon's criteria for a good friend?

CHOICES YIELD POSITIVE OR NEGATIVE CONSEQUENCES

Proverbs 20:1 – 22:16

Yesterday we considered how a moral lifestyle brings many benefits (Proverbs 17 – 19). Today we look at how choices can have positive or negative consequences.

Key concept. Living morally yields positive consequences; living immorally yields negative consequences.

The big picture. Solomon offered numerous proverbs loaded with ethical and moral advice (Proverbs 20:1 – 22:16): "A gossip goes around telling secrets, so don't hang around with chatterers" (20:19). "People may be right in their own eyes, but the LORD examines their heart" (21:2). "True humility and fear of the LORD lead to riches, honor, and long life" (22:4).

Transformational truth. Proverbs 22:6 indicates that if we train or direct our children in God's ways, they won't depart from them when they grow older. The Hebrew word for "train" or "direct" comes from a root word that means "palate" or "roof of the mouth." Ancient midwives rubbed the palate of a newborn child with olive oil to give it a desire for food. Christian parents should seek to develop in their children a desire for the things of God.

A verse for meditation. "Direct your children onto the right path, and when they are older, they will not leave it" (Proverbs 22:6).

A question to ponder. Do you think Proverbs 22:6 is a promise or a principle? Does that make any difference?

ETHICS AND THE GOOD LIFE

Proverbs 22:17 – 24:34

Yesterday we considered how choices can have positive or negative consequences (Proverbs 20:1 – 22:16). Today we continue along this same line, focusing on how one's life will be better if one lives ethically.

Key concept. Living ethically can lead to the good life.

The big picture. Solomon provided many proverbs brimming with great moral and ethical guidelines (Proverbs 22:17 – 24:34): "Don't befriend angry people or associate with hot-tempered people, or you will learn to be like them and endanger your soul" (22:24-25). "Don't wear yourself out trying to get rich. Be wise enough to know when to quit" (23:4). "Don't excuse yourself by saying, 'Look, we didn't know.' For God understands all hearts, and he sees you" (24:12).

Transformational truth. A lazy person lays around doing nothing, unconcerned with necessary chores (Proverbs 24:30-34; 21:25). He never prepares for the future (20:4). He's always making excuses to avoid work (22:13). He never listens to the advice of those who could help put him on the right track (26:16).

A verse for meditation. "A little extra sleep, a little more slumber, a little folding of the hands to rest—then poverty will pounce on you like a bandit; scarcity will attack you like an armed robber" (Proverbs 24:33-34).

A question to ponder. How is Solomon himself the antithesis of a lazy person?

THE JOY OF MARITAL LOVE

Song of Songs 1–8

In the previous lesson, we explored how a person's life will be better if he lives ethically (Proverbs 22:17–24:34). Today we consider the joy of marital love.

Key concept. Marital love is one of God's greatest gifts to humankind.

The big picture. Solomon wrote the Song of Solomon in 968 BC, during the era of the united monarchy. It is an extended poem full of metaphors and imagery, showing the richness of sexual love between husband (lover) and wife (his beloved) (1:8–2:7). Of course, in any deep relationship, there is both joy and pain. The Song reflects this, pointing to both the joys and heartaches of wedded love (5:2–7:9).

Transformational truth. In the Song of Solomon, the young woman had worked for hours in the vineyard under the blazing sun. Yet she was beautiful beyond description (Song of Solomon 1). She felt likewise about her beloved. She dreamed of him coming to be with her (2:16). She felt desolate apart from him and was intoxicated with love for him (3:1-5).

A verse for meditation. "I am my lover's, and he claims me as his own" (Song of Solomon 7:10).

A question to ponder. In what ways do you think sin can disrupt this deepest of bonds?

SOLOMON SINS

1 Kings 11; 2 Chronicles 9:29-31; Ecclesiastes 1:1-11

Yesterday we considered the joy of married love (Song of Songs 1–8). Today we read about Solomon's late-life sin and his conclusions about life.

Key concept. Solomon sinned by worshipping false deities late in life. He also concluded that life is futile without the one true God.

The big picture. Solomon wrote Ecclesiastes in 935 BC, during the era of the united monarchy. In his old age, some of his foreign wives tragically led him into worshipping false gods (1 Kings 11). Solomon later determined there is no meaning in engaging in a seemingly endless cycle of doing the same old things day in and day out. Meaning is found in fearing and obeying God.

Transformational truth. Monogamy is God's standard for the human race. In the beginning, God created one man and one woman for each other (Genesis 1:27; 2:21-25). Jesus spoke of a man leaving his mother and father and joining to his wife (singular) (Matthew 19:4-6). Paul said, "Each man should have his own wife" (1 Corinthians 7:2).

A verse for meditation. "Everything is wearisome beyond description. No matter how much we see, we are never satisfied. No matter how much we hear, we are not content" (Ecclesiastes 1:8).

A question to ponder. Do you ever feel like life is meaningless? Why or why not?

MEANINGLESS EARTHLY PURSUITS

Ecclesiastes 1:12 – 6:12

Yesterday we gave attention to Solomon's sin and his conclusions about life (1 Kings 11; 2 Chronicles 9:29-31; Ecclesiastes 1:1-11). Today we turn our attention to how earthly pursuits do not bring meaning in life.

Key concept. The things of this world cannot bring meaning to life.

The big picture. Solomon investigated whether he could find meaning in knowledge and wisdom (Ecclesiastes 1:17-18), laughter and pleasure (2:2), wine (2:3), constructing great works (2:4-6), pursuing great wealth (2:7-8; 5:8-17), music and women (2:8), worldly recognition (2:9), and worldly pleasures (2:10). In the end, he found that all was futile (2:11). One should simply enjoy life and be content with the providences and blessings of God (2:24 – 3:13; 5:18-20; 6:1-9).

Transformational truth. Solomon affirmed that God "has planted eternity in the human heart" (Ecclesiastes 3:11). We all have a sense in our hearts that this life is not all there is—that life continues beyond the grave. From the first book in the Bible to the last, we read of great men and women of God who gave evidence that eternity permeated their hearts (see Hebrews 11:13-16).

A verse for meditation. "For everything there is a season, a time for every activity under heaven" (Ecclesiastes 3:1).

A question to ponder. What brings meaning to your life?

ENJOY LIFE AS
MUCH AS POSSIBLE

Ecclesiastes 7:1 – 11:6

Yesterday we considered how earthly pursuits do not bring meaning in life (Ecclesiastes 1:12 – 6:12). Today we review how one should try to enjoy life.

Key concept. Life can be hard. Try to enjoy it for as long as you can.

The big picture. Solomon said humans cannot fathom God's inscrutable plan (Ecclesiastes 7:1-15). Life does not seem to add up. The problem of evil is difficult to figure out. The best advice is to choose to enjoy life, despite its enigmas and mysteries (8). Death awaits us all (9:11-12), and hence it's best to work hard and enjoy life for as long as possible (9:7-10). The path of wisdom is the best game plan (9:15 – 11:6).

Transformational truth. Solomon said, "Don't long for 'the good old days.' This is not wise" (Ecclesiastes 7:10). Don't live in the past. It's better to keep your eyes on what's in front of you. As Paul put it, "I focus on this one thing: Forgetting the past and looking forward to what lies ahead" (Philippians 3:13).

A verse for meditation. "A wise person thinks a lot about death, while a fool thinks only about having a good time" (Ecclesiastes 7:3).

A question to ponder. What takes the "sting" out of death for you? (Hint: See 1 Corinthians 15:54-57.)

FEAR AND OBEY GOD

Ecclesiastes 11:7 – 12:14

In the previous lesson, we explored how one should try to enjoy life (Ecclesiastes 7:1–11:6). Today we consider the importance of fearing and obeying God.

Key concept. Fear and obey God, for we'll all face the judgment.

The big picture. We ought to live joyfully, for death awaits us all (Ecclesiastes 11:7-8). It is especially important to enjoy life in one's youth, while still remembering the future judgment (11:9-10). We should fear God and keep His commandments (12:13-14).

Transformational truth. God will judge us for everything we do (Ecclesiastes 12:14). Believers will stand before the judgment seat of Christ (Romans 14:8-10). Each believer's life will be examined in regard to deeds done while in the body. Personal motives and intents of the heart will also be weighed. This judgment has to do with the reception or loss of rewards, based on whether we lived faithfully or unfaithfully after becoming Christians (1 Corinthians 3:10-15).

A verse for meditation. "Here now is my final conclusion: Fear God and obey his commands, for this is everyone's duty. God will judge us for everything we do, including every secret thing, whether good or bad" (Ecclesiastes 12:13-14).

A question to ponder. How does your biblical knowledge of the judgment seat of Christ motivate you toward change in your life?

ERA 5: THE KINGDOM DIVIDED
930 – 586 BC

Books in whole or in part: 1 Kings • 2 Kings
2 Chronicles • Psalms • Proverbs • Isaiah • Jeremiah
Ezekiel • Daniel • Hosea • Amos • Jonah
Micah • Nahum • Habakkuk • Zephaniah

Today we begin our study of a new biblical era—titled "The King-dom Divided," dated 930–586 BC. Bible books pertinent to our study of this era include 1 Kings, 2 Kings, 2 Chronicles, Psalms, Proverbs, Isaiah, Jeremiah, Ezekiel, Daniel, Hosea, Amos, Jonah, Micah, Nahum, Habakkuk, and Zephaniah. A lot happened during this era.

Things had been going so well for Israel. The people enjoyed many military victories under the able leadership of the shepherd-king David. After David's son Solomon became king, a wonderful temple was built. Solomon made many treaties with foreign nations. But then the cancer of spiritual compromise emerged and did tremendous damage to the nation. Even Solomon took part in this by marrying pagan women. Following his death, things deteriorated quickly.

The problem was that it took significant material wealth not just to build the temple, but also to build Solomon's luxurious palace and other buildings. This resulted in burdensome taxation for the common folk. They were barely surviving.

When Solomon died, his son Rehoboam took over leadership of the nation. The people promptly approached him and asked for tax relief (1 Kings 12:2-5). He turned a deaf ear toward their request. He was used to living in luxury, and was not open to change (12:12-15). As a result, the nation split into two kingdoms. The ten northern tribes revolted and set up Jeroboam as their king (12:16-20). This left only two tribes under Rehoboam's leadership—the southern kingdom of Judah. God's people were now splintered into two nations that would be at odds with each another for an extended time.

Of course, God attempted to reach the people, sending one prophet after another. But these prophets were ignored and persecuted. The people in both kingdoms didn't want to hear messages of repentance.

Things went from bad to worse. In 722 BC, the northern kingdom of Israel fell to the Assyrians, who destroyed the capital city of Samaria. Sometime later, the southern kingdom of Judah fell to the Babylonians. There were three deportations involved in Babylon's victory over Judah. The first took place in 605 BC and included Daniel and his friends. The second took place in 597 BC and included Ezekiel. The third took place in 586, when the Babylonians destroyed Jerusalem and the temple. Judah would remain in captivity for some 70 years. The Assyrians and the Babylonians were God's whipping rods to chasten His sinful people.

While the people were in captivity, God continued to speak to them through the prophets. But now His messages focused on comfort in view of a future restoration and a future hope. I'll talk more about these captivities when we survey Era 6, titled "Living in Exile," dated 586–538 BC.

In the coming chapters, we will journey through 1 Kings, 2 Kings, 2 Chronicles, Psalms, Proverbs, Isaiah, Jeremiah, Ezekiel, Daniel, Hosea, Amos, Jonah, Micah, Nahum, Habakkuk, and Zephaniah. In case you're wondering which prophets spoke to which of the two kingdoms, here's a helpful summary:

The Great Divide

- The kingdom was divided into the northern kingdom (Israel) and the southern kingdom (Judah) in 930 BC.

- First Kings provides a history of the kings of Israel (the northern kingdom) and Judah (the southern kingdom) (12:1–22:53).

- Second Kings is part 2 of 1 Kings—they were originally a single book.

- Second Chronicles documents all of Judah's kings, from

Rehoboam through Zedekiah. The divided kingdom is in full swing in these books.

Prophets to the Northern Kingdom of Israel

- Jonah's prophetic ministry began in 793 BC. His purpose was to point to God's magnificent grace and His concern for all people.

- Amos's prophetic ministry began in 760 BC. His purpose was to pronounce judgment on the northern kingdom for its complacency, idolatry, and oppression of the poor.

- Hosea's prophetic ministry began in 753 BC. The purpose of his book was to illustrate the tremendous love of God for His sinful people.

- The northern kingdom was taken into exile by the Assyrians in 722 BC.

Prophets to the Southern Kingdom of Judah

- Micah's prophetic ministry began in 750 BC. His purpose was to warn God's people that judgment was imminent.

- Isaiah's prophetic ministry began in 740 BC. His purpose was to call the southern kingdom back to God and prophesy of God's coming salvation through the future divine Messiah.

- Habakkuk's prophetic ministry began in 612 BC. His purpose was to demonstrate that God was still in control of the world, even though there was pervasive evil everywhere.

- Nahum's prophetic ministry began in the mid-600s BC. His purpose was to pronounce God's judgment on the wicked Assyrians, and thereby bring comfort to Judah with this truth.

- Jeremiah's prophetic ministry began in 627 BC. His

ERA 5: THE KINGDOM DIVIDED 930 – 586 BC

purpose was to motivate God's people to repent and turn back to God.

- Zephaniah's prophetic ministry began about 625 BC. His purpose was to motivate the people of Judah to stop being complacent and turn back to God.

- Daniel's prophetic ministry began around 600 BC. His prophecies have relevance for three biblical eras—the kingdom divided, living in exile, and the return from exile. We will see that he helped the exiled Jews in Babylon understand God's long-term plan for Israel.

- Ezekiel's prophetic ministry began in 593 BC. His purpose was to speak words of hope and comfort to Judah's people.

- The southern kingdom's deportation to Babylon (the Babylonian captivity) took place in three phases—in 605, 597, and 586 BC.

The Psalms and Proverbs

- Meanwhile, there were many psalms written or rediscovered during this era. These psalms were collected during the time of King Hezekiah, a well-respected king of Judah who began ruling in about 726 BC (2 Kings 18:20; Isaiah 36–39; 2 Chronicles 29–32). It's possible some of them were written prior to this time and then rediscovered. But many were likely written during Hezekiah's reign. Some were written by descendants of Korah, but most were anonymous.

- There were also a number of proverbs collected during the time of King Hezekiah. They are thus properly included in this era.

As you go through the various biblical books associated with this era, it's important to note a technique often used by the prophets. Sometimes they spoke in the present tense as if an event were presently happening, or they spoke in the past tense as if the event had already happened, *even though the event had not yet taken place.* They did this to emphasize the certainty that the prophesied event would, in fact, take place. More specifically, the prophets sometimes spoke as if the Babylonian captivity had already occurred, or that the exiles in Babylon were now being released, when in fact neither of these events had taken place from the perspective of the prophet. The prophets did this to indicate the *certainty* of the captivity and the *certainty* of a surviving remnant.

One additional fact worth noting is that the prophets often seemed like broken records because they repeatedly talked about sin, the need for repentance, and the threat of punishment. They addressed these themes relentlessly. Underlying all this was the fact that God wanted to bless His people. *But the only way He can bless His people is if they first become blessable—by turning from sin.* So if the prophets seem repetitious, it was because of God's relentless desire for His people's ultimate good.

Preview: In Day 165, we will consider specific details about why God's people split into two kingdoms.

THE KINGDOM DIVIDES

1 Kings 12 – 15; 2 Chronicles 10:1 – 15:19

Yesterday we introduced Era 5, titled "The Kingdom Divided," dated 930 – 586 BC. Today we consider the circumstances of the division.

Key concept. The northern and southern tribes split into two kingdoms in 930 BC.

The big picture. King Rehoboam became increasingly harsh. The northern tribes revolted against him and made Jeroboam their king (1 Kings 12:1-15). The kingdom was now split between the northern tribes (Israel) and the southern tribes (Judah), with two different kings (12:16-24). During this era, kings died and their sons replaced them (13 – 15). Asa, Abijah's son, was notable because he pleased God by removing idols and pagan shrines from Judah (15:9-24).

Transformational truth. David — now long dead — had been known as an obedient and heartfelt follower of God (1 Kings 14:8). Yet he broke four of the Ten Commandments in his adultery with Bathsheba (2 Samuel 11). Even great men of God can fall (see 1 Corinthians 10:12)!

A verse for meditation. "I ripped the kingdom away from the family of David and gave it to you. But you have not been like my servant David, who obeyed my commands and followed me with all his heart and always did whatever I wanted" (1 Kings 14:8).

A question to ponder. Does it surprise you that even the most devout followers of God can fall into deep sin?

BAD KINGS AND GOOD KINGS

1 Kings 15:16 – 17:7; 2 Chronicles 16 – 17

Yesterday we looked at the dividing of Israel into two kingdoms (1 Kings 12 – 15; 2 Chronicles 10:1 – 15:19). Today we consider the various kings — both good and bad.

Key concept. Bad kings violated God's will and promoted idolatry. Good kings sought repentance and reform.

The big picture. Asa, king of Judah, became the first of four later Davidic kings to initiate religious reform against idolatry (1 Kings 15:16-24). Baasha became the king of Israel, and reigned for 24 years, from 909 – 886 BC. Like Jeroboam, Baasha did evil in the sight of the Lord (15:33 – 16:7). Baasha's reign was followed by that of Omri and then Ahab, both wicked kings (16:21-28).

Transformational truth. Nadab, the son of Jeroboam, followed his father's example in wickedness (1 Kings 15:26). Scripture reveals that many sons and daughters followed the wickedness of a parent (Genesis 26:6-11; 37:3-4; 1 Kings 22:52; 2 Chronicles 22:3; Jeremiah 9:14). Other sons and daughters followed the righteousness of a parent (2 Chronicles 17:3; 26:4; 2 Timothy 1:5).

A verse for meditation. Nadab "did what was evil in the LORD's sight and followed the example of his father" (1 Kings 15:26).

A question to ponder. Are you acquainted with any Christians who have picked up either good or bad habits from a parent?

GOD'S SUPERIORITY OVER BAAL

1 Kings 17:8 – 20:22

Yesterday we focused on various kings—both good and bad (1 Kings 15:16–17:7; 2 Chronicles 16–17). Today we turn our attention to God's superiority over Baal.

Key concept. The false god Baal was shown to be woefully inferior to the one true God.

The big picture. When God demonstrated His superiority over Baal, Baal's priests were humiliated (1 Kings 17:8–18:46). Following God's triumph, the wicked queen Jezebel threatened the prophet Elijah's life, and he fled to southern Judah and then on to Horeb (19:1-9). The Lord promptly appeared to him and commissioned him for further service (19:9-18). Elisha was then anointed as Elijah's successor (19:19-21).

Transformational truth. In 1 Kings 18:40 we witness a contest between the one true God, represented by Elijah, and Baal, represented by 850 priests. Baal was silent when called upon to bring fire to consume a sacrifice, but the one true God instantly burned the sacrifice. God is incomparable: "There is no one like the God of Israel" (Deuteronomy 33:26).

A verse for meditation. "How much longer will you waver, hobbling between two opinions? If the Lord is God, follow him! But if Baal is God, then follow him! But the people were completely silent" (1 Kings 18:21).

A question to ponder. What kinds of things might cause people to be spiritually blind?

AHAB AVERTS JUDGMENT

1 Kings 20:23 – 22:9; 2 Chronicles 18:1-8

In the previous lesson, we explored God's superiority over Baal (1 Kings 17:8 – 20:22). Today we consider how King Ahab of Israel averted judgment.

Key concept. King Ahab deserved judgment for his wickedness, but he averted it by humbling himself before God.

The big picture. Ahab damaged Israel by leading the people into apostasy and marrying the wicked Jezebel. He then sought to appropriate the property of his neighbor, Naboth (1 Kings 21:1-2). Naboth refused, and Ahab became downcast (21:3-4). Jezebel then took matters into her own hands and Naboth was murdered (21:13). God subsequently spoke judgment against Ahab through Elijah (21:17-24). Ahab humbled himself before God, however, and avoided judgment (21:29).

Transformational truth. Ahab "was evil in the LORD's sight, even more than any of the kings before him" (1 Kings 16:30). Yet when he humbled himself before God, God mercifully chose to withhold judgment (21:29). When people humble themselves before God, He always responds in mercy and grace. *It's never too late.*

A verse for meditation. "Do you see how Ahab has humbled himself before me? Because he has done this, I will not do what I promised during his lifetime" (1 Kings 21:29).

A question to ponder. Have you ever sinned so badly that you feared it might put you beyond God's mercy and forgiveness?

GOOD LEADERS CAN FAIL

1 Kings 22:10-43,51-53; 2 Chronicles 18:9 – 20:30

Yesterday we considered how King Ahab avoided judgment by repentance (1 Kings 20:23 – 22:9). Today we focus on how it's possible for even good leaders to fail.

Key concept. Good leaders can fail God and bring injury to His people.

The big picture. Micaiah the prophet announced that Ahab—who had humbled himself before God—would lose his life if he battled against the Syrians (1 Kings 22:10-28). As predicted, he indeed was killed in the battle at Ramoth-gilead (22:29-40). Ahab was succeeded by his son Ahaziah, who was wicked (22:51-53).

Transformational truth. King Jehoshaphat of Judah was commended for seeking God, and for urging people to return to Him. But he failed to get rid of all the pagan shrines (2 Chronicles 19; 1 Kings 22:43). It has been said that the only thing necessary for the triumph of evil is for good men to do nothing.

A verse for meditation. "Jehoshaphat was a good king, following the example of his father, Asa. He did what was pleasing in the LORD's sight. During his reign, however, he failed to remove all the pagan shrines, and the people still offered sacrifices and burned incense there" (1 Kings 22:43).

A question to ponder. Why do you think a good man like Jehoshaphat failed in this way?

GENERATIONAL WICKEDNESS AMONG KINGS

2 Kings 1; 3; 8:16-22; 22:41-50;
2 Chronicles 20:31-37; 21:1-7

Yesterday we considered how good leaders can fail (1 Kings 22:10-43,51-53). Today we read about generational wickedness among kings.

Key concept. As kingship was passed from father to son, trickle-down generational wickedness continued.

The big picture. Elijah carried out his ministry from 862 to 852 BC, during the era of the kingdom divided. Second Kings focuses on the kings of the northern kingdom of Israel and the southern kingdom of Judah. More specifically, it traces the continued decline of these two kingdoms, with kings passing down wickedness to each successive generation of kings. The kings addressed in today's reading include Ahaziah and Jehoram (2 Kings 1; 3).

Transformational truth. Music can open the heart to spiritual things. An example of this is how Elisha the prophet experienced God's anointing at the sound of music (2 Kings 3:15). In Bible times, God's people typically celebrated before the Lord by "singing songs and playing all kinds of musical instruments—lyres, harps, tambourines, castanets, and cymbals" (2 Samuel 6:5; Psalm 150:3-4).

A verse for meditation. "While the harp was being played, the power of the LORD came upon Elisha" (2 Kings 3:15).

A question to ponder. Does music play a significant role in your own worship of the Lord?

ELISHA BECOMES ELIJAH'S SUCCESSOR

2 Kings 2; 4

Yesterday we considered generational wickedness among kings (2 Kings 1; 3; 8:16-22; 22:41-50; 2 Chronicles 20:31-37; 21:1-7). Today we look at how Elisha became Elijah's successor.

Key concept. Elisha succeeded Elijah's prophetic ministry.

The big picture. Elisha was publicly recognized as the legitimate successor to Elijah (2 Kings 2:12-18). Some youths mocked him as a divinely appointed prophet of God. They rejected the one who represented Yahweh in a pagan culture. This jeering ultimately represented a challenge to God. The youths paid for this mockery of God and his servant by forfeiting their lives (2:24). Elisha then engaged in further miracles (4).

Transformational truth. Elisha requested of Elijah "a double share of your spirit" (2 Kings 2:9). He was not being self-focused in this request. He was God-focused, with pure motives, seeking to accomplish even more for God. We should never fear asking God for His power or blessing when our motives are God-focused.

A verse for meditation. "Elijah said to Elisha, 'Tell me what I can do for you before I am taken away.' And Elisha replied, 'Please let me inherit a double share of your spirit and become your successor'" (2 Kings 2:9).

A question to ponder. Are you ever hesitant to request great things from God?

ELISHA'S MIRACLES

2 Kings 5 – 8

In the previous lesson, we saw how Elisha became Elijah's successor (2 Kings 2; 4). Today we consider the miraculous nature of Elisha's ministry.

Key concept. Elisha's ministry was characterized by many astounding miracles.

The big picture. Elisha cured a Syrian commander of leprosy. The commander offered gifts to Elisha, which Elisha declined. Elisha's servant, however, claimed the gifts for himself. Elisha then declared that the leprosy which had afflicted the Syrian commander would now afflict his servant (1 Kings 5). Chapters 6 and 7 feature a variety of Elisha's miracles. Chapter 8 reports on dying kings and their replacements.

Transformational truth. Elisha and a young man with him, under threat by hostile forces, were surrounded and protected by powerful guardian angels (2 Kings 6:17). A key ministry of angels is to act as guardians over the heirs of salvation (Matthew 18:10; Acts 12:15; Hebrews 2:14). As Psalm 91:11 puts it, "He will order his angels to protect you wherever you go."

A verse for meditation. "Elisha prayed, 'O LORD, open his eyes and let him see!' The Lord opened the young man's eyes, and when he looked up, he saw that the hillside around Elisha was filled with horses and chariots of fire" (2 Kings 6:17).

A question to ponder. How does it make you feel to know that God's guardian angels are watching over you?

JEHU'S PARTIAL REFORMS IN ISRAEL

2 Kings 9:1 – 10:31; 2 Chronicles 21:8 – 22:9

Yesterday we considered the miraculous nature of Elisha's ministry (2 Kings 5 – 8). Today we look at Jehu's partial reforms in Israel.

Key concept. King Jehu, the son of Jehoshaphat, brought partial reforms in the northern kingdom of Israel.

The big picture. Jehu was anointed as king by Elisha (2 Kings 9:1-10). He eradicated many of Israel's Baal worshippers and destroyed the temple of Baal (10:18-28). He made a good start, but his reforms were only partial because he still permitted some false religion in Israel (10:29-31).

Transformational truth. In 2 Kings 9:6, the people of Israel are referred to as "the LORD's people." This is despite the fact that the Israelites had consistently fallen into deep sin. This sin had been going on for generations. God could have just annihilated them. But He still held on to them as His precious people. *That's amazing grace!*

A verse for meditation. "Jehoram was thirty-two years old when he became king, and he reigned in Jerusalem eight years. No one was sorry when he died. They buried him in the City of David, but not in the royal cemetery" (2 Chronicles 21:20).

A question to ponder. Unlike Jehoram's sorry end, what positive legacy can you leave for those who come after you?

THE FAILURE OF RELIGIOUS REFORMS

2 Kings 10:32 – 12:21; 2 Chronicles 22:10 – 24:22

Yesterday we considered Jehu's partial reforms in Israel (2 Kings 9:1 – 10:31; 2 Chronicles 21:8 – 22:9). Today we turn our attention to Joash's attempted reforms.

Key concept. Joash, king of Judah (the southern kingdom), attempted reforms but failed in the face of overwhelming paganism.

The big picture. Joash attempted to restore true worship of the Lord in Judah and Jerusalem. He sought to repair the temple, which had fallen into ruin (2 Kings 12:4-16). His attempted reforms, however, didn't stick. The negative momentum of pagan worship was just too great to overcome. The people continued to offer sacrifices at pagan shrines (12:3). Resistance to Joash continued to grow until his own officials assassinated him (12:20).

Transformational truth. "Jehoash did what was right in the eyes of the Lord all his days, because Jehoiada the priest instructed him" (2 Kings 12:2 ESV). King Jehoash received good spiritual advice from the priest Jehoiada, and he acted upon it. It is wise to be open to good advice from respected spiritual leaders (see Proverbs 12:15; 13:10).

A verse for meditation. "This is what God says: Why do you disobey the Lord's commands and keep yourselves from prospering? You have abandoned the Lord, and now he has abandoned you!" (2 Chronicles 24:20).

A question to ponder. Do you seek and follow the advice of spiritually mature believers? Why is it good to do this?

A PATTERN OF SINFUL REBELLION

2 Kings 13:1-11,14-25; 2 Chronicles 24:23-27; Joel 1 – 3

Yesterday we considered Joash's attempted reforms (2 Kings 10:32 – 12:16; 2 Chronicles 22:10 – 24:22). Today we read about Israel's ongoing pattern of sinful rebellion.

Key concept. While there were brief times of commitment to the Lord in Israel (the northern kingdom), the overall momentum was downward and sinful.

The big picture. Jehoahaz succeeded his father Jehu on Israel's throne. He followed the example of Jeroboam and did what was evil in the Lord's sight (2 Kings 13:1-3). But he did turn to God for rescue from the neighboring Arameans (13:4-5). Nevertheless, the people "continued to sin, following the evil example of Jeroboam" (13:6).

Transformational truth. God withheld His judgment on the Israelites when they turned to Him (2 Kings 13:4-6). But their commitment didn't last long. "They continued to sin" (13:6). The Israelites had periodic times of faithfulness sprinkled into longer periods of disobedience. Their overall momentum was in the wrong direction. Let's learn from their example how *not* to live as God's people.

A verse for meditation. "The LORD was very angry with Israel, and he allowed King Hazael of Aram and his son Ben-hadad to defeat them repeatedly" (2 Kings 13:3).

A question to ponder. How would you assess the overall momentum of your life these days?

GOD'S UNIVERSAL COMPASSION

Jonah 1–4; 2 Kings 13:12-13; 14:1-27;
15:1-5; 2 Chronicles 25:1–26:21

In the previous lesson, we explored Israel's ongoing pattern of sinful rebellion (2 Kings 13:1-11,14-25; 2 Chronicles 24:23-27). Today we consider God's universal compassion.

Key concept. God shows compassion toward all people everywhere.

The big picture. Jonah wrote his book in 760 BC. He was a prophet of the northern kingdom of Israel, and was commanded by God to preach to Nineveh's inhabitants. Because these people had previously attacked and destroyed Israel, Jonah abhorred the idea of preaching to them. He tried to run from God to get out of this assignment. God providentially manipulated circumstances to bring Jonah to Nineveh. The Ninevites listened to Jonah's message and promptly repented, thereby averting judgment (Jonah 1–4).

Transformational truth. God is compassionate. He showed compassion for the Ninevites by sending Jonah to preach to them (Jonah 4:11). He showed compassion for the ship's mariners, sparing them from a life-threatening storm (1:15). He showed compassion toward Jonah by rescuing him from drowning (1:17).

A verse for meditation. "Nineveh has more than 120,000 people living in spiritual darkness…Shouldn't I feel sorry for such a great city?" (Jonah 4:11).

A question to ponder. What evidences do you see in the book of Jonah for God's sovereign control of nature?

GOD CARES FOR THE POOR

Amos 1–6

Yesterday we considered God's universal compassion (Jonah 1–4). Today we focus on God's care for the poor and the oppressed.

Key concept. God will judge those engaged in social injustice.

The big picture. Amos was written by a prophet of the same name in 755 BC. He was a prophet to the northern kingdom of Israel (Amos 7:14-15), and focused on the rampant sin and social injustices of his day (5:24). During his time the land was prosperous, yet the rich did not aid the disadvantaged. He prophesied that a day of judgment was forthcoming (7:1–9:10). Not long after this, the Assyrians took the people into captivity.

Transformational truth. Because God cares for the poor, you and I must also care for them. Amos spoke against those "who oppress the poor and crush the needy" (Amos 4:1). God smiles upon those who help the poor.

A verse for meditation. "Listen to this message that the LORD has spoken against you, O people of Israel...'From among all the families on the earth, I have been intimate with you alone. That is why I must punish you for all your sins'" (Amos 3:1-2).

A question to ponder. Is there a Christian shelter or mission nearby where you might consider volunteering to help the poor and needy?

JUDGMENT IS IMMINENT

*Amos 7–9; 2 Kings 14:28-29; 15:6-29;
2 Chronicles 26:22-23; Isaiah 6:1-13*

Yesterday we considered God's care for the poor and the oppressed (Amos 1–6). Today we turn our attention toward imminent judgment.

Key concept. Judgment was coming in view of the people's unrepentant sin.

The big picture. Amos had five visions of judgment against his spiritually lethargic people in the northern kingdom—locust swarms (Amos 7:1-3), a consuming fire (7:4-6), a plumb line (7:7-17), a basket of summer fruit (8:1-14), and the Lord beside the altar (9:1-10). Each vision pointed to the catastrophic nature of the coming judgment. God also promised eventual restoration and blessing (9:13-15).

Transformational truth. By trade, Amos was a lowly shepherd and a dresser of fig trees. God often uses lowly servants in His work (1 Corinthians 1:26-27). David was a simple shepherd boy, but became king (2 Samuel 5). Peter was a simple fisherman, but became an apostle (Matthew 4:18-22). God can use you and me too!

A verse for meditation. "In that day I will restore the fallen house of David. I will repair its damaged walls. From the ruins I will rebuild it and restore its former glory" (Amos 9:11).

A question to ponder. What is the most important spiritual lesson you learn from the pages of Amos?

PAGANISM ENTRENCHED

2 Kings 15:32 – 16:9; 2 Chronicles 27:1 – 28:15;
Micah 1:1-16; Isaiah 7

Yesterday we focused on imminent judgment (Amos 7–9). Today we turn our attention to how entrenched paganism was in Judah, the southern kingdom.

Key concept. Paganism essentially remained unchallenged, even during the reign of a righteous king.

The big picture. Jotham was 25 years old when he became king of Judah. He reigned 16 years. While he pleased the Lord in some ways, he failed by not destroying pagan shrines. When he died, his son Ahaz became king at age 20 (2 Kings 15:32-38). He reigned for 16 years. He displeased the Lord, even sacrificing his son in a fire and offering sacrifices at pagan shrines (16:1-4).

Transformational truth. "Jotham did what was pleasing in the Lord's sight…But he did not destroy the pagan shrines, and the people still offered sacrifices and burned incense there" (2 Kings 15:34). God desires not *partial* obedience but *complete*. Meditate on Psalm 119:1-4.

A verse for meditation. [A prophecy of the Messiah:] "Look! The virgin will conceive a child! She will give birth to a son and will call him Immanuel (which means 'God is with us')" (Isaiah 7:14).

A question to ponder. What does Jesus's name, *Immanuel*, mean to you on a personal level?

JUDGMENT IS COMING

Isaiah 8 – 11

In the previous lesson we explored how entrenched paganism had become in the southern kingdom of Judah (2 Kings 15:32 – 16:9; Isaiah 7). Today we consider how judgment was imminent.

Key concept. Judgment was coming, but a remnant would survive — and there would be blessing and restoration in the end.

The big picture. Isaiah warned Judah of swift judgment should the people refuse to repent. They indeed failed to repent, and judgment fell. But God promised that a remnant would survive and be blessed (Isaiah 8 – 10). A future Messiah was also promised who would bring blessing and peace to the people (9; 11). His would be a perfect government.

Transformational truth. God's people were called to preserve "the teaching of God" and hand it down, generation by generation (Isaiah 8:16). You and I must do the same. We as Christian parents must pass God's truths from Scripture down to our children, just as they will one day pass it on to their children (see 2 Timothy 3:17; Deuteronomy 6:6-9).

A verse for meditation. [A prophecy of the Messiah:] "His government and its peace will never end. He will rule with fairness and justice from the throne of his ancestor David for all eternity" (Isaiah 9:7).

A question to ponder. Do you think it possible that the world will ever attain true and lasting peace without Christ being at the helm?

GOD'S RELENTLESS LOVE

Hosea 1 – 2; Isaiah 12:1-6; 17:1-14;
2 Chronicles 28:16-25; 29:1-2;
2 Kings 15:30-31; 16:10-18; 17:1-4; 18:1-8

Yesterday we considered how judgment was imminent (Isaiah 8 –11). Today we examine God's relentless love for His people.

Key concept. God loves His people, despite their spiritual infidelity.

The big picture. Hosea's prophetic ministry began to the northern kingdom of Israel in 753 BC. Hosea wrote his book during the closing days of Jeroboam II in about 710 BC. It depicts the heartfelt pain Hosea suffered at the unfaithfulness of his own wife Gomer. This, in turn, gave the prophet deep insight to the way God feels when His own people are unfaithful to Him (Hosea 2:2-5; 6:4-11; 8:1-14).

Transformational truth. Just as Gomer ran after other men, so Israel (the northern kingdom) ran after other gods (Hosea 1 – 2). And yet, just as Hosea chose to redeem Gomer, so God chose to redeem His people (see Romans 5:8).

A verse for meditation. "Go and marry a prostitute, so that some of her children will be conceived in prostitution. This will illustrate how Israel has acted like a prostitute by turning against the LORD and worshiping other gods" (Hosea 2:2).

A question to ponder. What "false gods" (or idols) might people turn to today in their infidelity to the Lord?

GOD'S AMAZING LOVE

Hosea 2:14 – 8:14

Yesterday we considered God's relentless love for His people (Hosea 1–2). Today we continue our study of God's love.

Key concept. God loves Israel, despite her perpetual unfaithfulness.

The big picture. Gomer was forced to sell herself as a bondservant, but Hosea was willing to redeem her (Hosea 3:1-3). God likewise continued to redeem Israel (3:4-5). Hosea 4–8 provides significant detail on Israel's ongoing infidelity and impending judgment.

Transformational truth. Hosea declared, "There is no faithfulness, no kindness, no knowledge of God in your land" (Hosea 4:1). Because there was no knowledge of God, sin was running rampant and Hosea's people were on the fast track to judgment. Hosea also proclaimed, "My people are being destroyed because they don't know me" (Hosea 4:6). The priests were not ministering God's Word to the people, and ended up on a fast slide into the gutter, morally speaking.

A verse for meditation. "Then the LORD said to me, 'Go and love your wife again, even though she commits adultery with another lover. This will illustrate that the LORD still loves Israel, even though the people have turned to other gods and love to worship them'" (Hosea 3:1).

A question to ponder. Does God's relentless love *for you* motivate your fidelity toward Him?

PUNISHMENT FOLLOWED BY RESTORATION

Hosea 9 – 14

Yesterday we continued our study of God's love (Hosea 2:14 – 8:14). Today we consider how God's judgment will be followed by restoration.

Key concept. Bad times were coming. But God hadn't forgotten His people. Good times would one day return.

The big picture. God provided details about His impending judgment against Israel (Hosea 9:1 – 10:15). He then spoke of His great love for Israel (11:1-12). Judgment was coming, but God would not abandon His people. While Israel's history was permeated with examples of infidelity (12:1 – 13:6), God nevertheless promised to restore His people in the future (14:1-9).

Transformational truth. Hosea 10:2 reveals, "The hearts of the people are fickle." The Amplified Bible renders this, "Their heart is divided (faithless)." A divided heart will always lead to a downfall. God is looking for people whose hearts are totally committed to Him (see Psalm 119). It is only total commitment that will bring God's complete blessing.

A verse for meditation. "Come, let us return to the LORD. He has torn us to pieces; now he will heal us. He has injured us; now he will bandage our wounds. In just a short time he will restore us, so that we may live in his presence" (Hosea 6:1-2).

A question to ponder. Do you ever struggle with a divided heart in your relationship with God?

SIN AND CAPTIVITY

Isaiah 1:1-20; 28; 2 Kings 17:5-41; 18:9-12

In the previous lesson we explored how God's judgment will be followed by restoration (Hosea 9–14). Today we consider how unrepentant sin yields captivity.

Key concept. As promised in God's covenant with the Israelites, unrepentant sin results in captivity.

The big picture. In Deuteronomy, God promised, through Moses, great blessings if the Israelites lived in obedience to the covenant. God also warned that if they disobeyed His commands, they would experience the punishments listed in the covenant—including exile from the land (Deuteronomy 28:15-68). Old Testament history is replete with illustrations of how unfaithful the Israelites were. They would soon be taken captive by Assyria.

Transformational truth. In 2 Kings 17:33 we read of those who "though they worshiped the LORD, they continued to follow their own gods according to the religious customs of the nations from which they came." What absolute folly! What an insult to the one true God (Deuteronomy 5:29; 6:13; Job 28:28; Psalm 111:10; Proverbs 1:7; 3:7; 8:13; 16:6; Ecclesiastes 12:13).

A verse for meditation. "Again and again the LORD had sent his prophets and seers to warn both Israel and Judah…But the Israelites would not listen" (2 Kings 17:13-14).

A question to ponder. Why do you think the Israelites were so stubborn in their folly?

JUDGMENT PRECEDES BLESSING

Isaiah 1:21-31; 2 – 5

Yesterday we considered how unrepentant sin yields captivity (Isaiah 1:1-20; 28; 2 Kings 17:5-41; 18:9-12). Today we focus on how God's present judgment precedes His future blessing.

Key concept. God's blessing will come following His judgment.

The big picture. Isaiah foresaw the distant eschatological future when Christ's perfect kingdom of peace will be established (Isaiah 2:1-4; 4:2-6). Isaiah also foresaw the judgment of rebellious sinners—both in his time (3:1–4:1) and in the future (2:5-22). Judah is metaphorically viewed as a vineyard which—despite fertile soil and careful cultivation—has failed to produce the desired fruit (5).

Transformational truth. God was grieved by His people's moral degradation, social injustice, and religious hypocrisy. Isaiah warned Judah of swift judgment should they refuse to repent (Isaiah 2–5). They did indeed refuse, and judgment fell, as promised. If there's one thing we witness in Isaiah, it's that God blesses obedience and punishes disobedience.

A verse for meditation. "Tell the godly that all will be well for them. They will enjoy the rich reward they have earned! But the wicked are doomed, for they will get exactly what they deserve" (Isaiah 3:10-11).

A question to ponder. Why do you think some of God's people choose to ignore His warnings and promises?

GOD THE DIVINE JUDGE

Isaiah 13 – 16; 2 Kings 16:19-20; 2 Chronicles 28:26-27

Yesterday we considered how God's present judgment precedes His future blessing (Isaiah 1:21-31; 2 – 5). Today we consider how God judges both humans and fallen angels.

Key concept. God is both the Judge of human beings and fallen angels.

The big picture. God is the Judge of the whole earth. God's judgment will extend far beyond Israel and Judah to include many of the nations around them. This includes God's judgments against Babylon (13:1 –14:23), Assyria (14:24-27), Philistia (14:28-32), Moab (15:1 –16:14), and others.

Transformational truth. Isaiah 14:4-11 reveals that Lucifer became prideful and sought exaltation and godhood for himself. He became corrupt, and his name changed to Satan (meaning "adversary"). One third of the angelic realm apparently followed him in rebellion (Revelation 12:4). God cast Lucifer/Satan to the earth in judgment. Today, Satan and demons stand against Christians in a variety of ways (Matthew 13:38-39; Acts 5:3; 1 Corinthians 7:5; Ephesians 2:1-3; 6:11-12). Christian beware!

A verse for meditation. "For you [Lucifer] said to yourself, 'I will ascend to heaven…and be like the Most High'" (Isaiah 14:13-14).

A question to ponder. Do you daily make efforts to "resist the devil" so that he will "flee from you" (James 4:7)?

HEZEKIAH'S REVIVAL

2 Chronicles 29:3 – 31:21

Yesterday we looked at how God judges both humans and fallen angels (Isaiah 13–16). Today we consider how Hezekiah brought revival to the people of the southern kingdom of Judah.

Key concept. Hezekiah brought about major reforms and revival for his people.

The big picture. Hezekiah ordered the priests to restore and purify God's temple because it had been desecrated during the reign of his father Ahaz. He then led the people in rededicating the temple (2 Chronicles 29:3-31). The celebration of the Passover was reinstated (30:1-27), and pagan altars and idols were destroyed throughout the land (31:1). Hezekiah then ordered his people to bring first fruits and offerings to make provisions for the priests and Levites (31:2-21).

Transformational truth. Second Chronicles summarizes Jehoshaphat's revival (17:1-19), Hezekiah's revival (29:1–31:21), and Josiah's reforms (34:1-13). God's people were up and down, up and down—a spiritual revival followed by spiritual decline, on and on. This can be true of us as individuals as well—up and down, up and down. *Let's seek consistency with the Lord!*

A verse for meditation. "Listen to me, you Levites! Purify yourselves, and purify the Temple of the LORD, the God of your ancestors. Remove all the defiled things from the sanctuary" (2 Chronicles 29:5).

A question to ponder. What do you think might bring about *continuous* revival in our lives?

SOME PROVERBS OF SOLOMON

Proverbs 25 – 29

In the previous lesson we explored how Hezekiah brought revival to his people (2 Chronicles 29:3 – 31:21). Today we consider some proverbs of Solomon that guide us in relating to others.

Key concept. Solomon provides wisdom on relationships.

The big picture. Solomon composed his proverbs between 970 and 931 BC. King Hezekiah's scribes compiled Solomon's proverbs for the book of Proverbs from 729 to 686 BC. Today's reading provides wisdom on relating to others—including kings, neighbors, unreliable people, enemies, quarrelsome spouses, fools, sluggards, friends, and gossipers (Proverbs 25:1 – 26:28). We also find tidbits of wisdom on life (27:1-27), the law (28:1-10), wealth (28:11-28), and stubbornness (29:1-27).

Transformational truth. Death could come at any time. Solomon thus urges, "Don't brag about tomorrow, since you don't know what the day will bring" (Proverbs 27:1; compare with Luke 12:16-21). This reminds us of James 4:14: "How do you know what your life will be like tomorrow? Your life is like the morning fog—it's here a little while, then it's gone." We ought to live with eternity in view (Colossians 3:1-2).

A verse for meditation. "People who conceal their sins will not prosper, but if they confess and turn from them, they will receive mercy" (Proverbs 28:13).

A question to ponder. Does your mortality motivate you to maintain an eternal perspective?

A VIRTUOUS AND CAPABLE WIFE

Proverbs 30 – 31

Yesterday we considered some proverbs that guide us in relating to others (Proverbs 25 – 29). Today we will focus on the virtuous and capable wife.

Key concept. A virtuous wife is more precious than rubies.

The big picture. The book of Proverbs closes with wisdom from Agur (Proverbs 30:1-33) and Lemuel (31:1-9). Then we come to a great description of the good and capable wife in Proverbs 31:10-31.

Transformational truth. The virtuous wife is resourceful and hardworking, and takes care of her husband and household. She values inner virtue more than external beauty. "When she speaks, her words are wise, and she gives instructions with kindness. She carefully watches everything in her household and suffers nothing from laziness" (Proverbs 31:26-27).

A verse for meditation. "Who can find a virtuous and capable wife? She is more precious than rubies. Her husband can trust her, and she will greatly enrich his life. She brings him good, not harm, all the days of her life" (Proverbs 31:10-12).

A question to ponder. Can you see the wisdom of involving God (by prayer) in the selection of your future spouse?

YEARNING FOR GOD

Psalms 42 – 46

Yesterday we considered the good and virtuous wife (Proverbs 30 – 31). Today we turn our attention to the psalmist's yearning for God.

Key concept. The psalmist yearned to return to Jerusalem's temple and enjoy God.

The big picture. Psalms 42 and 43 are parts 1 and 2 of a beautiful poem in which the psalmist—apparently away from Jerusalem—yearned to return to Jerusalem's temple and enjoy God's presence there. In Psalm 44, the Israelites recall God's past acts of deliverance as they bring before Him a present need for deliverance. Psalm 45 is a royal wedding psalm, while Psalm 46 is a psalm of trust and thanksgiving celebrating the God of Israel.

Transformational truth. Those who are rightly related to God yearn for His presence (Psalm 42:1). The psalmist elsewhere affirmed, "O God, you are my God; I earnestly search for you. My soul thirsts for you; my whole body longs for you in this parched and weary land where there is no water" (63:1). He asked, "Whom have I in heaven but you? I desire you more than anything on earth" (73:25).

A verse for meditation. "As the deer longs for streams of water, so I long for you, O God" (Psalm 42:1).

A question to ponder. What kinds of circumstances cause you to yearn most for God?

GOD IS SOVEREIGN

Psalms 47 – 49; 84 – 85; 87

Yesterday we focused on the psalmist's yearning for God (Psalms 42 – 46). Today we consider God's sovereignty.

Key concept. God is sovereign over all things.

The big picture. Psalm 47 celebrates God's sovereign kingship over all the earth. Psalm 48 praises God for His greatness. Psalm 49 speaks of the folly of trusting in the temporal pleasures of riches instead of the everlasting blessings of God. Psalm 84 addresses the joy of being in God's presence in Jerusalem's temple. Psalm 85 recalls God's past faithfulness, states the present distress of God's people, and expresses hope in God's future deliverance. Psalm 87 focuses on the wondrous city of Jerusalem.

Transformational truth. God is sovereign over all the earth. Psalm 47:7-8 tells us, "God is the King over all the earth...God reigns above the nations, sitting on his holy throne." The psalmist elsewhere stated that "the LORD has made the heavens his throne; from there he rules over everything" (Psalm 103:19).

A verse for meditation. "The LORD Most High is awesome. He is the great King of all the earth" (Psalm 47:2).

A question to ponder. Does it give you a sense of security to know that God is the great King of all the earth?

MEDITATION ON GOD'S WORD

Psalms 1 – 2; 10; 33; 71; 91

In the previous lesson we explored God's sovereignty (Psalms 47 – 49; 84 – 85; 87). Today we consider the joys of meditating on God's Word.

Key concept. Meditating on God's Word yields a joyful spiritual experience.

The big picture. Psalm 1 reveals that those who meditate on and obey God's Word are blessed. Psalm 2 speaks of the supreme messianic King. Psalm 10 is a lament psalm that appeals to God to bring deliverance from the wicked. Psalm 33 calls on the righteous to praise the Lord. Psalm 71 is a cry for help, and Psalm 91 expresses trust in God's love and protection.

Transformational truth. Meditating on God's Word yields a joyful spiritual life (Psalm 1:2). The Hebrew word translated "meditate" often carries the basic idea of "murmuring." When one meditates on God's Word and His character, it's possible to concentrate so intensely that murmuring of the lips can occur.

A verse for meditation. "Oh, the joys of those who do not follow the advice of the wicked, or stand around with sinners, or join in with mockers. But they delight in the law of the LORD, meditating on it day and night" (Psalm 1:1-2).

A question to ponder. Would you say you're more of a *reader* of God's Word or a *meditator* on God's Word? Or perhaps both?

THE BOOMERANG EFFECT

Psalms 92 – 97

Yesterday we considered the joys of meditating on God's Word (Psalms 1 – 2). Today we look at the "boomerang effect."

Key concept. We reap what we sow.

The big picture. Psalm 92 offers thanks to God for His judgment of the wicked. Psalm 93 exults in God as sovereign King. Psalm 94 affirms there will be ultimate retribution against the wicked. Psalm 95 is a call to praise and worship God. Psalm 96 is a call to praise the Lord, worship Him, and rejoice in Him. Psalm 97 speaks of God as the supreme and exalted King of the universe.

Transformational truth. Psalm 94:23 affirms that "God will turn the sins of evil people back on them." Scripture consistently emphasizes that God allows the wicked to fall into the traps they themselves set for others. "If you set a trap for others, you will get caught in it yourself" (Proverbs 26:27). This is an example of the boomerang effect (Obadiah 1:15; Galatians 6:7).

A verse for meditation. "Come, let us worship and bow down. Let us kneel before the LORD our maker, for he is our God. We are the people he watches over, the flock under his care" (Psalm 95:6-7).

A question to ponder. Do you know any people who have experienced the boomerang effect?

THANKSGIVING TO GOD

Psalms 98 – 100; 102; 104

Yesterday we gave attention to the boomerang effect (Psalms 92 – 97). Today we consider thanksgiving to God.

Key concept. We ought always to be thankful to God.

The big picture. Psalm 98 praises God as Deliverer, King, and Ruler. Psalm 99 celebrates God's majestic kingship. Psalm 100 calls on all people to praise and worship God. Psalm 102 is a prayer in the midst of distress, all the while trusting in God's sovereign purposes. Psalm 104 celebrates how God is worthy of praise as Creator and Ruler of the earth.

Transformational truth. The psalmist urges, "Enter his gates with thanksgiving; go into his courts with praise. Give thanks to him and praise his name" (Psalm 100:4). Thankfulness is a common theme in the Psalms. We are to give thanks forever (30:12) and honor God with thanksgiving (69:30). We are to come before Him with thanksgiving (95:2), and even offer a sacrifice of thanksgiving (116:17). This is also a New Testament emphasis. We should always give thanks to God (Ephesians 5:20), and even overflow with thanksgiving (Colossians 2:7).

A verse for meditation. "Acknowledge that the LORD is God! He made us, and we are his. We are his people, the sheep of his pasture" (Psalm 100:3).

A question to ponder. What blessings can you thank God for today?

GOD'S WONDROUS WORKS

Psalms 105–106

Yesterday we considered thanksgiving to God (Psalms 98–100; 102; 104). Today we look at God's wondrous works among His people.

Key concept. Despite the many sins of God's people, He continues to do wondrous works among them.

The big picture. Psalm 105 is a call to praise in view of God's wondrous works among the Israelites. Included are summaries of Joseph's life and his rise to power in Egypt, Moses and his role in delivering Israel, God's care for the Israelites during the wilderness sojourn, and the entrance into Canaan. Psalm 106 is primarily a lament psalm depicting Israel's many sins, including murmuring during the wilderness sojourn, worship of the golden calf, participating in pagan worship, and continued disobedience upon entering Canaan.

Transformational truth. The psalmist exulted, "I will sing to the LORD as long as I live" (Psalm 104:33). Singing is often a great way of expressing praise. Psalm 69:30 says, "I will praise God's name with singing." Psalm 95:2 says, "Let us sing psalms of praise to him." We see the same thing in the New Testament (Ephesians 5:19-20).

A verse for meditation. "O LORD, what a variety of things you have made! In wisdom you have made them all. The earth is full of your creatures" (Psalm 104:24).

A question to ponder. What is your favorite praise song? Why not sing it now?

GOD'S WONDROUS WORKS

Psalms 107; 111–114

I n the previous lesson we explored God's wondrous works among His people (Psalms 105–106). More of the same today.

Key concept. God has done mighty and wondrous works throughout Israel's history.

The big picture. Psalm 107 presents four word pictures of deliverance. In each word picture, a problem is presented, the people pray, after which God renders help, and God is praised for His deliverance. Psalm 111 exhorts people to praise God because of His mighty works. Psalm 112 contrasts the blessings of the righteous with the woes of the wicked. Psalm 113 is another call to praise God. Psalm 114 commemorates God's mighty deeds during the exodus from Egypt.

Transformational truth. The psalmist affirmed, "Good comes to those who lend money generously" (Psalm 112:5). This is a common emphasis in Scripture. Proverbs 22:9 tells us that the generous man is blessed. The godly always give generous loans (Psalm 37:26; see also Romans 12:8; Ephesians 4:28).

A verse for meditation. "How joyful are those who fear the LORD and delight in obeying his commands" (Psalm 112:1).

A question to ponder. Do you think God's generosity toward us can serve as a motivation for us to be generous toward others?

LET US PRAISE AND THANK GOD

Psalms 115 – 118

Yesterday we continued our study of God's mighty works among His people (Psalms 107; 111–114). Today we see again how God is worthy of praise and thanksgiving.

Key concept. Praise and thanksgiving are rightly due to God for His wondrous deliverances and blessings.

The big picture. Psalm 115 contrasts the one true sovereign God of the universe with impotent earthly idols. Psalm 116 is a psalm of thanksgiving for the Lord's many deliverances in the midst of distressing situations. Psalm 117 is a simple call to praise. Psalm 118 is a psalm of thanksgiving to be sung as worshippers enter into the temple.

Transformational truth. The psalmist affirmed, "Not to us, O Lord, not to us, but to your name goes all the glory for your unfailing love and faithfulness" (Psalm 115:1). Human beings often love to hog the glory to make themselves look good before others. But God's glory belongs to Him alone. God affirmed, "I am the Lord; that is my name! I will not give my glory to anyone else" (Isaiah 42:8).

A verse for meditation. "This is the day the Lord has made. We will rejoice and be glad in it" (Psalm 118:24).

A question to ponder. How might your life change if you resolved to "rejoice and be glad" each new morning you wake up?

THE BLESSINGS OF GOD'S WORD

Psalm 119

Yesterday we considered how God is worthy of praise and thanksgiving (Psalms 115–118). Today we survey the many blessings of God's Word.

Key concept. God's Word blesses us in countless ways.

The big picture. Psalm 119 points to the numerous blessings of God's Word. This psalm is formatted as an alphabetic acrostic in which each stanza of eight verses is devoted to successive letters of the Hebrew alphabet. Such was considered an effective learning tool among the Hebrews.

Transformational truth. Psalm 119 is brimming with helpful spiritual gems. For example, God can use personal suffering to draw us closer to His Word: "I used to wander off until you disciplined me; but now I closely follow your word" (Psalm 119:67). The psalmist also affirmed, "My suffering was good for me, for it taught me to pay attention to your decrees" (119:71). A renewed commitment to God's Word can, in turn, reduce sin in our lives: "I have hidden your word in my heart, that I might not sin against you" (119:11). "How can a young person stay pure? By obeying your word" (119:9).

A verse for meditation. "Oh, that my actions would consistently reflect your decrees! Then I will not be ashamed when I compare my life with your commands" (Psalm 119:5-6).

A question to ponder. Can you think of a time in your life during which personal suffering caused you to recommit yourself to God's Word?

GOD OUR DELIVERER

Psalms 120 – 121; 123; 125 – 126

Yesterday we considered the blessings of God's Word (Psalm 119). Today we shift attention to God our Deliverer.

Key concept. God delivers and rescues His people.

The big picture. Psalm 120 is a lament psalm seeking God's deliverance as well as retribution upon enemies. Psalm 121 affirms that help comes from the Lord who "never slumbers or sleeps" (121:4). Psalm 123 is a prayer for deliverance. Psalm 125 is a song of trust affirming the security of God's people. Psalm 126 portrays the joy of restoration.

Transformational truth. The psalmist was a believer in prayer: "I took my troubles to the LORD; I cried out to him, and he answered my prayer" (Psalm 120:1). The psalmist made specific requests of God. Likewise, in the Lord's Prayer we are exhorted to pray for our daily needs (Matthew 6:11). The apostle Paul urged, "Don't worry about anything; instead, pray about everything. Tell God what you need, and thank him for all he has done" (Philippians 4:6).

A verse for meditation. "The LORD keeps you from all harm and watches over your life. The LORD keeps watch over you as you come and go, both now and forever" (Psalm 121:7-8).

A question to ponder. Are there any specific needs you need to bring before God today in prayer?

THANKS BE TO GOD

Psalms 128 – 130; 132; 134 – 135

In the previous lesson we explored God our Deliverer (Psalms 120 – 121; 123; 125 – 126). Today we again consider thanksgiving and praise to God, despite a painful past.

Key concept. There is much to be thankful for, no matter what happened in the past.

The big picture. Psalm 128 addresses the blessings of both home and community. Psalm 129 is a psalm of thanksgiving. Psalm 130 is a lament about Israel's enemies and Israel's future hope. Psalm 132 recalls David bringing the Ark of the Covenant to Jerusalem and reaffirms the Davidic covenant. Psalm 134 calls on the priests to bless the Lord. Psalm 135 is an anthology of praise.

Transformational truth. It is a wonderful thing to be forgiven of our sins by the Lord. The psalmist affirmed, "LORD, if you kept a record of our sins, who, O Lord, could ever survive? But you offer forgiveness" (Psalm 130:3-4). The psalmist elsewhere wrote, "He has removed our sins as far from us as the east is from the west" (103:12). "Oh, what joy for those…whose sin is put out of sight" (32:1).

A verse for meditation. "The LORD does whatever pleases him throughout all heaven and earth" (Psalm 135:6).

A question to ponder. Have you anchored your spiritual life on God's complete forgiveness of your sins?

PRAISE GOD

Psalms 136; 146–150

Yesterday we considered praise and thanksgiving to God (Psalms 128–130). Today we look at further reasons to praise God.

Key concept. God is truly worthy of our continued praise.

The big picture. Psalm 136 points to the evidences for God's steadfast love. Psalms 146 and 147 list reasons to praise God's greatness and graciousness. Psalm 148 is a call for the heavens and the earth to praise God. Psalm 149 is a summons to praise and a song of triumph. Psalm 150 is a final doxology of praise.

Transformational truth. The psalmist proclaimed, "How great is our Lord! His power is absolute! His understanding is beyond comprehension!" (Psalm 147:5). Our God is *omnipotent* (all-powerful) and *omniscient* (all-knowing). One great fact about God's omniscience is that when we trusted in Him for salvation, He was fully aware of every sin we had ever committed and ever would commit in the future. (He had no later regrets.) And one wonderful truth about His omnipotence is that He has the power to keep us saved (John 10:27-28).

A verse for meditation. "I will praise the LORD as long as I live. I will sing praises to my God with my dying breath" (Psalm 146:2).

A question to ponder. Does God's omnipotence and omniscience give you a sense of security in your salvation?

GOD DENOUNCES MULTIPLE SINFUL NATIONS

Isaiah 19 – 23

Yesterday we considered reasons for praising God (Psalms 136; 146–150). Today we return to the book of Isaiah and survey God's denunciations of multiple sinful nations.

Key concept. God denounced multiple nations for their relentless sins.

The big picture. After denouncing Judah (Isaiah 1:1–12:6), Isaiah proclaimed a series of oracles against other nations—including Babylon (13:1–14:23), Assyria (14:24-27), Philistia (14:28-32), Moab (15:1–16:14), Damascus (Syria) and her ally, Israel (17:1-14), Ethiopia (18:1-7), Egypt (19:1–20:6), Babylon (21:1-10), Edom (21:11-12), Arabia (21:13-17), Jerusalem (22:1-25), and Tyre (23:1-18).

Transformational truth. Egypt was well known for its many "wise counselors" (Isaiah 19:11). In reality, however, they were all deceived and full of foolishness. True wisdom comes from God. And God will give us wisdom if we simply ask Him for it (James 1:5; see also 1 Kings 3:9; 2 Chronicles 1:10; Psalm 27:11; 119:12,18,34,125; 2 Timothy 2:7).

A verse for meditation. "The LORD said, 'My servant Isaiah has been walking around naked and barefoot for the last three years. This is a sign—a symbol of the terrible troubles I will bring upon Egypt and Ethiopia'" (Isaiah 20:3).

A question to ponder. Are you presently facing difficult circumstances for which you could use God's wisdom?

JUDAH'S IMPENDING CAPTIVITY

Isaiah 24 – 27; 29

Yesterday we looked at God's denunciation of multiple nations (Isaiah 19 – 23). Today we consider Judah's future captivity in Babylon.

Key concept. Judah in the not-too-distant future would suffer captivity in Babylon that would last for 70 years. (Isaiah's prophetic ministry began in 740 BC and ended in 680 BC, long before the Babylonian captivity began in 605 BC. Isaiah was speaking *prophetically* of the future captivity and the survival of a remnant.)

The big picture. The nation of Judah, because of its continued unrepentant idolatry, would go into captivity in Babylon for 70 years. Nations around Judah would also fall to Babylon (Isaiah 25). Isaiah spoke of the prophet Jeremiah proclaiming that Jerusalem would fall because of sin. Judah's leaders resented Jeremiah and tried to have him executed (26). Jeremiah informed the people that their only hope was unconditional surrender to Babylon (27). Jeremiah later wrote a letter to Jewish captives already in Babylon, and told them to make the best of a bad situation (29). (There were three deportations involved in Babylon's captivity of Judah—605 BC, 597 BC, and 586 BC. Jeremiah apparently wrote a letter to those who became captive in the first wave.)

Transformational truth. God's judgment gets especially intense in Isaiah 24. But this one chapter on judgment is followed by three chapters on God's salvation and restoration (25 – 27). Joy awaits God's people on the other side of judgment (48:1-28). Many believe these chapters refer to the future seven-year tribulation period (judgment) followed by Christ's 1,000-year millennial kingdom (joy). What a day that will be!

A verse for meditation. "You will keep in perfect peace all who trust in you, all whose thoughts are fixed on you!" (Isaiah 26:3).

A question to ponder. Have you ever experienced "perfect peace"? How can it be found?

RESTORATION TO THE PROMISED LAND

Isaiah 30 – 33

I n the previous lesson we explored Judah's impending captivity in Babylon (Isaiah 24 – 27; 29). Today we consider how, following the captivity that will last 70 years, a remnant will be restored to the Promised Land.

Key concept. Restoration follows judgment.

The big picture. Isaiah prophesied that despite the punishment that Judah would endure in the Babylonian captivity, a remnant would survive and later be restored to the Promised Land. Even later, God would initiate a new covenant that would provide for the forgiveness of sins (Jeremiah 31:31-40). So confident was Jeremiah that a remnant would be restored that he purchased some land in Anathoth, his hometown (32:1-44). Isaiah 33 reminds the people that a descendant of David would one day rule on the throne of David in Judah (2 Samuel 7:12-16).

Transformational truth. People don't like to hear bad news—such as the warning of impending captivity in Babylon. In Isaiah's time, they said, "Tell us nice things. Tell us lies. Forget all this gloom. Get off your narrow path" (Isaiah 30:10-11). But it's better to hear the truth and face reality. It is foolish to build one's life on falsehoods and wishful thinking.

A verse for meditation. "Only in returning to me and resting in me will you be saved" (Isaiah 30:15).

A question to ponder. Do you ever resist hearing uncomfortable truths?

RESTORATION TO THE PROMISED LAND

Isaiah 34 – 35; Micah 2 – 5

Yesterday we considered how a remnant would be restored to the Promised Land following captivity (Isaiah 30 – 33). More of the same today.

Key concept. A remnant will survive captivity and go back to the Promised Land.

The big picture. Isaiah prophesied again that despite the devastating judgment that would come in the Babylonian captivity (Isaiah 34), the exiles would experience a refinement of their faith and eventually be released to return to the Promised Land. Isaiah therefore urged, "Say to those with fearful hearts, 'Be strong, and do not fear, for your God… is coming to save you'" (Isaiah 35:4).

Transformational truth. Micah—long before the Babylonian captivity began—warned of God's judgment on the rich and powerful leaders of Judah and Israel (both the southern and northern kingdoms) for their greed, oppression, and exploitation of the poor (Micah 2:2). One lesson these leaders would soon learn was that there is a direct cause-and-effect relationship between sins of injustice and God's just judgment.

A verse for meditation. [A messianic prophecy:] "When he comes, he will open the eyes of the blind and unplug the ears of the deaf. The lame will leap like a deer, and those who cannot speak will sing for joy!" (Isaiah 35:5-6).

A question to ponder. Are you ever outraged at sins of greed, exploitation, and injustice among the rich and powerful in our own day?

SENNACHERIB'S INTIMIDATION TACTICS

*Isaiah 36; Micah 6 – 7;
2 Chronicles 32:1 – 8; 2 Kings 18:13 – 37*

Yesterday we gave attention to how a remnant will be restored to the Promised Land after the Babylonian captivity (Isaiah 34 – 35). Today we consider Sennacherib and his intimidation tactics against Hezekiah, king of Judah (the southern kingdom) in 701 BC.

Key concept. Sennacherib and his Assyrian army engaged in psychological warfare against Hezekiah.

The big picture. Sennacherib and his army were outside of Jerusalem's walls. He tried to engage in psychological warfare prior to actual physical warfare. He sent a message to Hezekiah not only mocking Judah's ally, Egypt, but also mocking God's capacity to stop an invasion (Isaiah 36).

Transformational truth. Sennacherib was trying to mess with Hezekiah's mind prior to Assyria's physical invasion into Judah. If he succeeded, he might have gained a psychological advantage. When threatened, you and I should never be intimated. As 2 Timothy 1:7 puts it, "God has not given us a spirit of fear and timidity, but of power, love, and self-discipline."

A verse for meditation. [Sennacherib taunted those in Jerusalem:] "Don't let Hezekiah deceive you. He will never be able to rescue you. Don't let him fool you into trusting in the Lord by saying, 'The LORD will surely rescue us. This city will never fall into the hands of the Assyrian king!'" (Isaiah 36:14-15). (See Day 207 for God's response.)

A question to ponder. How do you normally respond when someone tries to intimidate you?

GOD'S RESPONSE
TO SENNACHERIB

Isaiah 37; 2 Kings 19; 2 Chronicles 32:9-23

Yesterday we read about Sennacherib's intimidation tactics against Hezekiah and Jerusalem's inhabitants (Isaiah 36). Today we consider God's response to Sennacherib's blasphemy.

Key concept. Judgment fell upon Sennacherib's army overnight.

The big picture. In view of Sennacherib's taunting, Hezekiah asked Isaiah to pray. Isaiah urged Hezekiah not to worry because God had heard Sennacherib's blasphemy. The angel of the Lord promptly killed 185,000 Assyrian warriors in a single night (Isaiah 37:36).

Transformational truth. Sennacherib defied the living God. He taunted, "Don't let Hezekiah deceive you…Don't let him fool you into trusting in the LORD…Have the gods of other nations rescued them?" (Isaiah 36:15; 37:12). Hezekiah appealed directly to God: "You alone are God of all the kingdoms of the earth…Bend down, O LORD, and listen!…Listen to Sennacherib's words of defiance against the living God" (37:16-17). God responded. Sennacherib didn't stand a chance.

A verse for meditation. "That night the angel of the LORD went out to the Assyrian camp and killed 185,000 Assyrian soldiers. When the surviving Assyrians woke up the next morning, they found corpses everywhere. Then King Sennacherib of Assyria broke camp and returned to his own land" (Isaiah 37:36).

A question to ponder. Have you ever been ridiculed for trusting God in the face of an overwhelmingly difficult circumstance?

GOD EXTENDS HEZEKIAH'S LIFE

Isaiah 38 – 39; 2 Kings 20:1-19; 2 Chronicles 32:24-31

In the previous lesson we witnessed God's response to Sennacherib's blasphemy (Isaiah 37). Today we consider how God extended Hezekiah's life.

Key concept. God granted Hezekiah several more years of life.

The big picture. Isaiah informed Hezekiah that his end was near. Hezekiah went to God in humble prayer, and God granted him an additional 15 years of life (Isaiah 38). Once in good health, he erred in naively showing kindness and accommodation to a royal emissary from Babylon—a nation that would soon attack Judah (39).

Transformational truth. After being informed that his life would soon end, Hezekiah prayed: "Remember, O LORD, how I have always been faithful to you and have served you single-mindedly, always doing what pleases you" (Isaiah 38:3). The Lord responded: "I have heard your prayer and seen your tears. I will add fifteen years to your life" (38:5). *God answers prayer* (James 4:2; Philippians 4:6-7)!

A verse for meditation. "Lord, your discipline is good, for it leads to life and health. You restore my health and allow me to live!" (Isaiah 38:16).

A question to ponder. Do you think Hezekiah's situation was unique, or do you think God might extend other people's lives today in answer to prayer?

THE REMNANT WILL BE RESCUED FOLLOWING CAPTIVITY

Isaiah 40 – 44:5

Yesterday we considered how God extended Hezekiah's life (Isaiah 38 – 39). Today we focus on God's rescue of the future remnant in captivity.

Key concept. God will make sure the remnant survives.

The big picture. Isaiah prophesied that God would engineer captivity as a discipline; He would also engineer the exiles' return to the Promised Land (Isaiah 40). God always rescues those who trust Him (41). Isaiah 42 prophetically fast-forwards to the more distant prophetic future and speaks of a coming "Servant"—ultimately fulfilled in the coming of Jesus the Messiah. Isaiah then summarized God's relentless love toward Israel (43 – 44:5).

Transformational truth. Isaiah 40:11 pictures God as a gentle and caring Shepherd who holds His sheep close to Himself and nourishes them. This reminds us of Jesus, the Good Shepherd: "I am the good shepherd; I know my own sheep, and they know me" (John 10:14). Here's an important lesson: It's always in the sheep's best interest to stay near the shepherd.

A verse for meditation. "Even youths will become weak and tired, and young men will fall in exhaustion. But those who trust in the LORD will find new strength. They will soar high on wings like eagles" (Isaiah 40:30-31).

A question to ponder. Why do you suppose God compares His people to sheep?

GOD'S PURPOSE FOR
THE COMING CAPTIVITY

Isaiah 44:6 – 48:11

Yesterday we considered God's rescue of the future remnant in captivity (Isaiah 40 – 44:5). Today we look at God's purpose for allowing the captivity.

Key concept. God allows the Babylonian captivity as a means of refining His people.

The big picture. Isaiah 44 presents God as sovereign over Israel's past and future. Isaiah prophesied that the Persian king Cyrus would be God's chosen instrument in destroying Babylon, and releasing the people from captivity so they could return home and rebuild their temple (45). God's people were urged to remain confident that He would care for them in the future (46). God would judge the Babylonians without mercy because they themselves showed no mercy (47). God would purposely allow this time of captivity in Babylon to refine His people and purge them of idolatry (Isaiah 48:1-11).

Transformational truth. God often affirmed that He alone is deity: "I am the First and the Last; there is no other God" (Isaiah 44:6). "Is there any other God? No!" (44:8). "I am the LORD; there is no other God" (45:5). *Let's serve Him alone* (see Jeremiah 9:24).

A verse for meditation. "I am God, and there is none like me. Only I can tell you the future before it even happens" (Isaiah 46:9-10).

A question to ponder. Why do you think some Israelites held on to idolatry even in the face of God's multiple pronouncements that He alone is God?

DELIVERANCE AND JOY

Isaiah 48:12 – 52:12

Yesterday we read about God's purpose for the Babylonian captivity (Isaiah 44:6 – 48:11). Today we consider the joy that will result upon release from captivity.

Key concept. Release from captivity will be celebrated with great joy.

The big picture. Despite Israel's stubborn unbelief, Isaiah prophesied that God, in the future, would free His people from Babylon for His own glory (Isaiah 48:12-22). Looking to the more distant prophetic future, Isaiah revealed that the Lord's Servant—the divine Messiah—would save His despairing people with a salvation available to everyone, Jew and Gentile (49:1 – 50:3). This salvation will last forever (50:4 – 52:12).

Transformational truth. In Isaiah 48:20 we read, "Be free from your captivity! Leave Babylon and the Babylonians." Following their future release from captivity, the people would shout for joy. Are you a captive to a sin, a bad habit, or a bad attitude? Trust the Lord to deliver you, and you too will soon be shouting for joy (Luke 4:18).

A verse for meditation. "I am the LORD your God, who teaches you what is good for you and leads you along the paths you should follow. Oh, that you had listened to my commands! Then you would have had peace flowing like a gentle river and righteousness rolling over you like waves in the sea" (Isaiah 48:17-18).

A question to ponder. Do God's words in Isaiah 48:17-18 motivate you to stay on His chosen paths?

YAHWEH'S SUFFERING SERVANT

Isaiah 52:13 – 57:21

In the previous lesson we explored the joy that results upon release from captivity (Isaiah 48:12 – 52:12). Today we consider how Yahweh's Suffering Servant — Jesus Christ — will bring full salvation.

Key concept. Yahweh's Servant will bring a complete salvation for all people.

The big picture. Yahweh's Servant is a suffering Savior — "a man of sorrows, acquainted with deepest grief" (Isaiah 53:3). This is a messianic prophecy of Jesus, who would suffer on the cross for humankind's sins (52:1 – 55:13; Matthew 8:17; Luke 22:37). While God will bring a complete salvation to His people, He still expects them to keep His laws and practice justice (56:1-12). People cannot worship God while at the same time worshipping idols (57:1-21).

Transformational truth. Jesus "was pierced for our rebellion, crushed for our sins. He was beaten so we could be whole. He was whipped so we could be healed" (Isaiah 53:5). Spiritual healing is in view here because "rebellion" and "sins" are mentioned. No spiritual disease is terminal when Jesus is in the picture.

A verse for meditation. "All of us, like sheep, have strayed away. We have left God's paths to follow our own. Yet the LORD laid on him the sins of us all" (Isaiah 53:6).

A question to ponder. Do you ever feel like your "spiritual disease" is so advanced that it's beyond a cure?

GLORY AHEAD FOR JUDAH

Isaiah 58:1 – 63:14

Yesterday we considered how Yahweh's Servant would bring ultimate salvation (Isaiah 52:13 – 57:21). Today we focus on the glory
that lay ahead for Judah.

Key concept. Despite a dismal past, there is great glory to come for
Judah.

The big picture. True religion does not consist of mere rituals. Obedience to God plays the key role (Isaiah 58). There were many sins that
had separated Judah's people from God (59:1-21). Yet there is a future
glory planned for Jerusalem. God will one day delight in His people.
They will be a bright light to the world (60:1 – 62:12).

Transformational truth. In Isaiah 51:7 we read, "Listen to me, you
who know right from wrong, you who cherish my law in your hearts.
Do not be afraid of people's scorn, nor fear their insults." My friend,
don't let scorn bother you. Let God handle it. Keep your attention
where it belongs: *Jesus!*

A verse for meditation. [A prophecy of the Messiah:] "The Spirit
of the Sovereign LORD is upon me, for the LORD has anointed me to
bring good news to the poor. He has sent me to comfort the broken-
hearted and to proclaim that captives will be released and prisoners will
be freed" (Isaiah 61:1).

A question to ponder. How did you respond the last time someone
made fun of you because of your faith?

TWO POSSIBLE PATHS

*Isaiah 63:15 – 66:24; 2 Kings 20:20-
21; 2 Chronicles 32:32-33*

Yesterday we considered the glory that lies ahead for Jerusalem (Isaiah 58:1–63:14). Today we look at two possible paths people can take in life.

Key concept. The wicked are on the path to destruction. The righteous are on the path to joy and peace.

The big picture. While glory lies ahead for God's people, they must first finish their course of punishment for sin and rebellion. Isaiah prayed that God would sustain them through their sufferings (63:15–64:12). He closed by contrasting two groups of people with two different eternal destinies: The wicked were on the path to destruction; the righteous were on the path to joy and peace (65:1–66:24).

Transformational truth. Because our attempted good deeds are sinstained, we should never try to earn salvation by works. Isaiah 64:6 states, "We are all infected and impure with sin. When we display our righteous deeds, they are nothing but filthy rags." Thankfully, our salvation is not based on good works, but on grace alone (Ephesians 2:8-9).

A verse for meditation. "My hands have made both heaven and earth; they and everything in them are mine. I, the LORD, have spoken!" (Isaiah 66:2).

A question to ponder. Scripture says we cannot earn God's favor by doing good works. What is a correct perspective of good works?

IDOLATRY AND
IMMINENT JUDGMENT

Jeremiah 1:1 – 2:22; 2 Kings 21:1 – 22:2;
2 Chronicles 33:1 – 34:7

Yesterday we considered two possible paths people can take in life (Isaiah 63:15 – 66:24). Today we turn to the book of Jeremiah and consider the imminence of judgment in view of unrepentant idolatry.

Key concept. God's people remained in idolatry. Judgment was therefore imminent.

The big picture. Jeremiah began his ministry in Judah (the southern kingdom) in 627 BC, during the reign of Josiah (640 – 609 BC). He continued through the reigns of four other kings: Jehoahaz (609 BC), Jehoiakim (609 – 598 BC), Jehoiachin (598 – 597 BC), and Zedekiah (597 – 586 BC). For decades Jeremiah warned the people of a judgment that was coming, but he was ignored (Jeremiah 1 – 2). The people continued in idol worship, injustice, tyranny against the helpless, dishonesty, and more. Such sins were causing the people to rush toward painful judgment (see 39 – 45). Captivity was coming.

Transformational truth. When God called Jeremiah to service, Jeremiah replied, "I can't speak for you! I'm too young!" (Jeremiah 1:6). God would not accept excuses. He promised to be with Jeremiah, protect him, and put His words in the prophet's mouth (1:7-8).

A verse for meditation. "Before you were born I set you apart and appointed you as my prophet to the nations" (Jeremiah 1:5).

A question to ponder. Do you ever feel inadequate to speak for God, like Jeremiah did?

IDOLATRY AND
IMMINENT JUDGMENT

Jeremiah 2:23 – 5:19

In the previous lesson we explored the imminence of judgment in view of unrepentant idolatry (Jeremiah 1:1 – 2:22). More of the same today.

Key concept. Judgment was imminent on Judah because the people were unrepentant.

The big picture. Jeremiah was instructed to charge the people with rebelling against God by turning to idolatry (Jeremiah 2). Israel was like a prostitute who had committed adultery with many false gods, and Israel's "sister," Judah, had followed her wicked example (3). For this reason, God would soon bring a disastrous judgment (4). Because the people had been unfaithful, God would use a distant nation as His whipping rod of discipline (5). He was referring to the Babylonian captivity.

Transformational truth. God doesn't like religious pretense. He declared, "Judah has never sincerely returned to me. She has only pretended to be sorry. I, the LORD, have spoken" (Jeremiah 3:10). The people of Judah were hypocrites. Hypocrisy pretends to possess a virtuous character—or moral/religious beliefs and principles—that one does not really have (Revelation 3:1). Don't be a hypocrite or a pretender.

A verse for meditation. "That treacherous sister Judah had no fear, and now she, too, has left me and given herself to prostitution" (Jeremiah 3:8).

A question to ponder. Have you ever caught yourself wearing a mask of hypocrisy?

GOD'S PEOPLE ARE ROBBING THEMSELVES OF BLESSING

Jeremiah 5:20 – 6:30; 2 Kings 22:3-20; 2 Chronicles 34:8-28

Yesterday we considered the imminence of judgment on Judah in view of unrepentant idolatry (Jeremiah 2:23–5:19). Today we focus on how God's people are virtually robbing themselves of God's blessing.

Key concept. By their unrepentant sin, the people were only doing injury to themselves. Judgment was coming.

The big picture. God's people had deprived themselves of wonderful blessings because of sin (Jeremiah 5:20-31). Judgment would soon come via a powerful army that would bring disaster and destruction (6:1-30).

Transformational truth. God said to the people, "Your sin has robbed you of all these good things" (Jeremiah 5:25). Perpetual sin kept God from blessing His people—such as bringing them good crops so they could eat well. This reminds us of Jeremiah 2:17, where God said to the people: "You have brought this upon yourselves by rebelling against the LORD your God." In Jeremiah 4:18 God said, "Your own actions have brought this upon you." *Choices have consequences.*

A verse for meditation. "Listen, you foolish and senseless people, with eyes that do not see and ears that do not hear. Have you no respect for me?" (Jeremiah 5:21-22).

A question to ponder. Do you think it possible that you may have forfeited past blessings from God because of unrepentant sin?

NINEVEH'S APPROACHING JUDGMENT

*Nahum 1–3; 2 Kings 23:1-28;
2 Chronicles 34:29–35:19*

Yesterday we considered how God's people were forfeiting blessing from God as a result of their sin (Jeremiah 5:20–6:30). Today we look at how judgment was on the horizon for Nineveh.

Key concept. The sins of Nineveh were like a judgment magnet. Judgment was on its way.

The big picture. Nahum's prophetic ministry began in 663 BC. Nahum—a contemporary of Zephaniah, Jeremiah, and Habakkuk—described the fall and destruction of Nineveh, the Assyrian capital. Nineveh had been brimming with idolatry, paganism, and brutality (Nahum 3:1-4). Believing itself invincible, Nineveh failed to recognize that God is the only true ultimate power in the universe. Nahum prophesied that even though the Assyrians might seem invincible, their days were numbered; judgment was rapidly approaching. Nineveh was destroyed, as prophesied by Nahum, in 612 BC.

Transformational truth. Our God is a jealous God—He desires His people to be faithful and obedient to Him, with not even a hint of infidelity (Nahum 1:2; see also Deuteronomy 4:24; 5:9; 6:15; 32:21). God will not allow another—an idol, for example—to have the honor that is due to Him alone (Isaiah 42:8; 48:11).

A verse for meditation. "What sorrow awaits Nineveh, the city of murder and lies!" (Nahum 3:1).

A question to ponder. In what ways might people commit "adultery" in their relationship with God today?

JUDAH'S SIN AND FORTHCOMING JUDGMENT

Habakkuk 1 – 3; Zephaniah 1:1 – 2:7

Yesterday we focused on how judgment was on the horizon for Nineveh (Nahum 1–3). Today we consider how Judah's unrepentant sin was rapidly leading to judgment.

Key concept. Because all calls to repentance in Judah were ignored, judgment was imminent.

The big picture. Habakkuk's ministry to Judah began in 612 BC. He was pained to witness what was going on. The nation had continuously been called to repentance, but the call had fallen on deaf ears. Habakkuk asked God, "How long will this state of affairs continue? How long will You be silent in the face of this escalating catastrophe?" God finally revealed to Habakkuk that the judgment of captivity would come soon enough—and that it would be exceedingly painful for Judah.

Transformational truth. Habakkuk ended his book with a psalm of praise to God (Habakkuk 3:1-5). He had come to see that God's plan is always best. He gained confidence in God's sovereign purposes, which caused him to express joy before the Lord (3:18). He had a great outlook!

A verse for meditation. "How foolish to trust in your own creation—a god that can't even talk!" (Habakkuk 2:18-19).

A question to ponder. Do you rejoice in God's sovereign purposes, even though you may not know why He is allowing certain circumstances in your life?

JUDGMENT ON THE PHILISTINES AND MOAB

*Jeremiah 47 – 48; Zephaniah 2:8 – 3:20;
2 Chronicles 35:20-27; 2 Kings 23:29-30*

In the previous lesson we explored how Judah's unrepentant sin was rapidly leading to judgment (Habakkuk 1–3). Today we consider how the Philistines and Moab would soon be judged.

Key concept. The Philistines and Moab were ripe for judgment!

The big picture. God would soon bring judgment against the Philistines (Jeremiah 47) and Moab (48). Of the Philistines, God said, "People will scream in terror...The time has come for the Philistines to be destroyed" (47:2,4). Of Moab, God said, "All the towns will be destroyed, and no one will escape" (48:8).

Transformational truth. Jeremiah issued prophetic proclamations against Egypt (Jeremiah 46:2-28), Philistia (47:1-7), Moab (48:1-47), Ammon (49:1-6), Edom (49:7-22), Damascus (49:23-27), Kedar and Hazor (49:28-33), Elam (49:34-39), and Babylon (50:1–51:64). No sinful and unrepentant nation escapes God's judgment. *All nations—indeed, all people—are held accountable.*

A verse for meditation. "'I will put an end to Moab,' says the LORD, 'for the people offer sacrifices at the pagan shrines and burn incense to their false gods'" (Jeremiah 48:35).

A question to ponder. In view of God's consistent judgment of the nations, are you ever concerned that God might one day judge America?

THE IMPENDING BABYLONIAN CAPTIVITY

Jeremiah 22:1-23; 25:1-14; 26; 2 Chronicles 36:1-5; 2 Kings 23:31 – 24:4

Yesterday we considered how the Philistines and Moab would soon be judged (Jeremiah 47 – 48). Today we focus on the impending Babylonian captivity.

Key concept. The Babylonian captivity was on the horizon because of Judah's relentless sin.

The big picture. Jeremiah prophesied disaster for three of Judah's kings: Jehoahaz (Jeremiah 22:10-12), Jehoiakim (22:13-23), and Jehoiachin (22:24-30). Because of idolatry, Judah's inhabitants would be carried away as captives to Babylon for 70 years (25:1-14). The priests were so angry at Jeremiah for all of this doomsday talk that they wanted him killed (26).

Transformational truth. It's hard to be continually rejected by the people you are preaching to, but that is exactly what Jeremiah experienced for 23 years in Judah. Jeremiah kept preaching, "Repent and turn from your evil." The people kept turning a deaf ear toward him. Jeremiah never gave up. Neither should we.

A verse for meditation. "Be fair-minded and just. Do what is right! Help those who have been robbed; rescue them from their oppressors. Quit your evil deeds! Do not mistreat foreigners, orphans, and widows. Stop murdering the innocent!" (Jeremiah 22:3).

A question to ponder. Are you aware of any forms of social injustice in your own community?

GOD'S WRATH ON THE NATIONS

Jeremiah 25:15-38; 36; 45 – 46

Yesterday we read about the impending Babylonian captivity of Judah (Jeremiah 22:1-23; 25:1-14; 26). Today we consider God's wrath coming upon other sinful nations.

Key concept. God's wrath will soon fall on various sinful nations.

The big picture. Because of the sins of the nations, they will be made to drink the cup of God's wrath (Jeremiah 25:15-38). Jeremiah — unable to go to the temple (35:5) — had his secretary, Baruch, read his words from a scroll in the temple. King Jehoiakim sent for Jeremiah's scroll and had it burned (36). Jeremiah assured Baruch he would be spared the devastating events that lay ahead. Jeremiah then recorded the Lord's messages for various sinful nations, beginning with Egypt (46).

Transformational truth. While King Jehoiakim burned Jeremiah's scroll, trying to destroy God's words to the people, the truth is that God's Word cannot truly be destroyed. Jesus said, "Heaven and earth will disappear, but my words will never disappear" (Matthew 24:35). Indeed, "the word of the Lord remains forever" (1 Peter 1:25).

A verse for meditation. "The LORD will bring his case against all the nations" (Jeremiah 25:31).

A question to ponder. How much thought have you given to the fact we are blessed to be able to own copies of God's Word?

JEREMIAH'S PERSECUTION AND DANIEL'S INTEGRITY

Jeremiah 19 – 20; Daniel 1

Yesterday we considered God's wrath coming upon sinful nations (Jeremiah 25:15-38; 36; 45–46). Today we read about Jeremiah's persecution and Daniel's integrity.

Key concept. Jeremiah was persecuted for preaching God's truth. Daniel openly displayed God-inspired integrity in Babylon.

The big picture. There were three deportations in Babylon's victory over Judah. The first took place in 605 BC and included Daniel and his friends. The second took place in 597 BC and included Ezekiel. The third took place in 586, when the Babylonians destroyed Jerusalem and the temple. While Daniel was in captivity (following the first deportation), most of Judah *was not*. Hence, Judah at this time is still properly categorized as being in the era of the divided kingdom (930–586 BC) instead of the era of living in exile (586–538 BC). Meanwhile, Jeremiah condemned his people's idolatry (Jeremiah 19). The priest in charge of the temple had him arrested and put in stocks. When Jeremiah was released, he spoke God's judgment upon the priest (20).

Transformational truth. Daniel was a man of integrity (Daniel 1:8-20). He lived the truth of 2 Corinthians 8:21: "We are careful to be honorable before the Lord, but we also want everyone else to see that we are honorable."

A verse for meditation. [Jeremiah's lament:] "Oh, that I had died in my mother's womb, that her body had been my grave!... My entire life has been filled with trouble, sorrow, and shame" (Jeremiah 20:17-18).

A question to ponder. Have you ever suffered persecution for speaking God's truth?

DANIEL INTERPRETS NEBUCHADNEZZAR'S DREAM

Daniel 2 – 3; Jeremiah 7:1 – 8:3

In the previous lesson we explored Jeremiah's persecution and Daniel's integrity (Jeremiah 19–20; Daniel 1). Today we consider how Daniel interpreted Nebuchadnezzar's dream.

Key concept. Daniel humbly served God and interpreted Nebuchadnezzar's dream.

The big picture. By God's power, Daniel revealed the meaning of Nebuchadnezzar's dream. God would raise up and then bring down four Gentile empires (Daniel 2). Nebuchadnezzar then set up a golden image and decreed that all bow to it (3:1-7). Daniel's friends refused, and were subsequently thrown into a fiery furnace as punishment. God delivered them, and they were all promoted (3:8-30).

Transformational truth. Daniel was a humble man who consistently pointed away from himself and instead pointed to God (Daniel 2:27-28). He had the same humility as John the Baptist: "He must become greater and greater, and I must become less and less" (John 3:30; see also Luke 1:52; James 4:10).

A verse for meditation. "There is a God in heaven who reveals secrets, and he has shown King Nebuchadnezzar what will happen in the future. Now I will tell you your dream and the visions you saw as you lay on your bed" (Daniel 2:28).

A question to ponder. What qualities in Daniel might you want to emulate in your life?

COVENANT VIOLATIONS AND JUDGMENT

Jeremiah 8:4–11:23

Yesterday we considered how Daniel interpreted Nebuchadnezzar's dream (Daniel 2–3; Jeremiah 7:1–8:3). Today we focus on imminent judgment in view of covenant violations.

Key concept. God's people had violated His covenant; judgment was imminent.

The big picture. The people of Jerusalem were on the wrong path and shamelessly refused to turn back to the Lord's way (Jeremiah 8). The Lord would soon scatter them in judgment, and wailing would be heard throughout the land (9). Idolatry always brings destruction (10). God's people had violated His covenant. The result: *disaster.* Jeremiah was instructed to not even pray for these people (11).

Transformational truth. In Jeremiah 8:4 we read, "When people fall down, don't they get up again? When they discover they're on the wrong road, don't they turn back?" Contrary to this statement, the people of Jerusalem *stayed* on the wrong road. Are there any areas of your life where you need to turn about and get on the right road?

A verse for meditation. "Don't let the wise boast in their wisdom, or the powerful boast in their power, or the rich boast in their riches. But those who wish to boast should boast in this alone: that they truly know me" (Jeremiah 9:23).

A question to ponder. Why is knowing God the single most important thing one can boast about?

JEREMIAH'S STRUGGLES

Jeremiah 12 – 15

Yesterday we gave attention to imminent judgment in view of covenant violations (Jeremiah 8:4 – 11:23). Today we consider some of Jeremiah's struggles.

Key concept. Jeremiah was struggling with the sorry state of affairs among his people.

The big picture. Jeremiah struggled over the fact the wicked seemed to prosper while the righteous suffered. God said things would be remedied when He brought judgment on the land of Judah (Jeremiah 12). He said He would soon "rot away the pride of Judah and Jerusalem" (13:9). Meanwhile, false prophets claimed there was nothing to worry about. God responded that Jeremiah—and not these smooth-talking phony prophets—spoke for Him (14). Jeremiah complained to God about how much mocking and persecution he had endured for speaking God's truth. God replied that He would protect the prophet (15).

Transformational truth. God described His people as "evil people" who "stubbornly follow their own heart" (Jeremiah 13:10). "The human heart is the most deceitful of all things, and desperately wicked" (17:9). The good news is that God is in the business of heart transformation (Romans 12:2; 2 Corinthians 3:18; Galatians 5:22).

A verse for meditation. "The LORD said to me, 'Do not pray for these people anymore'" (Jeremiah 14:11).

A question to ponder. Do you ever feel like complaining to God, like Jeremiah did?

JUDGMENT IMMINENT

Jeremiah 16 – 18; 35

Yesterday we focused on some of Jeremiah's struggles (Jeremiah 12 – 15). Today we again consider the imminence of judgment on God's people.

Key concept. God would not permit things to continue as they were. God's people were ripe for judgment.

The big picture. God instructed Jeremiah not to get married and have children. To do so would be foolish given the coming desolation (Jeremiah 16). Judah's sin-infection was pervasive. The only remedy was complete repentance (17). God declared that He would shape and mold Judah exactly as He saw fit. If Judah resisted, judgment was a sure thing (18).

Transformational truth. Judah sought Egypt's help against Babylon's attacks. God responded by stating, "Cursed are those who put their trust in mere humans, who rely on human strength and turn their hearts away from the LORD" (Jeremiah 17:5). It is much better to put *full* trust in the Lord (Proverbs 3:5-6).

A verse for meditation. "I, the LORD, search all hearts and examine secret motives. I give all people their due rewards, according to what their actions deserve" (Jeremiah 17:9-10).

A question to ponder. How is it both a comfort and a warning that God searches hearts and examines secret motives?

A REMNANT WILL SURVIVE

*Jeremiah 22:24 – 23:32; 49; 2 Kings
24:5-9; 2 Chronicles 36:6-9*

In the previous lesson, we explored how judgment was imminent for Judah (Jeremiah 16–18; 35). Today we again consider how a remnant of God's people would survive.

Key concept. Despite the coming judgment, a remnant would survive. Moreover, the Messiah would one day come and bring great blessing on all people.

The big picture. Jeremiah predicted that a faithful remnant would survive the captivity and return to the Promised Land. He also spoke of the coming of the Messiah, described as "The LORD Is Our Righteousness" (Jeremiah 23:1-6). Jeremiah then denounced the smooth-talking false prophets who denied judgment was drawing near (23:9-32).

Transformational truth. Jeremiah 23:9-14 reveals that the false prophets in the land contributed to the corrupt behavior of the people. They gave the people a false sense of security, assuring them all was well. Jeremiah told the truth: *You've sinned and judgment is coming!* Stay away from false prophets (see Matthew 7:15; 24:11,24; 2 Peter 2:1; 1 John 4:1)!

A verse for meditation. [A messianic prophecy:] " 'For the time is coming,' says the LORD, 'when I will raise up a righteous descendant from King David's line. He will be a King who rules with wisdom. He will do what is just and right throughout the land' " (Jeremiah 23:5).

A question to ponder. How does the Messiah—righteous, wise, and just—contrast with the leaders of God's people?

A REMNANT WILL SURVIVE

Jeremiah 23:33 – 24:10; 29:1 – 31:14

Yesterday we considered how a remnant of God's people would survive (Jeremiah 22:24 – 23:32,49). More of the same today.

Key concept. A faithful remnant would survive the Babylonian captivity and return to the land.

The big picture. Jeremiah continued denouncing the smooth-talking false prophets. Each of them would experience God's judgment (Jeremiah 23:33-40). God then showed Jeremiah a basket of good figs and bad figs. The good figs metaphorically represented the faithful remnant that would return to the land following captivity. The bad figs represented "King Zedekiah of Judah, his officials, all the people left in Jerusalem, and those who live in Egypt" (24:8). They would all be judged.

Transformational truth. God gave His sinful children a wonderful promise: "'I know the plans I have for you,' says the LORD. 'They are plans for good and not for disaster, to give you a future and a hope'" (Jeremiah 29:11). Blessing follows judgment (Jeremiah 30–33).

A verse for meditation. [A warning against false prophets:] "Stop using this phrase, 'prophecy from the LORD.' For people are using it to give authority to their own ideas, turning upside down the words of our God" (Jeremiah 23:35-36).

A question to ponder. Can you describe a time in your life when God brought blessing after experiencing a time of trial?

THE NEW COVENANT

Jeremiah 31:15-40; 49:34 – 51:14

Yesterday we considered how a remnant of God's people would survive (Jeremiah 23:33 – 24:10; 29:1 – 31:14). Today we zero in on the
new covenant.

Key concept. The new covenant makes provision for the total forgiveness of sins for all people.

The big picture. Under the old covenant, worshippers never enjoyed a
sense of total forgiveness. Under the new covenant, however, Christ our
High Priest made provisions for such forgiveness (Jeremiah 31:15-40).

Transformational truth. A final restoration would come through the
work of the coming Messiah. He would institute a new covenant that
would provide for complete forgiveness of sins (Jeremiah 31:31-34).
When Jesus ate the Passover meal with the disciples in the upper room,
He said to them, "This cup is the new covenant between God and
his people—an agreement confirmed with my blood" (1 Corinthians
11:25). Jesus has done everything necessary for our forgiveness by His
once-for-all sacrifice on the cross.

A verse for meditation. "In the past I deliberately uprooted and tore
down this nation. I overthrew it, destroyed it, and brought disaster
upon it. But in the future I will just as deliberately plant it and build it
up. I, the LORD, have spoken!" (Jeremiah 31:28).

A question to ponder. How is the new covenant a game changer, to
use modern vernacular?

THE FUTURE DESTRUCTION OF BABYLON

Jeremiah 51:15 – 52:3; 37:1-10; 2 Kings 24:10-20; 2 Chronicles 36:10-14; 1 Chronicles 3:10-16

Yesterday we looked at the new covenant (Jeremiah 31:15-40). Today we consider the future destruction of Babylon.

Key concept. Babylon would be completely destroyed after being used by God as His whipping rod against Judah.

The big picture. Jeremiah offered a hymn of praise that contrasted dead idols with the living God (Jeremiah 51:15-19). This living God would use Babylon as His whipping rod to punish other nations, such as Judah. Once God finished using Babylon in this way, He would punish Babylon because of its treatment of Jerusalem (51:20-44). God instructed the remnant to be sure to exit Babylon before this judgment fell (51:45-53).

Transformational truth. While in exile, God's people would be paralyzed with guilt because of past sins (Jeremiah 51:51). No matter what happens in our lives, however, we ought to put the past behind us and concentrate on living for God in the present and the future (see Philippians 3:13).

A verse for meditation. "The craftsmen are disgraced by the idols they make, for their carefully shaped works are a fraud. These idols have no breath or power...But the God of Israel is no idol!" (Jeremiah 51:17-19).

A question to ponder. Do you ever struggle with present pain that is rooted in the past? What help does Philippians 3:13 offer?

GOD COMMISSIONS EZEKIEL

Jeremiah 37:11 – 38:28; Ezekiel 1:1 – 3:15

In the previous lesson, we explored God's future destruction of Babylon (Jeremiah 51:15 – 52:3). Today we consider God's commission of Ezekiel.

Key concept. Ezekiel was a prophet to the southern kingdom of Judah. Initially he preached judgment, but later he preached consolation.

The big picture. Ezekiel was born in 623 BC. He went into exile in Babylon in 597 BC, and began prophesying there in 593 BC. At that time, not all of Judah was yet in captivity, for Babylon's third wave of deportation wasn't until 586 BC. Ezekiel graphically communicated that God's judgment came because of human sin. Once Judah's inhabitants were all in exile, they were depressed, and Ezekiel began preaching a message of hope and comfort.

Transformational truth. God called the people of Judah "rebellious" and "hard-hearted"—not likely to listen (Ezekiel 2:3-4). Yet God called Ezekiel to speak to them anyway. We ought always to be willing to speak God's truth, regardless of the expected response.

A verse for meditation. [God's exhortation to Ezekiel:] "Don't be afraid of them or fear their angry looks, even though they are rebels" (Ezekiel 3:9).

A question to ponder. Have you ever felt a little "gun shy" about speaking God's truth, knowing that some people may react against you?

EZEKIEL ON THE BABYLONIAN SIEGE

Jeremiah 27–28; 51:59-64; Ezekiel 3:16–4:17

Yesterday we considered God's commission of Ezekiel to speak without fear (Jeremiah 37:11–38:28; Ezekiel 1:1–3:15). Today we focus on Ezekiel's message about the coming Babylonian siege.

Key concept. Ezekiel used graphic illustrations to communicate to the people about God's warnings of impending judgment.

The big picture. Ezekiel dramatically enacted the nearing Babylonian siege against Jerusalem. He also ate very little bread—cooked over dung—to depict the starvation conditions that would soon come upon Jerusalem (Ezekiel 4:1-17). *Things were about to get bad!*

Transformational truth. Jeremiah, like Ezekiel, told the truth about God's approaching judgment, which made him unpopular (Jeremiah 28:8-17). Hananiah spoke lies that gave people a false sense of security. People loved to hear from a "prophet" that everything was okay. The same is true today—people prefer to listen to comforting lies rather than face painful truth. *We must not give up telling the truth.*

A verse for meditation. "Do not listen to your false prophets, fortune-tellers, interpreters of dreams, mediums, and sorcerers who say, 'The king of Babylon will not conquer you.' They are all liars, and their lies will lead to your being driven out of your land" (Jeremiah 27:9-10).

A question to ponder. Can you think of any examples of modern-day false prophets who have led people astray?

A REMNANT WILL SURVIVE

Ezekiel 5 – 9

Yesterday we considered Ezekiel's dramatic message on the coming Babylonian siege (Jeremiah 27 – 28). Today we focus on a prophecy about the survival of a remnant following the captivity.

Key concept. Desolation was coming, but a remnant would survive.

The big picture. The hair from Ezekiel's shaved head prophetically represented four groups among God's people of Judah. Group 1 would be destroyed in the city; group 2 would be killed in battle; group 3 would go into exile; group 4 was the remnant that would survive (Ezekiel 5). Those slain by the sword would lie right next to the idols they had worshipped (6–7). The Jerusalem temple had been profaned through idolatry (8). God instructed that every person grieved by the temple's desecration receive a mark on the forehead. Those without the mark would be destroyed (9).

Transformational truth. God informed Ezekiel of the attitude of the sinful people: "The LORD doesn't see us" (Ezekiel 8:12). They thought God was unaware of their perpetual sin. The truth is, *God sees everything.* Nothing is hidden from His omniscient vision (Psalm 44:21; 139:4; Isaiah 40:28; Hebrews 4:13). Live your life accordingly!

A verse for meditation. "Is it nothing to the people of Judah that they commit these detestable sins, leading the whole nation into violence, thumbing their noses at me, and provoking my anger?" (Jeremiah 8:17).

A question to ponder. How does it make you feel that God knows *every sin you have committed* and *every sin you will yet commit,* and yet He has completely forgiven you in Jesus Christ (2 Corinthians 5:21)?

PROPHECIES OF JUDGMENT
SOON FULFILLED

Ezekiel 10 – 13

Yesterday we focused on the survival of a remnant (Ezekiel 5 – 9). Today we again consider how God's prophecies of judgment will soon come to pass. (I recognize some of the prophets sound like broken records. But God was relentless about sending warnings because He earnestly sought the people's repentance so He could bless them.)

Key concept. God's prophecies of judgment would soon come to pass.

The big picture. God's glory was leaving the temple because His people polluted it with pagan practices (Ezekiel 10). Ezekiel condemned Jerusalem's leaders, who taught prosperity instead of imminent judgment (11). He then acted out Jerusalem's fall and exile (12). He condemned the false prophets who told the people what they wanted to hear instead of speaking God's truth (13).

Transformational truth. A common proverb in Israel was, "Time passes, and prophecies come to nothing" (Ezekiel 12:21). The people ignored warnings of judgment and thought God's prophecies would come to nothing. God said, "I will put an end to this proverb, and you will soon stop quoting it" (12:23). In other words, judgment would soon fall. Today, scoffers mock the second coming (2 Peter 3:3-4). They ought to repent while there is yet time!

A verse for meditation. "I am the LORD! If I say it, it will happen. There will be no more delays" (Ezekiel 12:24-25).

A question to ponder. What is your attitude toward end-time prophecies?

LOYALTY AND FIDELITY

Ezekiel 14 – 16

In the previous lesson, we explored how God's prophecies of judgment would soon come to pass, despite scoffers saying the contrary (Ezekiel 10 – 13). Today we consider how God demands loyalty and fidelity.

Key concept. Loyalty and fidelity bring God's blessings. A lack of these brings judgment.

The big picture. God would not permit the worship of false gods by His people (Ezekiel 14). The people of Judah were like a vine that bears no fruit. Fruitless vines were cut down and thrust into the fire (15). God had given unbelievable blessings to His people, but they still turned to paganism. Even so, God would be faithful to His covenant promises in the end (16).

Transformational truth. Noah, Daniel, and Job were righteous and godly men (Genesis 6:8-9; Daniel 2:47-48; Job 1:1). But even their presence could not prevent the coming judgment on Judah (Ezekiel 14:14-19). Sinners suffer the consequences of their sins even when godly people are in the vicinity. If I attend a church with a godly pastor, I can still suffer consequences if I engage in unrepentant sin.

A verse for meditation. "You used the lovely things I gave you to make shrines for idols, where you played the prostitute. Unbelievable! How could such a thing ever happen?" (Ezekiel 16:16).

A question to ponder. Do you ever feel like a vine that bears no fruit? If so, what can you do to remedy this?

INDIVIDUAL RESPONSIBILITY FOR SIN

Ezekiel 17 – 19

Yesterday we considered how God demands loyalty and fidelity (Ezekiel 14 – 16). Today we turn our attention to individual responsibility for sin.

Key concept. Each person is responsible for his or her own sin.

The big picture. In 597 BC, Babylon's King Nebuchadnezzar took King Jehoiachin from Judah to Babylon. Nebuchadnezzar made Zedekiah a puppet king in Judah, with Judah continuing temporarily as a tributary kingdom. But Zedekiah broke his covenant with Nebuchadnezzar and appealed to Egypt for help. This spelled doom for Judah (Ezekiel 17). Judah's people then blamed their ancestors for their woes in life. Ezekiel responded that people are accountable for their own sins (18 – 19).

Transformational truth. God proclaimed, "The person who sins is the one who will die. The child will not be punished for the parent's sins, and the parent will not be punished for the child's sins" (Ezekiel 18:20). I can't blame anyone but myself when I stand before God to give an account of my life. This is a motivation to take responsibility and live righteously!

A verse for meditation. "Do you think that I like to see wicked people die? says the Sovereign LORD. Of course not! I want them to turn from their wicked ways and live" (Ezekiel 18:23).

A question to ponder. Do you think Ezekiel 18:23 might be a good motivation for evangelism?

CHOICES HAVE CONSEQUENCES

Ezekiel 20:1 – 22:16

Yesterday we considered individual responsibility for sin (Ezekiel 17–19). Today we ponder, yet again, how choices have consequences. *Key concept.* Choices always have consequences.

The big picture. Some of Judah's leaders asked Ezekiel for a message from God. The Lord responded, "How dare you come to ask me for a message? As surely as I live, says the Sovereign LORD, I will tell you nothing" (Ezekiel 20:3). Ezekiel then gave the people a history lesson documenting their consistent rebellion (20). Because of their history, God was sending His wrath upon the people, with the Babylonians as His instrument of wrath (20:45–21:32). God's people were ripe for judgment because of their rampant idolatry (22:1-16).

Transformational truth. Choices have consequences. This is thoroughly illustrated in Ezekiel's panoramic view of Israel's history of rebellion and sin (Ezekiel 20). Despite God's attempts to bring the people back on the right path, they consistently rebelled, sinned, and engaged in idolatry, which is spiritual adultery. Now they would suffer judgment. Let us learn from their folly!

A verse for meditation. "You are defiled because of the idols you have made. Your day of destruction has come! You have reached the end of your years" (Ezekiel 22:4).

A question to ponder. Can you think of any recent events in your life that confirm the maxim "Choices have consequences"?

SPIRITUAL ADULTERY

*Ezekiel 22:17–24:14; 2 Kings 24:20–25:2;
Jeremiah 52:3-5; 39:1*

Yesterday we focused on how choices have consequences (Ezekiel 20:1–22:16). Today we consider the consequences of spiritual adultery.

Key concept. Unrepentant spiritual adultery before God yields painful judgment.

The big picture. Israel and Judah—the northern and southern kingdoms—were compared to two adulterous sisters. They pursued "lovers" with reckless abandon. Both engaged in spiritual adultery before God, worshipping pagan idols (Ezekiel 23). God's people would therefore face the fire of His judgment, like stew in a cooking pot (24:1-14).

Transformational truth. Intense heat helps remove impurities from precious metals. When metals are heated, dross rises to the top and is skimmed away (see Ezekiel 22:17-22). By analogy, God uses trials to remove impurities from our lives. "These trials will show that your faith is genuine. It is being tested as fire tests and purifies gold—though your faith is far more precious than mere gold" (1 Peter 1:7).

A verse for meditation. "The time has come, and I won't hold back. I will not change my mind, and I will have no pity on you. You will be judged on the basis of all your wicked actions, says the Sovereign LORD" (Ezekiel 24:14).

A question to ponder. What attitude should you have when you experience trials?

THE HIGH PRICE
OF FOLLOWING GOD

Ezekiel 24:15 – 25:17; 29:1-16;
30:20 – 31:18; Jeremiah 21; 34

In the previous lesson we explored the consequences of spiritual adultery (Ezekiel 22:17 – 24:14). Today we consider how following God can entail great sacrifice.

Key concept. Ezekiel himself is an example of how following God can require immense sacrifice.

The big picture. God informed Ezekiel that his wife was going to die. When this happened, Ezekiel was not to mourn her death. This was presented as a sign to the Jewish exiles *already in* Babylon that their loved ones in Jerusalem would be slaughtered by the Babylonians. (Recall that there were three deportations from Judah to Babylon—in 605 BC, 597 BC, and finally, 586 BC, when the Babylonians assaulted Jerusalem and destroyed the temple. From Ezekiel's perspective, this last event had not yet happened.) Like Ezekiel, the exiles now in Babylon were not to outwardly mourn when this assault occurred. They would simply groan in all their evil (Ezekiel 24:15-27).

Transformational truth. Ezekiel's loss of his wife was part of a word picture about Judah coming under judgment. Following God can entail great sacrifice. Christians, too, can experience heavy sacrifice. Jesus Himself said, "If any of you wants to be my follower, you must give up your own way, take up your cross, and follow me" (Matthew 16:24).

A verse for meditation. "You will waste away because of your sins. You will groan among yourselves for all the evil you have done" (Ezekiel 24:23).

A question to ponder. How would you describe a balanced understanding of what it means to live sacrificially for Christ?

WHEN NOT TO REJOICE

Ezekiel 26:1-14; Jeremiah 32 – 33

Yesterday we considered how following God can entail great sacrifice (Ezekiel 24:15 – 25:17). Today we focus on *not* rejoicing over someone else's fall.

Key concept. Don't rejoice over another person's demise.

The big picture. Ezekiel was writing just prior to the Babylonian assault on Judah in 586 BC. Because Tyre was rejoicing over Babylon's impending assault on Jerusalem, God said He would bring King Nebuchadnezzar of Babylon against Tyre as well and destroy all its villages (Ezekiel 26:1-14). While the Babylonians were attacking Jerusalem, Jeremiah bought some land in Anathoth, his hometown, fully confident that his people would one day return from captivity (Jeremiah 32). Jeremiah then confirmed that one of David's descendants would reign from the throne of Judah (33). (This would be Jesus Christ.)

Transformational truth. God destroyed Tyre because Tyre rejoiced over the fall of Jerusalem (Ezekiel 26:1-14). God does not desire that anyone gloat over someone else's demise, even if they're an adversary. As Proverbs 24:17-18 puts it, "Don't rejoice when your enemies fall; don't be happy when they stumble. For the LORD will be displeased with you."

A verse for meditation. "The time will come when I will heal Jerusalem's wounds and give it prosperity and true peace. I will restore the fortunes of Judah and Israel and rebuild their towns" (Jeremiah 33:6-7).

A question to ponder. Have you ever been tempted to feel good about someone else's fall?

TYRE, SIDON, AND LUCIFER'S FALL

Ezekiel 26:15 – 28:26; 2 Kings 25:3-7;
Jeremiah 39:2-10; 52:6-11

Yesterday we focused on *not* rejoicing over someone else's fall (Ezekiel 26:1-14; Jeremiah 32–33). Today we consider God's condemnation of Tyre and Sidon, as well as Lucifer's fall.

Key concept. Tyre and Sidon were condemned, and the details of Lucifer's fall were provided.

The big picture. God continued to pronounce judgments against various nations, including Tyre (26:15–28:19) and Sidon (28:20–26). Today's reading addresses not only the King of Tyre, but also the spiritual king of Tyre operating behind the scenes—*Lucifer,* whose name changed to Satan (see 28:11-19).

Transformational truth. Ezekiel 28:11-19 tells us about the fall of Lucifer. The sin that corrupted him was self-generated pride. He desired the honor and glory that belonged to God alone. God then judged him and cast him to the earth (28:17-18). Christian, be forewarned: Satan seeks to bring you down. He will try to tempt you (1 Thessalonians 3:5), hinder you (1 Thessalonians 2:18), wage war against you (Ephesians 6:11-12), incite persecutions against you (Revelation 2:10), and much more.

A verse for meditation. "Your heart was filled with pride because of all your beauty. Your wisdom was corrupted by your love of splendor. So I threw you to the ground" (Ezekiel 28:17).

A question to ponder. Do you take spiritual warfare seriously? (Meditate on Ephesians 6:10-20.)

JUDGMENT FALLS, JEREMIAH SPARED

*Jeremiah 39:11 – 40:6; 52:12-27; 2 Kings
25:8-21; 2 Chronicles 36:15-21*

Yesterday we considered God's condemnation of Tyre and Sidon, and the fall of Lucifer (Ezekiel 26:15 – 28:26). Today we look at the judgment that finally fell on Jerusalem.

Key concept. As promised, God's judgment fell upon Jerusalem—just as the prophets predicted. Jeremiah's life was spared.

The big picture. Once Babylon's assault on Jerusalem began, Jeremiah's life was spared and he was given the freedom to remain in Judah (Jeremiah 39:11 – 40:6). The temple was destroyed. Valuable items from within it were taken as plunder to Babylon (Jeremiah 52:12-27; 2 Kings 25:8-21). Countless lives in Jerusalem were lost (2 Chronicles 36:15-21).

Transformational truth. God had given His people plenty of time to repent: "The Lord… repeatedly sent his prophets to warn them, for he had compassion on his people and his Temple. But the people mocked these messengers of God and despised their words. They scoffed at the prophets until the Lord's anger could no longer be restrained and nothing could be done" (2 Chronicles 36:15-16). *Repentance is the best way to avoid judgment.*

A verse for meditation. [God said to Jeremiah:] "Because you trusted me, I will give you your life as a reward. I will rescue you and keep you safe. I, the Lord, have spoken!" (Jeremiah 39:18).

A question to ponder. Can you think of any repentance that might be needed in your life so you can avoid God's loving disciplinary measures (Hebrews 12:5-6)?

ERA 6: LIVING IN EXILE
586 – 538 BC

Books in whole or in part:
2 Kings • Psalms • Jeremiah • Lamentations
Ezekiel • Daniel • Obadiah

Today we begin our study of a new biblical era—the era titled "Living in Exile," dated 586–538 BC. Bible books pertinent to our study of this era include 2 Kings, Psalms, Jeremiah, Lamentations, Ezekiel, Daniel, and Obadiah.

The book of Deuteronomy provides an important backdrop for our study. Through Moses, God promised great blessings if the nation lived in obedience to the Sinai covenant. God also warned that if the nation disobeyed His commands, it would experience the punishments listed in the covenant—*including exile from the land*: "The LORD will exile you and your king to a nation unknown to you and your ancestors" (Deuteronomy 28:36).

Despite this warning, sin predominated at every level of Jewish society over an extended time. A pattern we witness in 2 Kings is the preponderance of bad kings who ruled God's people—in both the northern kingdom of Israel and the southern kingdom of Judah (see 2 Kings 2–17). These wicked leaders caused a trickle-down effect—that is, evil trickled down from the throne to the general populace. The people took on *and maintained* the wicked character of their leadership. They were therefore ripe for judgment (17:7-41).

Old Testament history is replete with illustrations of how unfaithful Israel and Judah were to the Sinai covenant. The two most significant periods of exile for the Jewish people involved the fall of Israel to the Assyrians in 722 BC, and the collapse of Judah to the Babylonians in 605–586 BC. As God promised, disobedience brought exile to His people. Let's consider Judah as an illustration.

The first chapter of Isaiah takes the form of a lawsuit against Judah.

Judah was indicted by the Lord (through Isaiah) because of Judah's "breach of contract" in breaking the Sinai covenant, which had been given to the nation at the time of the exodus from Egypt. In this court-room scene, the Lord called upon heaven and earth to act as witnesses to the accusations leveled against the nation: "Listen, O heavens! Pay attention, earth! This is what the LORD says: 'The children I raised and cared for have rebelled against me'" (Isaiah 1:2). The whole universe was to bear witness that God's judgments are just.

The Lord indicted Judah for rebelling against Him. It is noteworthy that the Hebrew word for "rebel" in Isaiah 1:2 was often used among the ancients in reference to a subordinate state's violation of a treaty with a sovereign nation. In Isaiah 1, the word points to Judah's blatant violation of God's covenant. Hence, Judah suffered the just penalty of going into captivity.

In this case, the Babylonian captivity was God's means of chastening Judah. As noted earlier, there were three deportations involved in Babylon's captivity of Judah. The first took place in 605 BC and included Daniel and his friends. The second was in 597 BC and included Ezekiel and others. The third occurred in 586 BC, when the Babylonians destroyed both Jerusalem and its temple.

The Babylonians plundered all the sacred utensils found within the temple — "the gold altar; the gold table for the Bread of the Presence; the lampstands of solid gold…lamps, and tongs — all of gold; the small bowls, lamp snuffers, bowls, ladles, and incense burners — all of solid gold" (1 Kings 7:48-50). The seizing of these sacred objects as spoils were believed by the Babylonians to represent the victory of Babylon's gods over the God of Israel. Little did the Babylonians know that it was actually the one true God of Judah who had handed His people over to them for chastisement: "King Nebuchadnezzar of Babylon came to Jerusalem and besieged it. The Lord gave him victory over King Jehoiakim of Judah and permitted him to take some of the sacred objects from the Temple of God. So Nebuchadnezzar took them back to the land of Babylonia and placed them in the treasure-house of his god" (Daniel 1:2; see also Deuteronomy 28:64; Jeremiah 25:8-14). This was a painful chastening for Judah.

This punishment, of course, was intended as a corrective. Throughout both the Old and New Testaments, we find that God disciplines His children in order to purify them. Just as an earthly father disciplines his children, so God the Father disciplines His children to train and educate them (Hebrews 12:1-5).

During the time preceding exile, Judah's false prophets claimed repeatedly that no judgment was coming. The prophet Jeremiah countered, promising that the people would be in captivity in Babylon for 70 years. As a result of his dark prophecies, Jeremiah suffered harsh opposition and persecution (Jeremiah 26–45). The false prophets called for his death. But Judah's leaders spared him this destiny.

Opposition continued to escalate against Jeremiah (see Jeremiah 34–35). He was prohibited from entering the temple. His assistant, Baruch, therefore read his proclamations in the temple on his behalf. Jeremiah's prophetic scroll was burned by the king. All this, for telling God's truth.

Of course, once the people of Judah were in exile, Jeremiah felt compassion and sought to bring comfort to them. He emphasized that good things can happen when God's people seek Him with their whole heart:

> "If you look for me wholeheartedly, you will find me. I will
> be found by you," says the LORD. "I will end your captiv-
> ity and restore your fortunes. I will gather you out of the
> nations where I sent you and will bring you home again to
> your own land" (Jeremiah 29:13-14).

In the coming chapters, we will journey through 2 Kings, Psalms, Jeremiah, Lamentations, Ezekiel, Daniel, and Obadiah as we learn interesting details about the era of living in exile. Some of the lessons from these books focus on familiar themes, such as the need for repentance, lamenting Jerusalem's destruction, and prayers for restoration. However, an interesting fact about two of the books—Ezekiel and Daniel—is that they focus heavily on prophecies to be fulfilled in the more distant end times, such as prophecies of Israel's rebirth as a nation after a long and worldwide dispersion, the future tribulation, the role of the antichrist, and Christ's future millennial kingdom. To give Israel a firm hope for the future, Daniel and Ezekiel set forth God's long-term plans for Israel via end-times prophecies. It's as if they were saying to the exiles, "We've already shown you the short-term future. Now we'll pull back the veil to give you a glimpse of the long-term future."

Following are some dates that provide a helpful chronological orientation for this era:

930 BC—The kingdom was divided into the northern kingdom (Israel) and southern kingdom (Judah).

722 BC—The northern kingdom was taken into exile by the Assyrians.

627 BC—Jeremiah's prophetic ministry to Judah began.

605 BC—Deportation 1 in Judah's Babylonian captivity took place. Daniel and his friends were among the captives and became powerful witnesses for God in Babylon.

597 BC—Deportation 2 in Judah's Babylonian captivity took place. Ezekiel was among the captives.

593 BC—Ezekiel prophesied to the exiles in Babylon.

586 BC—Deportation 3 in Judah's Babylonian captivity took place; Jerusalem's temple was destroyed; Jeremiah wrote Lamentations as he mourned for his people; Jeremiah's ministry ended.

571 BC—Ezekiel's ministry ended.

535 BC—Daniel's ministry ended.

Preview: In Day 245, we will consider the people's anguish over Jerusalem's destruction.

ANGUISH AT JERUSALEM'S DESTRUCTION

Lamentations 1–4

In the previous lesson, we introduced Era 6, titled "Living in Exile," dated 586–538 BC. Today we consider the people's anguish over Jerusalem's destruction.

Key concept. The destruction of Jerusalem was a catastrophic heartbreak to the people of Judah.

The big picture. Jeremiah's prophetic ministry began in 627 BC. The Babylonians destroyed Jerusalem in 586 BC. Jeremiah wrote Lamentations later that same year. *Lamentations* means "funeral songs" and is descriptive of the book's contents. It expresses the anguish of God's people over the destruction of Jerusalem by the Babylonians. Jeremiah appears to have witnessed the destruction firsthand. The temple was destroyed, and the people were deported to live in exile. This book depicts the funeral of a city.

Transformational truth. For more than four decades, Jeremiah functioned as a prophet when warning his people of impending judgment. He then acted as a fellow brother when he expressed grief over Jerusalem's destruction. He would now act as a spiritual father when praying for God's mercy and the restoration of his people (Lamentations 3:1-66). Spiritual leaders often wear many hats.

A verse for meditation. "The faithful love of the LORD never ends! His mercies never cease. Great is his faithfulness; his mercies begin afresh each morning" (Jeremiah 3:22-23).

A question to ponder. What are some of the new mercies God shows you each day?

PRAYING FOR RESTORATION

*Lamentations 5; Obadiah 1; 2 Kings
25:22-26; Jeremiah 40:7 – 41:18*

Yesterday we considered the people's anguish over Jerusalem's destruction (Lamentations 1–4). Today we focus on the captives lamenting and praying for restoration.

Key concept. The captive Jews — depressed and discouraged — pray for restoration.

The big picture. Lamentations 1 expresses Jeremiah's mourning over Jerusalem's destruction by Babylon. Chapter 2 reveals that Babylon was the whipping rod of the Lord. Chapter 3 portrays Jeremiah praying for God's mercy and the restoration of his people. Chapter 4 points to how severely Jerusalem had been judged by the Lord in His anger. Today's reading, chapter 5, shows the Jews reflecting on their horrific state of affairs, and praying for restoration.

Transformational truth. When life throws you a punch, your first best response is to turn to the Lord in prayer. The Jews in captivity yearned for and prayed for deliverance and restoration. These prayers included both confession of sin and an appeal to God's grace (Lamentations 5). Jeremiah's people would indeed be restored, but not until their trial yielded its proper fruit — thorough repentance and recommitment to the Lord.

A verse for meditation. "Restore us, O LORD, and bring us back to you again! Give us back the joys we once had!" (Lamentations 5:21).

A question to ponder. What motivates your prayers?

ATTEMPTED REFUGE IN EGYPT

Jeremiah 42–44; Ezekiel 33:21-33

Yesterday we considered the captive Jews lamenting and praying for restoration (Lamentations 5). Today we explore how some of Judah's inhabitants sought refuge in Egypt.

Key concept. The Jews who were intended by God to watch over Judah during the exile fled for Egypt.

The big picture. Jeremiah informed these Jews they would be safe if they stayed in Judah, despite Babylon's threat. If they moved to Egypt, however, they would be destroyed (Jeremiah 42). They rejected Jeremiah's words. They departed for Egypt and forced Jeremiah to accompany them. Jeremiah prophesied that Babylon would conquer Egypt and that the people who fled there would die (43). Those who fled to Egypt would never see Judah again (44).

Transformational truth. The Jews in Judah had a bogus commitment to the Lord. As summed up by Jeremiah, "You said, 'Just tell us what the LORD our God says, and we will do it!' And today I have told you exactly what he said, but you will not obey the LORD your God any better now than you have in the past" (Jeremiah 42:20-21). For a better policy, consult James 1:22.

A verse for meditation. "To this very hour you have shown no remorse or reverence" (Jeremiah 44:10).

A question to ponder. What do you think motivates such "bogus commitment" among so many of God's people?

REPENT AND LIVE

*Ezekiel 32:17 – 33:20; Jeremiah 52:28-
30; 1 Chronicles 4:24 – 5:17; Psalm 137*

Yesterday we considered how some of Judah's inhabitants foolishly sought refuge in Egypt (Jeremiah 42 – 44; Ezekiel 33:21-33). Today we focus on the choice to repent and live—an important lesson in view of Jerusalem's fall to the Babylonians.

Key concept. The righteous will live and be blessed. The wicked will come to ruin.

The big picture. God called Ezekiel to be His watchman (Ezekiel 33:1-9). The watchman's message was that God takes no pleasure in the death of the wicked but wants them to repent. Those who choose righteousness will live and be blessed. Those who choose and remain in wickedness will come to ruin (33:10-20).

Transformational truth. God pleads for the wicked to repent. He does not want them to perish (Ezekiel 33:11). This brings to mind 2 Peter 3:9: "He does not want anyone to be destroyed, but wants everyone to repent."

A verse for meditation. "As surely as I live, says the Sovereign LORD, I take no pleasure in the death of wicked people. I only want them to turn from their wicked ways so they can live. Turn! Turn from your wickedness, O people of Israel! Why should you die?" (Ezekiel 33:11).

A question to ponder. Has this repetitious theme from the Old Testament prophets drilled into you the reality that *choices have consequences?*

THERE IS HOPE FOR THE FUTURE

1 Chronicles 5:18-26; 6:3-15; 7:1 - 8:28

Yesterday we considered the choice to repent and live—an important lesson in view of Jerusalem's fall to the Babylonians (Ezekiel 32:17 – 33:20; Jeremiah 52:28-30; 1 Chronicles 4:24 – 5:17; Psalm 137). Today we explore hope for the future.

Key concept. There was hope for those who had gone into exile, for a remnant would survive and go back to the Promised Land.

The big picture. First Chronicles is presented from the vantage point of Jews going into exile, and then a remnant eventually returning from Babylon to Jerusalem. The future at present looked bleak, but 1 Chronicles gave the people hope. It reminded everyone of God's promises about their land, temple, priesthood, and that they were God's chosen people. It also reminded them of their genealogical connection with God's past purposes in general and with the Davidic covenant in particular (1 Chronicles 5:18-26; 6:3-15; 7:1 – 8:28).

Transformational truth. People can't last long without hope. Once hope is lost, people just give up. In today's Scripture reading, hope is given to the exiles about their future. You and I have a future hope as well. It's all based on the inheritance awaiting us in heaven (1 Peter 1:4).

A verse for meditation. Various tribes "went into exile when the LORD sent the people of Judah and Jerusalem into captivity under Nebuchadnezzar" (1 Chronicles 6:15).

A question to ponder. Do you think much about your future hope and inheritance?

THE HUMBLING OF NEBUCHADNEZZAR

Daniel 4; 1 Chronicles 8:29 – 9:1

Yesterday we focused on the choice to repent and live (1 Chronicles 5:18-26; 6:3-15; 7:1 – 8:28). Today we consider how God — during Judah's time of captivity — humbled Nebuchadnezzar in Babylon and later restored him to his kingdom.

Key concept. God brought Nebuchadnezzar down in Babylon, but later restored him.

The big picture. The prideful Nebuchadnezzar had a dream indicating that God was going to bring him down and humiliate him for a time, causing him to dwell with animals. He was eventually restored and afterward offered praises to God: "I praised and worshiped the Most High and honored the one who lives forever" (Daniel 4:34).

Transformational truth. Daniel urged Nebuchadnezzar, "Stop sinning and do what is right" (Daniel 4:27). Daniel's comment was motivated by two spiritual realities: (1) sin leads to destruction and death; (2) righteousness leads to blessing and long life. Daniel knew it was in the king's best interest to turn from sin and pursue righteousness. The same is true for us (Exodus 19:5; Deuteronomy 4:40; Matthew 5:2-12).

A verse for meditation. "How great are his signs, how powerful his wonders! His kingdom will last forever, his rule through all generations" (Daniel 4:3).

A question to ponder. Are there any areas of your life where you need to "stop sinning and do what is right"?

DANIEL AND THE LIONS' DEN

Daniel 6; 9

In the previous lesson we explored how God humbled Nebuchadnezzar in Babylon and later restored him to his kingdom (Daniel 4; 1 Chronicles 8:29–9:1). Today we consider how Daniel survived the lions' den.

Key concept. God rescued Daniel in the lions' den.

The big picture. During Judah's captivity in Babylon, a plot was launched against Daniel by unscrupulous government officials (Daniel 6:1-9). The result was that Daniel was thrown into a lions' den (6:10-17). God protected Daniel throughout the night (6:18-23). This took place in 539 BC. Later, Daniel revealed Israel's prophetic timetable—70 groups of seven years, or 490 years. The final "week" of seven years will be the future seven-year tribulation period in the end times (9:20-27).

Transformational truth. God blessed Daniel because he lived faultlessly before God and other human beings (Daniel 6:4). Faultless living is described for us in Psalm 119—the psalmist boasted, "Blessed are those whose way is blameless" (verse 1 ESV; see also verses 2-6). We should all seek to be "Psalm 119 Christians."

A verse for meditation. "My God sent his angel to shut the lions' mouths so that they would not hurt me, for I have been found innocent in his sight" (Daniel 6:22).

A question to ponder. Do you think you've ever been protected by an angel in a dangerous circumstance?

BLESSINGS LIE AHEAD FOR ISRAEL

Ezekiel 34 – 36

Yesterday we focused on how Daniel survived the lions' den (Daniel 6; 9). Today we consider the blessings that lie ahead for God's people in the more distant prophetic future.

Key concept. Captivity in Babylon would be followed by great blessings for God's people.

The big picture. The shepherds of God's people had treated them badly. How much better will be the Good Shepherd—the Messiah—who will truly care for His people (Ezekiel 34). In addition to restoring His people to the land following the Babylonian captivity, God also promised to restore His people to the Promised Land in the distant end times and draw Jews back to the land from all the nations of the world (after being dispersed in AD 70 by Rome). This is what makes the year 1948 significant, for Israel was reborn as a nation that year, and Jews have been streaming back to the land ever since. (My books on Bible prophecy address this issue in great detail.) God also promised to give His people a new heart and a new spirit (36).

Transformational truth. God's pattern is to restore His people after chastening them for a time (Ezekiel 36:24). God likewise restores you and me following our individual trials (1 Peter 5:10). Always be watching for the light at the end of the tunnel!

A verse for meditation. "I will give you a new heart, and I will put a new spirit in you. I will take out your stony, stubborn heart and give you a tender, responsive heart" (Ezekiel 36:26).

A question to ponder. What effect do you think the words in Ezekiel 36:26 would have had on the Jews in exile in Babylon?

GOD THE GREAT DELIVERER

Ezekiel 37 – 39; 32:1-16

In the previous lesson we explored the blessings that lie ahead for God's people in the more distant prophetic future (Ezekiel 34 – 36). Today we consider how God will be the great Deliverer of His people in the end times.

Key concept. God will deliver His people from a massive invasion force in the last days.

The big picture. Ezekiel prophesied that Israel would become a nation again and that the Jews would be regathered from "many nations" to Israel in the end times (Ezekiel 36 – 37). This happened in 1948 and after. Ezekiel then prophesied that, sometime later, there would be an all-out invasion of Israel by a massive northern assault force, with Russia heading up a coalition of Muslim nations, including modern Iran, Sudan, Turkey, and Libya. Israel will have virtually no chance of defending herself. God, however, will intervene and supernaturally destroy the invaders (38 – 39). (See my book *Northern Storm Rising*, Harvest House Publishers.)

Transformational truth. Despite the overwhelming large coalition of nations attacking Israel, God Himself will destroy the invaders (Ezekiel 39; Psalm 121:4; Isaiah 54:17). Just as God will rescue Israel in this seemingly impossible situation, so God can rescue you and me (see Ephesians 3:20; Hebrews 13:5).

A verse for meditation. "I will bring you back to the land of Israel. When this happens, O my people, you will know that I am the LORD" (Ezekiel 37:12-13).

A question to ponder. How do you think these end-times prophecies made the exiles in Babylon feel?

A REVIVED ROMAN EMPIRE

Daniel 7–8; 5

Yesterday we focused on how God will be the great Deliverer of His people in the end times (Ezekiel 37–39; 32:1-16). Today we consider the antichrist's rule over a future revived Roman Empire during the future tribulation period.

Key concept. A wicked end-times ruler—the antichrist—will one day rise to power in a revived Roman Empire during the seven-year tribulation period that precedes Christ's second coming.

The big picture. Daniel had a vision of four strange beasts, representing four kingdoms that would play an important role in biblical prophecy. These were Babylon, Medo-Persia, Greece under Alexander the Great, and a revived Roman Empire, which is yet future. It is over this empire that the antichrist will one day rule during the future tribulation period (Daniel 7–8).

Transformational truth. Daniel 7:10 refers to "millions of angels" that serve God. Their number is elsewhere described as "thousands and millions of angels around the throne" (Revelation 5:11). Job 25:3 understandably asks, "Who is able to count his heavenly army?" There are more than enough angels to serve as "ministering spirits" for Christians (Hebrews 1:14 ESV).

A verse for meditation. [A messianic prophecy:] "I saw someone like a son of man coming with the clouds of heaven…His rule is eternal—it will never end" (Daniel 7:13-14).

A question to ponder. Has your study of biblical prophecy bolstered your faith in God and your confidence in Scripture? Do you think prophecy would have done the same for the Jews in exile?

THE MILLENNIAL TEMPLE

Ezekiel 40:1 – 43:27

In the previous lesson we explored the antichrist's rule over a future revived Roman Empire during the tribulation period (Daniel 7 – 8; 5). Today we consider the future end-times millennial temple.

Key concept. Ezekiel informs the exiles of the future millennial temple.

The big picture. Ezekiel 40:38 – 43:27 provides details about Christ's future millennial kingdom—a 1,000-year kingdom of perfect peace and righteousness on earth. During this time, God will fulfill all His covenant land promises to Israel. Today's reading provides details on the millennial temple. The sacrifices in this temple should not be seen as a return to the Mosaic law. Rather, they serve only one purpose—to remove any ceremonial uncleanness in the temple itself.

Transformational truth. Worship will be a central feature of Christ's millennial kingdom (Ezekiel 43:13 – 46:24). Ezekiel provided a strong prophetic hope to those who were in exile. You and I can also have a strong prophetic hope—a hope that motivates righteous living (Titus 2:12-14; 2 Peter 3:11-12; 1 John 3:2-3).

A verse for meditation. "The glory of the God of Israel appeared from the east. The sound of his coming was like the roar of rushing waters, and the whole landscape shone with his glory" (Ezekiel 43:2).

A question to ponder. Do you have a strong prophetic hope? How does it change the way you live?

THE MILLENNIAL SACRIFICES

Ezekiel 44 – 46

Yesterday we considered the future end-times millennial temple (Ezekiel 40:1 – 43:27). Today we focus on the purpose of the millennial sacrifices.

Key concept. The millennial sacrifices serve only to remove ceremonial uncleanness and prevent defilement in the temple itself.

The big picture. Ezekiel informed the exiles about the priests, the Levites, and the services at the future millennial temple. The priests will offer sacrifices in the temple. The purpose of the sacrifices is apparently to remove ceremonial uncleanness and prevent defilement from polluting the purity of the temple environment. Such will be necessary because Yahweh will again be dwelling on the earth in the midst of mortal people (still with their sin natures) who have entered into the millennial kingdom (see Matthew 25:31-46). It's also possible that the sacrifices may serve as memorials of the finished sacrifice of Christ.

Transformational truth. Ezekiel 44:4 illustrates how human beings in their mortal bodies fall on their faces when witnessing God's tremendous glory. In the afterlife, we'll have glorified resurrection bodies suited to dwelling in the direct presence of God (1 Corinthians 13:12; see also Psalm 17:15; Revelation 21:3). *I can't wait!*

A verse for meditation. "I looked and saw that the glory of the LORD filled the Temple of the LORD, and I fell face down on the ground" (Ezekiel 44:4).

A question to ponder. Have you ever thought about what it will be like to dwell face to face with God in heaven?

LAND ALLOTMENTS IN
THE MILLENNIAL KINGDOM

*Ezekiel 47–48; 29:17–30:19; 2 Kings
25:27-30; Jeremiah 52:31-34*

Yesterday we considered the purpose of the millennial sacrifices
(Ezekiel 44–46). Today we look at the land allotments for Israel
in the millennial kingdom.

Key concept. In ultimate fulfillment of the Abrahamic covenant,
land allotments for Israel in the millennial kingdom are described.

The big picture. Ezekiel prophetically witnessed the specific borders
of Israel in the millennial kingdom (Ezekiel 47:13-20). Seven of Israel's tribes will be given portions of the land north of the temple area
(48:1-7). A sacred portion of the land will be allotted for the temple,
the priests, and the Levites (48:8-22). Five of Israel's tribes will then
be given land south of the temple area (48:23-29). All of this will be
according to God's directions.

Transformational truth. Christians raptured before the tribulation
will participate in the heavenly government during this millennial
kingdom (check out Revelation 5:10; 20:6; 2 Timothy 2:12). What an
honor and privilege!

A verse for meditation. "This is what the Sovereign LORD says: 'Divide
the land in this way for the twelve tribes of Israel'" (Ezekiel 47:13).

A question to ponder. Can you imagine a perfect living environment
on earth where Christ personally reigns over and dwells among people?

ERA 7: THE RETURN FROM EXILE
538 – 6 BC

*Books in whole or in part: 1 Chronicles
2 Chronicles • Ezra • Nehemiah • Esther • Psalms
Daniel • Joel • Haggai • Zechariah • Malachi*

Today we begin our study of a new biblical era—the era titled "The Return from Exile," dated 538–6 BC. Bible books pertinent to our study of this era include 1 Chronicles, 2 Chronicles, Ezra, Nehemiah, Esther, Psalms, Daniel, Joel, Haggai, Zechariah, and Malachi. This is the final era in the Old Testament.

The Jews had been in captivity in Babylon for 70 years. Early during the captivity, King Nebuchadnezzar had a dream which—interpreted by Daniel—indicated that the Medo-Persian Empire would one day conquer Babylon (Daniel 2:39). Historically, the Medes and Persians conquered Babylon in 539 BC. King Cyrus of Persia then issued a decree that allowed the Jews to go back to their homeland.

The Jewish people did not return to their homeland all at once. They went in waves. Under Zerubbabel's leadership, a first remnant of Jewish captives left Babylon for Jerusalem in 538 BC, just a year after the Medes and Persians conquered Babylon. Upon arriving in their homeland, they built an altar, offered sacrifices to God, and celebrated the feast of tabernacles. They then laid the foundation of the temple and established themselves in the land.

Their work in building the temple was hindered by enemies who convinced the Persian king to stop reconstruction of the temple (see Ezra 4). Moreover, the people had become spiritually complacent and emotionally despondent at how ruined their former habitat had become. They were in no mood to rebuild the temple.

The prophet Haggai promptly reprimanded the people for procrastinating in building the temple (Haggai 1:2-6). They had built their own houses, but now they were indifferent about building God's house.

Haggai exhorted them to make haste and get busy (1:7-8). He reminded them that the reason God had not blessed them was because they had forgotten Him (1:9-11). That needed to be remedied immediately. They heeded Haggai's words and resumed building the temple (1:12-15).

Haggai also instructed the returned exiles not to get all bent out of shape by the smaller size of this temple (it was much smaller than Solomon's). Haggai gave them a promise from the Lord that the glory of this temple would be greater than that of the former temple (Haggai 2:4-5,9). Moreover, restoring God to first place in their lives would bring great blessing (2:18-19).

Meanwhile, the prophet Zechariah—a contemporary of Haggai—communicated four messages to the people designed to end their spiritual lethargy: (1) empty ritualism was rebuked (Zechariah 7:4-7); (2) divine retribution always follows disobedience (7:8-14); (3) God promised a regathering, restoration, and blessing for Israel (8:1-17); and (4) there would be much joy among God's people (8:18-23).

Motivated by the prophets Haggai and Zechariah, the people worked steadily to complete the temple. As for the enemies who convinced the Persian king to stop reconstruction of the temple, the king investigated matters and ruled in favor of the returned remnant of Jews. The temple was completed in 516 BC, more than two decades after they arrived in their homeland.

A second wave of Jews—nearly six decades later—returned to their homeland in 458 BC under the leadership of Ezra. This involved some 2,000 families. When Ezra arrived, he found that the returnees' spiritual lives were in utter ruins. Ezra's goal was to bring spiritual healing. He was instrumental in teaching the Jews about God's law. He sought to revive his people according to this law (Ezra 9:1–10:44). He called for repentance and renewal.

A few years later, the prophet Nehemiah came to the homeland with a small group of people. Nehemiah's goal was to rebuild and repair the city walls (Nehemiah 2–3). Samaria's king opposed the repairs, but Nehemiah refused to be slowed. He assigned half the people to engage in rebuilding the walls, while the others remained on military watch for any outside interference (4). Through Nehemiah's prayers and decisive leadership, the construction work continued (5) and was finally completed in 52 days (6). During this time, Nehemiah also called on the people to repent of their sins and spiritual lethargy.

The prophets Joel and Malachi were also on the scene, rebuking sin, calling for faithfulness to God, and reminding the returnees of God's love. The Israelites were so encumbered by difficulties that they seemed blind to God's love for them. God assured the people through Malachi that His love for them was unending. Malachi also powerfully urged repentance—for more judgment would surely come if sin continued.

In the coming chapters, we will journey through 1 Chronicles, 2 Chronicles, Ezra, Nehemiah, Esther, Psalms, Daniel, Joel, Haggai, Zechariah, and Malachi as we learn interesting details about the era of the return from exile. The following dates provide a helpful chronological orientation:

539—Cyrus decreed Jewish liberation.

538–457—The events described in the book of Ezra transpired.

538—People began returning to their homeland from exile.

536—Construction of the temple began.

530—Work on the temple halted.

522–486—Haggai ministered during these years.

520—Haggai wrote his little book; Zechariah began his prophetic ministry; work on the temple resumed.

516—The temple was completed.

465—Artaxerxes I became king of Persia.

458—Ezra went to Jerusalem.

457–444—The book of Ezra was written.

445—Nehemiah went to Jerusalem and became governor; the wall of Jerusalem was rebuilt.

433–400—Malachi wrote his short book.

Preview: In Day 259, we begin our study of exiles returning to their land.

RETURN FROM EXILE

Ezra 1-4:5; 2 Chronicles 36:22-23; 1 Chronicles 3:17-24

Yesterday we introduced Era 7, titled "The Return from Exile," dated 538–6 BC. Today we focus on the first of the exiles to return to Jerusalem.

Key concept. The first wave of exiles arrived in Jerusalem.

The big picture. In the book of Ezra, there were two returns from Babylon—one led by Zerubbabel (Ezra 1–6), and then nearly six decades later, one under Ezra (7–10). The first return aimed at rebuilding the temple (1:1–2:70). The second return had as its aim Ezra's rebuilding of his people's spiritual lives (7:1–8:36). All of this followed the Persian King Cyrus's decree of Jewish liberation in 539 BC.

Transformational truth. By returning from Babylon to Israel, the Jews were demonstrating their faith in God's promises: "The LORD fulfilled the prophecy he had given through Jeremiah" (Ezra 1:1). A common theme in Scripture is that God is a promise keeper (Numbers 23:19; Joshua 23:14). What He promises, *He fulfills.* So take Him at His word!

A verse for meditation. "All the people gave a great shout, praising the LORD because the foundation of the LORD's Temple had been laid" (Ezra 3:11).

A question to ponder. Why was the rebuilding of the temple so critically important for the returned Jews?

ANGELIC ASSISTANCE IN ANSWER TO PRAYER

Daniel 10 – 12; Ezra 4:24 – 5:1; Haggai 1

Yesterday we considered the first of the exiles returning to Jerusalem (Ezra 1–4:5). Today we read about how an angel showed up to help Daniel in answer to Daniel's prayer.

Key concept. Though the Jews were free to return to their homeland, Daniel chose to remain in Babylon. According to today's Scripture reading, he encountered an angel that helped him interpret a prophecy.

The big picture. In answer to prayer, God sent an angel to explain further details to Daniel about the prophetic future. These details largely related to the antichrist's role in the future tribulation period (Daniel 10; 11:44; 12:1,4). Meanwhile, the prophet Haggai sought to shake his people out of their despondency and rejuvenate their spiritual commitment (Haggai 1).

Transformational truth. Angels are sometimes dispatched by God to take care of our prayer requests (Acts 12:6-19). Fallen angels sometimes seek to thwart the angels God dispatches to answer a particular prayer. This happened when Daniel prayed (Daniel 10:13). When you pray, keep your faith strong, even if there seems to be a delay in God's answer. You never know what's going on behind the scenes in the spiritual world!

A verse for meditation. "Don't be afraid, Daniel. Since the first day you began to pray for understanding and to humble yourself before your God, your request has been heard in heaven. I have come in answer to your prayer" (Daniel 10:12).

A question to ponder. Does today's lesson embolden you to pray more fervently without discouragement when answers seem delayed?

MOTIVATION TO REBUILD THE TEMPLE

Zechariah 1–5; Haggai 2; Ezra 5:2

Yesterday we focused on how an angel showed up to help Daniel in answer to his prayer (Daniel 10–12; Haggai 1). Today we consider the encouragement offered to the returned Jews to finish rebuilding the temple.

Key concept. The stagnating Jews were motivated to finish rebuilding their temple.

The big picture. The Jews began returning to their homeland in 538 BC. Construction of the temple began in 536 BC, but halted in 530 BC (Ezra 4:4-5). God called Zechariah to get the people on their feet again and finish the task. Zechariah's approach was to demonstrate the importance of the temple: It was the religious center of Jewish life, and it represented God's presence among His people.

Transformational truth. God affirmed, "Return to me, and I will return to you" (Zechariah 1:3). This reminds us of James 4:8: "Come close to God, and God will come close to you." If you feel distant from God, take the first step today by moving closer to God.

A verse for meditation. "The LORD says, 'Come away! Flee from Babylon…Come away, people of Zion, you who are exiled in Babylon!'" (Zechariah 2:6).

A question to ponder. Why should you make it a daily habit to draw near to God?

NO EMPTY RITUALISM

Zechariah 6 – 8; Ezra 5:3 – 6:14

In the previous lesson, we considered the encouragement offered to the returned Jews to finish rebuilding the temple (Zechariah 1 – 5; Haggai 2). Today we focus on avoiding empty ritualism.

Key concept. The returned Jews were merely going through the motions with God. They needed to "get real."

The big picture. Zechariah gave four messages representing his burden for the returned remnant: (1) empty ritualism was rebuked (Zechariah 7:4-7); (2) divine retribution follows disobedience (7:8-14); (3) God has promised a regathering, restoration, and blessing for Israel (8:1-17); and (4) there will be much joy among God's people (8:18-23).

Transformational truth. God dislikes it when people merely go through the motions with Him, not pouring their hearts into a relationship with Him (Zechariah 7:4-7). God desires authentic believers who show their commitment not only in how they relate to Him, but in how they relate to others (7:9-10). This reminds us of James 1:22: "Don't just listen to God's word. You must do what it says."

A verse for meditation. "Judge fairly, and show mercy and kindness to one another. Do not oppress widows, orphans, foreigners, and the poor. And do not scheme against each other" (Zechariah 7:9-10).

A question to ponder. Why are God's instructions in Zechariah 7:9 so critically important?

THE LORD IS MY SHEPHERD

Zechariah 9 – 14

Yesterday we considered empty ritualism (Zechariah 6 – 8; Ezra 5:3–6:14). Today we focus on God as the divine Shepherd of His people.

Key concept. God, as the divine Shepherd, takes care of His people.

The big picture. Zechariah closed his book with two oracles about the future Messiah: (1) The Messiah would be rejected in His first coming, betrayed for thirty pieces of silver (Zechariah 11:13); (2) just before the second coming, the Jews would be under attack and cry out to the Messiah for deliverance (12). Zechariah said Israel will be redeemed and delivered by the Messiah (13), and He will then set foot on the Mount of Olives, after which He will judge the nations and reign on earth (14).

Transformational truth. Zechariah 11:1-17 portrays God as bringing judgment upon wicked shepherds who had "no pity" on the people (11:5). How much better is the care of the divine Shepherd (11:7)! In the New Testament, Jesus is called the Good Shepherd (John 15:1-10), the Great Shepherd (Hebrews 13:20), and the Chief Shepherd (1 Peter 5:4 NIV). As Shepherd, He is our Leader and Companion.

A verse for meditation. "I cared for the flock intended for slaughter—the flock that was oppressed" (Zechariah 11:7).

A question to ponder. What does it mean to you personally that the divine Shepherd is your daily companion?

ESTHER INTERCEDED
FOR HER PEOPLE

Esther 1–4; Ezra 6:14-22; 4:6

Yesterday we focused on God as the divine Shepherd who cares for His people (Zechariah 9–14). Today we consider Esther interceding for her people.

Key concept. Esther used her high position to prevent her people's destruction.

The big picture. Queen Vashti had been deposed as queen in Persia (Esther 1). Esther, a Jew, subsequently became queen in 479 BC, almost 60 years after the Jews were released from bondage in Babylon. She found great favor in the king's eyes (2). Haman, the evil chief officer of King Ahasuerus, hated the Jews and sought to annihilate them. He set a plan in motion to do so (3). Under Mordecai's encouragement—and in God's providence—Esther used her high position to make an appeal to the king on behalf of her people (4).

Transformational truth. God has the ability to sovereignly and purposefully place His people in high and strategic positions of authority. Esther is a good example of this (Esther 2). We are also reminded of how God providentially elevated Joseph to great authority in Egypt (Genesis 38–39; 41; 50:20).

A verse for meditation. "Who knows if perhaps you were made queen for just such a time as this?" (Esther 4:14).

A question to ponder. What insights have you gleaned from the book of Esther on God's sovereignty over individual human lives?

THE JEWS ARE PROVIDENTIALLY RESCUED

Esther 5–10

Yesterday we focused on Esther using her high position to intercede on behalf of her people (Esther 1–4; Ezra 6:14-22; 4:6). Today we consider how God providentially used Esther in preventing the destruction of her people.

Key concept. God sovereignly used Esther to prevent the annihilation of the Jews.

The big picture. At a banquet arranged by Esther, the king offered to give her anything up to half his kingdom. She asked only that her people—the Jews—be saved, and that the one behind the plot to attack them be judged. Haman was promptly hanged. The king then issued a decree prohibiting the killing of the Jews (Esther 5–10).

Transformational truth. The king asked Esther: "Tell me what you want, Queen Esther. What is your request?" (Esther 7:2). Esther then boldly interceded before the king on behalf of her people, implicating the wicked Haman as the one seeking the destruction of her people. It is not always easy for us to speak up when we need to. May the Lord grant us boldness!

A verse for meditation. "If I have found favor with the king, and if it pleases the king to grant my request, I ask that my life and the lives of my people will be spared" (Esther 7:3).

A question to ponder. Do you trust God's providential oversight of your life?

REBUILDING SPIRITUAL LIVES

Ezra 4:7-23; 7-8

In the previous lesson we explored how God providentially used Esther in preventing the destruction of her people (Esther 5–10). Today we consider how Ezra sought to rebuild his people's spiritual lives.

Key concept. It wasn't just the temple that needed rebuilding. The people's spiritual lives also needed to be rebuilt.

The big picture. There were two "returns" from Babylon—one led by Zerubbabel (Ezra 1–6), and then six decades later, one under Ezra (7–10). The first return had as its aim the rebuilding of the temple (1:1–2:70). The second return had the goal of rebuilding the people's spiritual lives (7:1–8:36). In today's lesson, we see that Ezra is concerned with the latter.

Transformational truth. Ezra "studied and taught the commands and decrees of the LORD to Israel" (Ezra 7:11). The Jews were not just returning to their land, they were now also finally returning to the Word of God! You and I need the life-changing influence of God's Word as well (see 2 Timothy 3:15-17; Psalm 119:25,37).

A verse for meditation. "Praise him for demonstrating such unfailing love to me by honoring me before the king, his council, and all his mighty nobles! I felt encouraged because the gracious hand of the LORD my God was on me" (Ezra 7:28).

A question to ponder. Do you make it a high priority to immerse yourself in Scripture daily? What happens to your spiritual life when you fall away from God's Word?

JERUSALEM'S CITY WALLS REBUILT

Nehemiah 1 – 2; Ezra 9 – 10

Yesterday we considered Ezra's goal of rebuilding his people's spiritual lives (Ezra 4:7-23; 7 – 8). Today we turn our attention to the rebuilding of Jerusalem's city walls.

Key concept. Nehemiah oversaw the reconstruction of the city wall.

The big picture. Nehemiah prayed for his people, confessed their sins, and asked God for blessing in exchange for repentance (Nehemiah 1). Nehemiah was then permitted by Artaxerxes I to visit Jerusalem to assess the city's condition. He reported back that the city walls needed repairs (2). Nehemiah became governor in Jerusalem in 445 BC, and Jerusalem's shattered wall was rebuilt that same year.

Transformational truth. One reason God answered Nehemiah's prayers was that he was a righteous man (Nehemiah 1:4-6). This reminds us of James 5:16: "The earnest prayer of a righteous person has great power and produces wonderful results." The Lord "hears the prayers of the righteous" (Proverbs 15:29).

A verse for meditation. "O LORD, please hear my prayer! Listen to the prayers of those of us who delight in honoring you. Please grant me success today by making the king favorable to me. Put it into his heart to be kind to me" (Nehemiah 1:11).

A question to ponder. Have you ever considered asking the Lord to grant you favor in the eyes of an important person?

REBUILDING JERUSALEM'S CITY WALLS

Nehemiah 3:1 – 7:3

Yesterday we read about the repairs needed for Jerusalem's city wall (Nehemiah 1–2; Ezra 9–10). More of the same today.

Key concept. Despite some resistance, Nehemiah oversaw the process of getting Jerusalem's walls rebuilt.

The big picture. Nehemiah headed up a group of people who rendered repairs to Jerusalem's city walls (Nehemiah 3). Samaria's king opposed the repairs, but Nehemiah refused to be slowed. He assigned half the people to rebuild, while the others remained on military watch (4). Through Nehemiah's prayers and decisive leadership, the construction work continued (5) and was eventually completed in just 52 days (6).

Transformational truth. Many of the Jews were experiencing economic hardship and had to borrow from wealthy Jews to survive, using their land and even their children as collateral. The children would become slaves of the wealthy Jews if the debts were not repaid (Nehemiah 5:1-5). Nehemiah confronted the wealthy Jews and put an end to this exploitation (5:6-13). Taking a stand for social justice is important.

A verse for meditation. [Nehemiah's words to the exploiters:] "What you are doing is not right! Should you not walk in the fear of our God…?" (Nehemiah 5:9).

A question to ponder. What do you think are some of the more serious forms of social injustice in our country today?

REVIVED BY THE WORD

Nehemiah 7:4 – 8:12

Yesterday we focused on the rebuilding of Jerusalem's walls (Nehemiah 3:1–7:3). Today we consider how God's Word revived the people.

Key concept. The people were revived by hearing God's Word read and explained.

The big picture. Nehemiah discovered a genealogical record that enabled his people to be restored to the cities that had been their family inheritance (Nehemiah 7). The people soon requested that Ezra read the law of Moses to them. The Levites made sure everyone understood the Scriptures. The hearing of God's Word initially caused the people to weep, but then they rejoiced that they now understood it (8).

Transformational truth. The understanding of God's Word had a life-changing effect on Ezra's people. They "had all been weeping as they listened to the words of the Law," but now had "great joy" because they understood it (Nehemiah 8:9,12). The people then "confessed their own sins and the sins of their ancestors" (9:2). A revival swept through the nation (9:3-37).

A verse for meditation. "He faced the square just inside the Water Gate from early morning until noon and read aloud to everyone who could understand. All the people listened closely to the Book of the Law" (Nehemiah 8:3).

A question to ponder. Why do you think so many professing Christians today spend so little time reading God's Word?

A COMMITMENT TO OBEY

Nehemiah 8:13 – 10:39

In the previous lesson we explored how God's Word revived the people (Nehemiah 7:4 – 8:12). Today we consider the people's consequent commitment to obey.

Key concept. The revival experienced by the people moved them to obedience.

The big picture. Ezra read the law of Moses to the people, and the Levites made sure they understood it. The people rejoiced (Nehemiah 8) and experienced a revival (9). They then resolved to obey the Lord's commands (10): "They swore a curse on themselves if they failed to obey the Law of God as issued by his servant Moses" (verse 29).

Transformational truth. Nehemiah's people were fearful of surrounding peoples who might invade their land (Nehemiah 9). Nehemiah had earlier urged, "Don't be afraid of the enemy! Remember the LORD, who is great and glorious" (4:14). This brings to mind Romans 8:31: "If God is for us, who can ever be against us?" (see also Psalms 3:6; 27:3; 56:4).

A verse for meditation. "They remained standing in place for three hours while the Book of the Law of the LORD their God was read aloud to them. Then for three more hours they confessed their sins and worshiped the LORD their God" (Nehemiah 9:3).

A question to ponder. Do confession and worship play a role in your daily prayer life?

A DEDICATION CEREMONY

Nehemiah 11 – 12; 1 Chronicles 9:1-34

Yesterday we considered the people's commitment to obey God's Word (Nehemiah 8:13–10:39). Today we focus on a meaningful dedication ceremony.

Key concept. A dedication ceremony was held for Jerusalem's new wall.

The big picture. Jerusalem's inhabitants now included Israel's leaders, a small number of people from the towns of Judah and Benjamin, and some provincial officials (Nehemiah 11). There was a dedication ceremony held for the new walls of Jerusalem. Levites, singers, priests, and choirs participated in this joyous celebration (12).

Transformational truth. Choirs accompanied by musical instruments were a big part of the dedication ceremony (Nehemiah 12:35-36; see also 1 Chronicles 25; Psalms 4; 5; 6). Today's believers are likewise encouraged to sing "psalms and hymns and spiritual songs," and to make "music to the Lord in your hearts" (Ephesians 5:19).

A verse for meditation. "For the dedication of the new wall of Jerusalem, the Levites throughout the land were asked to come to Jerusalem to assist in the ceremonies. They were to take part in the joyous occasion with their songs of thanksgiving and with the music of cymbals, harps, and lyres" (Nehemiah 12:27).

A question to ponder. Have you ever considered how you can have a celebratory attitude all the year through in view of the blessings the Lord continually pours upon you?

DISILLUSIONMENT AND APATHY

Malachi 1:1 – 2:9; Nehemiah 12:27 – 13:31; 5:14-19

Yesterday we considered a meaningful dedication ceremony (Nehemiah 11–12). Today we focus on the priests' and the people's spiritual apathy.

Key concept. Malachi sought to shake the people loose from the spiritual apathy they developed *following* the temple's rebuilding. The spiritual lives of the people seemed to fluctuate up and down, up and down.

The big picture. The rebuilding of the temple began in 536 BC, halted in 530 BC, resumed in 520 BC, and was completed in 515 BC. The people had returned to their homeland, but this had not translated into a desire to walk closely with God. Spiritual lethargy was at an all-time high. God thus assured them through Malachi that He loved them (Malachi 1:1-5). But Malachi also issued a stern warning because the people had succumbed to social corruption and empty worship. The priests were particularly corrupt (1:6–2:16).

Transformational truth. A principle we learn from today's reading is that we should never doubt God's love—even when things seem to be going haywire in our lives (Malachi 1:1-5). Romans 5:8 tells us, "God showed his great love for us by sending Christ to die for us while we were still sinners."

A verse for meditation. " 'I have always loved you,' says the LORD" (Malachi 1:2).

A question to ponder. Are you ever tempted to doubt God's love for you when life throws you a punch?

DISILLUSIONMENT AND APATHY CONTINUE

Malachi 2:10 – 4:6

Yesterday we focused on the priests' and the people's spiritual apathy (Malachi 1:1–2:9). Today we consider more of the same.

Key concept. Spiritual lethargy, disillusionment, and apathy remained at an all-time high. Such lethargy had translated into faithless ritual. God's people were in a bad place.

The big picture. It was not only the priests who had been sinful (Malachi 1:6–2:9). The common folk had been just as bad, for they had married foreign women, robbed God of tithes and offerings, and arrogantly challenged God's character (2:10–3:15). The Lord responded that the time was coming when judgment would fall. Because of the presence of sin among God's people, the need for the coming Messiah was greater than ever (3:16–4:6). Of particular significance is a prophecy of John the Baptist preparing the way for the coming of Jesus Christ (3:1; see also Matthew 11:10).

Transformational truth. The people seemed to be functional atheists—that is, they acted as if God did not exist. Men were marrying foreign women who worshipped idols, divorced whenever they wanted, and acted as if they could do whatever they desired with no fear of judgment (Malachi 2:10-16). We simply cannot leave God out of the picture and live any way we want (1 Peter 1:13-25).

A verse for meditation. "I am the LORD, and I do not change" (Malachi 3:6).

A question to ponder. In what ways do we sometimes slip into living as functional atheists (acting as if God does not exist by the way we live)?

ERA 8: THE COMING OF JESUS CHRIST 6 BC – AD 30

Matthew • Mark • Luke • John

Today we begin our study of a new biblical era—the era titled "The Coming of Jesus Christ." Bible books pertinent to our study of this era include the four Gospels—Matthew, Mark, Luke, and John.

The New Testament is a collection of 27 books composed over a 50-year period by a number of different authors. The primary personality of the New Testament is Jesus Christ. The primary theme is salvation in Jesus Christ, based on the new covenant.

The word *testament* carries the idea of covenant, or agreement. The Old Testament focused on the old covenant between God and the Israelites. According to that covenant (the Sinai covenant), the Jews were to be God's people and were to be obedient to Him, and in return, God would bless them (Exodus 19:3-25). Israel failed over and over again and continually violated this covenant. Hence, even in Old Testament times, the prophets began to speak of a new covenant that would focus not on keeping external laws but on an inner reality and change in the human heart (Jeremiah 31:31). Unlike the old covenant, the new covenant was to make full provision for the forgiveness of sins. The New Testament tells us all about Jesus and the new covenant.

When Jesus ate the Passover meal with the disciples in the upper room, He spoke of the cup as "the new covenant between God and his people—an agreement confirmed with my blood" (Luke 22:20; see also 1 Corinthians 11:25). Hebrews 7 demonstrates that Christ's priesthood is superior to the old, and it thus logically follows that such a superior priesthood would have a superior ministry, which is provided for in the new covenant. Jesus has done all that is necessary for the forgiveness of sins by His once-for-all sacrifice on the cross. This new covenant is the basis for our relationship with God.

The first four books of the New Testament are the Gospels—Matthew, Mark, Luke, and John. Each of these contains an account of the life of Christ. While none of these portray all the details of His life, taken together, we can reconstruct a fairly full composite account.

Each author included different details about Christ's life depending upon the purpose of that Gospel. For example, the Gospel of Matthew has more allusions and citations from the Old Testament than any other Gospel because Matthew sought to prove to the Jews that Jesus was the promised Messiah of the Old Testament. Mark's Gospel, by contrast, had no such Jewish motivation, but rather sought to portray Jesus in action rather than as a teacher. Luke's Gospel stresses the wonderful blessings of salvation for all people. John's Gospel focuses heavily on the identity of Jesus, and thoroughly demonstrates His divine origin and deity. Jesus's deity is affirmed all throughout the Bible, especially in the New Testament. It is important that we thoroughly grasp this as we proceed in our study of the New Testament.

Jesus's Deity. There are numerous evidences for the deity of Christ in Scripture. For example, His deity is proven by the names ascribed to Him in the Bible, including God (Hebrews 1:8), Lord (Matthew 22:43-44), and King of kings and Lord of lords (Revelation 19:16). He also has all the attributes of deity, including being all-powerful (Matthew 28:18), all-knowing (John 1:48), and everywhere present (Matthew 18:20).

Certainly Jesus was worshipped as God many times according to the Gospel accounts and epistles. He accepted worship from Thomas (John 20:28), the angels (Hebrews 1:6), some wise men (Matthew 2:11), a leper (8:2), a ruler (9:18), a blind man (John 9:38), an anonymous woman (Matthew 15:25), Mary Magdalene (28:9), and the disciples (28:17). The fact that Jesus willingly received (and condoned) worship says a lot about His true identity, for it is the consistent testimony of Scripture that only God can be worshipped (Exodus 34:14).

Jesus is the Son of God. Jesus is also the divine Son of God. Perhaps no name or title of Christ has been so misunderstood as "Son of God." Some have taken the term to mean that Christ came into existence at a point in time and that He is in some way inferior to the Father. Some believe that because Christ is the Son of God, He cannot possibly be God in the same sense as the Father.

Such an understanding is based on a faulty conception of what "Son of…" meant among the ancients. Ancient Semitics and Orientals used the phrase "Son of…" to indicate *likeness or sameness of nature* and *equality of being*. So when Jesus claimed to be the Son of God, His Jewish contemporaries fully understood that He was making a claim to be God in an unqualified sense. Indeed, the Jews insisted, "By our law he ought to die because he called himself the Son of God" (John 19:7; see also 5:18). Recognizing that Jesus was identifying Himself as God, the Jews wanted to kill Him for committing blasphemy.

The Miracles of Jesus. The miracles of Jesus provide further evidence about His divine identity. Jesus's miracles are often called "signs" in the New Testament, for signs always signify something—in this case, that Jesus is the divine Messiah. Some of Jesus's more notable miracles include turning water into wine (John 2:7-8); walking on the sea (Matthew 14:25; Mark 6:48; John 6:19); calming a stormy sea (Matthew 8:26; Mark 4:39; Luke 8:24); feeding 5,000 men and their families (Matthew 14:19; Mark 6:41; Luke 9:16; John 6:11); raising Lazarus from the dead (John 11:43-44); and enabling the disciples to catch a great number of fish (Luke 5:5-6).

Jesus's Words. Jesus's words lend further support to His deity. His teachings were always presented as being ultimate and final. He never wavered in this. He unflinchingly placed His teachings above those of Moses and the prophets—and in a Jewish culture at that! He always spoke in His own authority. He never said, "Thus says the Lord…" as did the prophets; He always said, "Verily, verily, I say unto you…" He never retracted anything He said, never guessed or spoke with uncertainty, never made revisions, never contradicted Himself, and never apologized for what He said. He even asserted that "heaven and earth will disappear, but my words will never disappear" (Mark 13:31), hence elevating His words directly to the realm of heaven.

Jesus's teachings had a profound effect on people. His listeners always seemed to surmise that these were not the words of an ordinary man. When Jesus taught in Capernaum on the Sabbath, the people "were amazed at his teaching, for he spoke with authority" (Luke 4:32). After the Sermon on the Mount, "the crowds were amazed at his teaching, for he taught with real authority—quite unlike their teachers of religious law" (Matthew 7:28-29). When some Jewish leaders asked the temple guards why they had not arrested Jesus when He spoke, they responded: "We have never heard anyone speak like this" (John 7:46).

One cannot read the Gospels long before recognizing that Jesus regarded Himself and His message as inseparable. The reason Jesus's teachings had ultimate authority was because He was (is) God. The words of Jesus were the very words of God!

Jesus's Offices. Jesus, as the divine Messiah, fulfilled the three primary offices of Prophet, Priest, and King. As a Prophet, Jesus gave major discourses such as the Upper Room Discourse (John 14–16), the Olivet Discourse (Matthew 24–25), and the Sermon on the Mount (Matthew 5–7). He also spoke as a prophet on many occasions about the kingdom of God.

As our divine High Priest, Jesus represents God the Father to us and represents us to God the Father. He is our mediator (1 Timothy 2:5). As the ultimate High Priest, Jesus performed the ultimate sacrifice—He shed His own blood on our behalf (Hebrews 7:27). Jesus also prays on our behalf (7:25), just as Old Testament high priests prayed for the people.

Jesus's kingship is addressed throughout Scripture—from Genesis to Revelation. Genesis 49:10 prophesied that the Messiah would come from the tribe of Judah and reign as a king. The Davidic covenant in 2 Samuel 7:16 promised a Messiah who would have a dynasty, a people over whom He would rule, and an eternal throne. In Psalm 2:6, God the Father is portrayed announcing the installation of God the Son as King in Jerusalem. Psalm 110 affirms that the Messiah will subjugate His enemies and rule over them. Daniel 7:13-14 tells us that the Messiah-King will have an everlasting dominion. These and many other Old Testament passages point to Christ's role as sovereign King.

When we get to the New Testament, we find that before Jesus was born, an angel appeared to Mary and informed her that her son would "reign over Israel forever; his Kingdom will never end" (Luke 1:32-33). After Jesus was born in Bethlehem, some Magi from the east came to Jerusalem and asked, "Where is the newborn king of the Jews? We saw his star as it rose, and we have come to worship him" (Matthew 2:1-2). When Jesus comes again, He will come as the King of kings and Lord of lords (Revelation 19:16). Christ will truly rule forever.

In the coming chapters, we will journey through Matthew, Mark, Luke, and John as we learn interesting details about the era of the coming of Jesus Christ. We will witness Christ in the roles of Prophet, Priest, and King.

The following dates will provide you with a helpful chronological orientation:

6 BC—Jesus was born.

6 BC–AD 7—Jesus grew through infancy and His boyhood years.

AD 8–26—Jesus grew through adolescence and entered early manhood.

AD 26–27—Jesus was baptized by John the Baptist.

AD 27—Jesus began His ministry.

AD 28—A sinful woman anointed Jesus with expensive perfume; He taught some parables of the kingdom.

AD 29—Jesus commissioned 12 apostles to spread His message; John the Baptist was executed; Jesus miraculously fed more than 5,000; urged Christians to take up their crosses to follow Him; healed a man born blind; miraculously fed more than 4,000; defended a woman caught in adultery; sent out 70 followers to spread His message; taught the parable of the good Samaritan; and revealed He is the Good Shepherd.

AD 30—Jesus warned about the danger of wealth; taught a parable on prayer; taught the parable of the prodigal son; taught the parable of the rich man and Lazarus;

encountered an unfruitful fig tree; pronounced woes on the scribes and Pharisees; and spoke about signs of the end times.

AD 30 (Passion Week, Thursday, April 2)—Jesus celebrated His final Passover with the disciples, instituted the Lord's Supper, taught on the coming of the Holy Spirit, predicted Peter's denial, and prayed in Gethsemane.

AD 30 (Passion Week, Friday, April 3)—Jesus was crucified.

AD 30 (Sunday, April 5-May 14)—Jesus resurrected from the dead and made many appearances to His followers.

AD 30 (May 14)—Jesus ascended into heaven.

AD 50–60—Matthew wrote his Gospel.

AD 55—Mark wrote his Gospel.

AD 60—Luke wrote his Gospel.

AD 85–90—John wrote his Gospel.

Preview: On Day 275, we'll consider the birth of Jesus, and His identity as "God with us."

"GOD WITH US"

Matthew 1; Luke 1; 3:23-38; John 1:1-5

Yesterday we introduced Era 8 of biblical history, titled "The Coming of Jesus Christ," dated 6 BC–AD 30. Today we focus on the birth of Jesus.

Key concept. Jesus—eternal God—took on human flesh, and hence was called "God is with us."

The big picture. The incarnation of Jesus involved God's sovereign and providential oversight over the messianic line for ages and ages (Matthew 1:1-17; Luke 3:23-38). Mary's pregnancy was unlike any other. The Holy Spirit overshadowed her to produce a human nature within her womb for Jesus. Jesus was subsequently born as a human without a sin nature. Biblical scholars believe Mary became pregnant in 7 BC, and Jesus was born in 6 BC.

Transformational truth. God often uses less-than-perfect people to accomplish His purposes on earth. This is illustrated in the fact that there were three women who had been involved in worldly sin who are in Jesus's genealogy (Matthew 1:3,5,6; see also 1 Corinthians 1:26-30). Because God uses imperfect people, that means there's hope for you and me!

A verse for meditation. "The virgin will conceive a child! She will give birth to a son, and they will call him Immanuel, which means 'God is with us'" (Matthew 1:23).

A question to ponder. Have you ever thought about what might have happened had the incarnation of Jesus never occurred?

JESUS AS AN INFANT AND YOUNG BOY

Matthew 2; Luke 2

In the previous lesson, we explored the coming of Jesus into the world (Matthew 1; Luke 1; 3:23-38; John 1:1-5). Today we consider the infancy and boyhood of Jesus.

Key concept. Jesus's birth caused some to rejoice, others to seek His death.

The big picture. Jesus was born on earth in lowly conditions. And yet, even as a babe, He was recognized as the Messiah-Savior (Luke 2:21-38) and as King (Matthew 2:1-23; Luke 2:39-40). The evil Herod, feeling threatened at the prospect of a challenging king, sought to kill the babe (see Revelation 12:4). Later, as a 12-year-old boy, Jesus highly impressed temple leaders with His knowledge of Scripture (Luke 2:41-52). Since Jesus was born in 6 BC, His boyhood would have lasted till around AD 7. He began His ministry as an adult about AD 27.

Transformational truth. As soon as the Magi saw Jesus, they immediately "bowed down and worshiped him" (Matthew 2:11). Jesus was worshipped many times during His three-year ministry (Matthew 2:11; 8:2; 9:18; 15:25; John 9:38; 20:28; Hebrews 1:6). Worshipping Jesus will also be a common activity in heaven (Revelation 5:8,14; 19:4). We should get into the habit now!

A verse for meditation. "Jesus grew in wisdom and in stature and in favor with God and all the people" (Luke 2:52).

A question to ponder. Why do you think some people respond lovingly to Jesus while others respond with hate?

JOHN THE BAPTIST

Matthew 3; Mark 1:1-11; Luke 3:1-22; John 1:6-34

Yesterday we considered the infancy and boyhood of Jesus (Matthew 2; Luke 2). Today we focus on John the Baptist preparing the way for Jesus's ministry.

Key concept. John the Baptist called for repentance as he prepared the way for Jesus, the promised Messiah.

The big picture. John called people to repent of sin. He ministered in the winter and spring of AD 26 in preparation for the beginning of Jesus's ministry in AD 27. Some indeed did repent (Matthew 3:5-6), but others—the Pharisees and Sadducees—considered themselves righteous and not in need of repentance (verses 7-9). Those who repented and turned to God became the children of God.

Transformational truth. John the Baptist urged, "Prove by the way you live that you have repented of your sins and turned to God" (Matthew 3:8). He said this specifically to the Pharisees and Sadducees who gave lip service to living for God, but in reality were full of hypocrisy. It's easy to fall into this trap. People need to "prove they have changed by the good things they do" (Acts 26:20).

A verse for meditation. "To all who believed him and accepted him, he gave the right to become children of God" (John 1:12).

A question to ponder. How do you think John the Baptist's call for repentance would go over today?

JESUS TEMPTED BY THE DEVIL

Matthew 4:1-22; Mark 1:12-20; Luke 4:1-15; 5:1-11; John 1:35 – 2:25

Yesterday we considered John the Baptist preparing the way for Jesus's ministry (Matthew 3; Mark 1:1-11; Luke 3:1-22; John 1:6-34). Today we turn our attention to Jesus being tempted by the devil.

Key concept. Jesus was tempted by the devil in order to prove He could not be led into sin.

The big picture. Jesus experienced temptation by the devil near the beginning of His ministry in AD 27. Through His temptation experience, Jesus proved He could not be made to sin. The devil waited until 40 days had gone by, when Jesus was at His weakest from hunger. It was to no avail. Jesus defeated the devil via the Word of God (Matthew 4:1-17; Luke 4:1-15). Because He experienced temptation, He is able to help us in our temptations (Hebrews 2:17-18; 4:15).

Transformational truth. Each of us ought to beware of temptation (Galatians 6:1). Paul exhorts us, "Do not give in to sinful desires" (Romans 6:12). Scripture promises, "God is faithful. He will not allow the temptation to be more than you can stand. When you are tempted, he will show you a way out so that you can endure" (1 Corinthians 10:13).

A verse for meditation. "People do not live by bread alone, but by every word that comes from the mouth of God" (Matthew 4:4).

A question to ponder. What do you learn from Matthew 4 about how Jesus defended Himself against the devil's temptations?

YOU MUST BE BORN AGAIN

John 3

In the previous lesson, we explored Jesus's temptation by the devil (Matthew 4:1-22; Mark 1:12-20; Luke 4:1-15; 5:1-11; John 1:35–2:25). Today we consider Jesus's teaching about being born again.

Key concept. Human beings must be spiritually born again ("born from above") by faith in order to enter the kingdom of God.

The big picture. Jesus spoke to Nicodemus about the necessity of being born again. Our earthly birth enables us to live on earth, but then we eventually die. A second birth—a spiritual birth from above—enables us to go to heaven (John 3:1-21). The "new birth" refers to the act of God by which He gives eternal life to the one who believes in Christ (Titus 3:5). In heaven, we will never die.

Transformational truth. Each of us as Christians are promised "eternal life" (John 3:16). That means that once we trust in Christ for salvation, we can count on living with Him in heaven for all eternity. How glorious it will be for Christians! God "will wipe every tear from their eyes, and there will be no more death or sorrow or crying or pain. All these things are gone forever" (Revelation 21:4).

A verse for meditation. "I tell you the truth, unless you are born again, you cannot see the Kingdom of God" (John 3:3).

A question to ponder. How do you know you have been born again?

NEW LIFE IN THE SPIRIT

John 4:4-42,46-54

In the previous lesson, we explored Jesus's teaching about being born again (John 3). Today we consider new life in the Spirit.

Key concept. Jesus Himself is the source of new life in the Holy Spirit.

The big picture. While traveling, Jesus encountered a Samaritan woman. He asked her for some water, for He was thirsty. But the thing He desired more than water was her salvation. He offered her "living water" (new life—John 4:10). The woman expressed a desire for this living water. But before she could receive it, she needed to be confronted about her sin (John 4:16-24). After Jesus did this, He revealed to her that He was the promised divine Messiah who could give her eternal salvation.

Transformational truth. God is Spirit (John 4:24). A spirit does not have flesh and bones (Luke 24:39). Because God is Spirit, He is "the invisible God" (Colossians 1:15) and is "the unseen one who never dies" (1 Timothy 1:17). God is also omnipresent, or everywhere-present (Psalm 139:2-12). This means that even though God is invisible and you can't see Him, He is nevertheless always present with you wherever you go.

A verse for meditation. "Those who drink the water I give will never be thirsty again. It becomes a fresh, bubbling spring within them, giving them eternal life" (John 4:14).

A question to ponder. If you are experiencing thirst in your spiritual life, what have you learned in this lesson that might help you?

JESUS'S DIVINE AUTHORITY

*Matthew 4:23-25; 8:1-4,14-17; 9:1-8; Mark
1:21–2:12; Luke 4:31-44; 5:12-26*

Yesterday we considered new life in the Spirit (John 4:4-42,46-54).
Today we focus on the divine authority of Jesus.

Key concept. Jesus demonstrated His divine authority in convincing ways.

The big picture. In early AD 28, Jesus demonstrated His authority
as the divine prophesied Messiah in three ways: He cast out demonic
spirits (Mark 1:21-28; Luke 4:31-44); He exercised His divine prerogative to forgive people's sins (Mark 2:5-10; Matthew 9:2-6); and He
healed people of various diseases (Mark 1:29-34; 1:40–2:12; Luke 5:12-
26; Matthew 4:23-25; 8:1-4,14-17; 9:1-8).

Transformational truth. Despite being incredibly busy, Jesus always
took the time to pray (Mark 1:35). He often prayed for other people
(Matthew 19:13). Sometimes He prayed by Himself (Luke 5:16); other
times with other people (Luke 9:28). Most importantly, Jesus prayed
regularly (Luke 5:16). You and I need to do the same (Luke 9:18; 11:1-4;
18:1; 22:32). Here are some great verses to explore: Daniel 6:10; Matthew 7:7-8; John 14:13-14; James 5:17-18; Philippians 4:4-6; 1 Thessalonians 5:17.

A verse for meditation. [Jesus said:] " 'I will prove to you that the Son
of Man has the authority on earth to forgive sins.' Then Jesus turned
to the paralyzed man and said, 'Stand up, pick up your mat, and go
home!' " (Luke 5:24).

A question to ponder. How is Jesus's complete authority over all
things a comfort to you?

FOLLOWING JESUS

Matthew 9:9-17; Mark 2:13-22; Luke 5:27-39; John 5

Yesterday we gave attention to Jesus's divine authority (Matthew 4:23-25; 8:1-4,14-17; 9:1-8; Mark 1:21–2:12; Luke 4:31-44; 5:12-26). Today we turn our attention to the call to follow Jesus.

Key concept. Jesus invites any who are responsive to "Follow Me."

The big picture. In early AD 28, Jesus began calling disciples to follow Him. Notice that Jesus did not call upon religious leaders or the societal elite. He called common people—such as fishermen and tax collectors (Matthew 9:9-13; Mark 2:13-17; Luke 5:27-32). The religious elite—the Pharisees and the Sadducees—snubbed their noses at Jesus. They looked down on Him for associating with the lower class in society. Jesus replied that He came not to call the hypocritically self-righteous, but repentant sinners. Some of Jesus's harshest words were reserved for self-righteous hypocrites.

Transformational truth. Sin is like a disease. But Jesus is our spiritual physician and healer: "Healthy people don't need a doctor," Jesus said, but "sick people do" (Mark 2:17; see also Matthew 9:12; Luke 5:31). Sin makes us sick. But Jesus heals that sickness by His blood shed at the cross. If you are spiritually ailing because of sin, turn to Jesus immediately.

A verse for meditation. "Follow me and be my disciple" (Matthew 9:9).

A question to ponder. Do you think there is a difference between being a Christian and being a follower of Jesus Christ?

TRUE HAPPINESS IN LIFE

Matthew 5:1-16; 12:1-21; Mark 2:23 – 3:19; Luke 6:1-26

Yesterday we focused on the call to follow Jesus (Matthew 9:9-17; Mark 2:13-22; Luke 5:27-39; John 5). Today we turn our attention to Jesus's teaching on true happiness.

Key concept. Happiness is found not in obeying man-made rules, but rather by living one's life according to Jesus's beatitudes.

The big picture. Jesus taught people how to be truly happy. In sum: Happy are those who are humble, patient, yearn for righteousness, full of mercy, pure, and peace-seeking (Matthew 5:1-12; Luke 6:20-26). Christ also challenged His followers to proactively stand for Him and Christian values in the world around them. Every Christian ought to function as "salt" in society (Matthew 5:13-16).

Transformational truth. The word *blessed* means "happy," "fortunate," or "blissful." The word conveys a sense of well-being. In the beatitudes, Jesus depicted the means of a person attaining a divinely bestowed sense of well-being and happiness in daily life (Matthew 5:1-12). Such blessings give us a little foretaste of heaven. If you want to be truly happy in life, your single best course of action is to root yourself in Jesus's beatitudes.

A verse for meditation. "God blesses those whose hearts are pure, for they will see God" (Matthew 5:8).

A question to ponder. Has your understanding of happiness changed as a result of today's lesson?

TRANSFORMATIONAL TEACHINGS

Matthew 5:17 – 7:6; Luke 6:27-42

I n the previous lesson, we explored Jesus's teaching on true happiness (Matthew 5:1-16; 12:1-21; Mark 2:23 – 3:19; Luke 6:1-26). Today we consider more of His transformational teachings.

Key concept. Christ's teachings are life-changing.

The big picture. Jesus taught numerous transformational truths, including these: Stifle anger; it will cause bad behavior (Matthew 5:21-26). Take drastic steps in dealing with sin (5:27-30). You shouldn't have to take an oath for others to believe you are telling the truth (5:33-37). Give charitably not to gain praise from people, but to please God (6:1-4). Seek to earn heavenly rewards instead of earthly rewards that are temporal and will pass away (6:19-34).

Transformational truth. The Jewish leaders of Jesus's day taught that we should love those near and dear to us (Leviticus 19:18), but hate our enemies. Jesus refuted this idea, instructing us to love even our enemies. Matthew 5:48 instructs us, "You are to be perfect, even as your Father in heaven is perfect." In context, Jesus was talking about love. We are to be perfectly loving just as the Father is.

A verse for meditation. "You have heard the law that says, 'Love your neighbor' and hate your enemy. But I say, love your enemies! Pray for those who persecute you!" (Matthew 5:43-44).

A question to ponder. Do you think Jesus's teaching on love is workable in real life?

THE RIGHT FOUNDATION

Matthew 7:7-29; 8:5-13; 11:1-19; Luke 6:43 – 7:35

Yesterday we considered some of Christ's transformational teachings (Matthew 5:17 – 7:6; Luke 6:27-42). Today we focus on building life on the right foundation.

Key concept. It is wise to build our lives on Christ's teachings.

The big picture. Jesus emphasized the critical importance of putting His teachings into action. We need to *hear* His words, *understand* His words, and *obey* His words (compare with James 1:22-25). We should be persistent in prayer (Matthew 7:7-11) and always live according to the Golden Rule (7:12). Our goal should be to allow our commitment to Christ to show itself in the fruit we bear in daily life (Matthew 7:15-20). We should avoid being "fakers" at all costs. To such fakers, Jesus will one day say, "I never knew you."

Transformational truth. Jesus's Golden Rule contains the essence of God's requirements in the law and the prophets (Matthew 7:12). It ought to be a guiding rule for the family, the workplace, and social gatherings of all types.

A verse for meditation. "Do to others whatever you would like them to do to you. This is the essence of all that is taught in the law and the prophets" (Matthew 7:12).

A question to ponder. How well built is your "house" according to Jesus's teaching in Matthew 7:24-27?

MORE TRANSFORMATIONAL TEACHINGS

Matthew 11:20-30; 12:22-45; Mark 3:20–30; Luke 7:36 – 8:3; 11:14-32

Yesterday we gave attention to building life on the right foundation (Matthew 7:7-29; 8:5-13; 11:1-19; Luke 6:43 – 7:35). Today we turn our attention to additional transforming teachings of Christ.

Key concept. Jesus's teachings are life-changing.

The big picture. Jesus taught there will be varying degrees of punishment handed out to the wicked at the future judgment (Matthew 11:20-30). He invited all who were burdened by religious legalism to come to Him for rest (Matthew 11:28). He warned against misjudging another person's character (Luke 7:36-50). He also noted that some people have such hardened hearts against Him that no miracle will suffice to convince them otherwise (Matthew 12:38-45; Luke 11:24-32).

Transformational truth. Jesus promised rest for all who were weary and burdened (Matthew 11:28). If you are burdened by sin, come to Jesus. If you are burdened about your future, come to Jesus. If you are burdened by emotional or physical distress, come to Jesus. No matter what you face, come to Jesus! He promises, "I will give you rest" (verse 28), and "you will find rest for your souls" (verse 29).

A verse for meditation. "Come to me, all of you who are weary and carry heavy burdens, and I will give you rest" (Matthew 11:28).

A question to ponder. Are you weary and burdened? What are you waiting for?

PARABLES OF THE KINGDOM

Matthew 12:46 – 13:30; Mark 3:31 – 4:29; Luke 8:4-21

Yesterday we focused on additional transforming teachings of Christ (Matthew 11:20-30; 12:22-45; Mark 3:20-30; Luke 7:36 – 8:3; 11:14-32). Today we turn our attention to some of Jesus's teachings on the kingdom.

Key concept. People will have different responses to the preaching of God's Word.

The big picture. Jesus indicated that His true family members are those who do His Father's will. Eternal allegiance to God is far more important than earthly loyalties (Matthew 12:46-50). Jesus also taught that people will have different responses to God's Word. In some cases, the Word takes root and bears fruit. In other cases, it does not take root at all (Matthew 13:1-23; Mark 4:1-20; Luke 8:4-15).

Transformational truth. Jesus urged, "Anyone with ears to hear should listen and understand" (Matthew 13:9,16). Jesus often made this statement after making an important spiritual point (see Revelation 2 – 3). Jesus's intended meaning was that the mere hearing of the Word of God is not enough. One must personally appropriate what one has heard. As James 1:22 put it, "Don't just listen to God's word. You must do what it says."

A verse for meditation. "My mother and my brothers are all those who hear God's word and obey it" (Luke 8:21).

A question to ponder. Are you ever distracted by the cares of this world (Matthew 13:22)? Are there any thorns choking your commitment to Christ that you want to excise?

MORE PARABLES OF
THE KINGDOM

*Matthew 8:23-34; 13:31-52; Mark
4:30–5:20; Luke 8:22-39; 13:18-21*

In the previous lesson, we explored some of Jesus's teachings on the kingdom (Matthew 12:46–13:30; Mark 3:31–4:29; Luke 8:4-21). Today we consider further parables of the kingdom.

Key concept. God's kingdom will grow exponentially, and has incredible value to people.

The big picture. The kingdom of God started small through the disciples' preaching, but will grow to be very large (Matthew 13:31-32; Mark 4:30-32; Luke 13:18-21). Believers and unbelievers will coexist in the world until the end times, when God's angels will separate them (Matthew 13:36-43). The kingdom of God has incredible value (Matthew 13:44-46).

Transformational truth. Jesus taught people "as much as they could understand" (Mark 4:33). This brings to mind Jesus's words in John 16:12: "There is so much more I want to tell you, but you can't bear it now." We should always be sensitive about the learning capacity of the people we speak spiritual truths to. For example, Paul said to the Corinthians, "I had to feed you with milk, not with solid food, because you weren't ready for anything stronger" (1 Corinthians 3:2).

A verse for meditation. "'Who is this man?' they asked each other. 'When he gives a command, even the wind and waves obey him!'" (Luke 8:25).

A question to ponder. Are you presently facing any storms in your life that you need the Lord to calm? Why not turn to Him in prayer now?

FAITH AND HEALING

*Matthew 9:18-34; 13:53-58; Mark
5:21 – 6:6; Luke 4:16-30; 8:40-56*

Yesterday we considered some of Jesus's parables about the kingdom (Matthew 8:23-34; 13:31-52; Mark 4:30 – 5:20; Luke 8:22-39; 13:18-21). Today we focus on the role of faith in healing.

Key concept. Jesus healed many people. He said a person's faith plays a critical role in such healings.

The big picture. Jesus was now ministering in early AD 29. He started the year with two miracles—a healing and a resurrection (Matthew 9:18-26; Mark 5:21-43; Luke 8:40-56). These miracles were signs that Jesus was the promised Messiah. The Old Testament prophets spoke of the signs, affirming that when the divine Messiah came, the blind would see, the deaf would hear, and the lame would walk (Isaiah 35:5-6).

Transformational truth. A common thread that runs through the New Testament is that there is a direct correlation between faith and experiencing the miraculous (Mark 5:34; Hebrews 11:6). Those who do not experience miracles—as was the case with the residents of Nazareth (Matthew 13:58)—are those who do not have faith in Jesus.

A verse for meditation. "The Spirit of the Lord is upon me, for he has anointed me to bring Good News to the poor. He has sent me to proclaim that captives will be released, that the blind will see, that the oppressed will be set free" (Luke 4:18).

A question to ponder. Do you think miracles still happen today? Why or why not?

JESUS SENDS OUT 12 APOSTLES

*Matthew 9:35–10:42; 14:3-12; Mark
6:6-13,17-29; Luke 9:1-6*

Yesterday we gave attention to the role of faith in healing (Matthew
9:18-34; 13:53-58; Mark 5:21–6:6; Luke 4:16-30; 8:40-56). Today
we turn our attention to Jesus sending out 12 apostles.

Key concept. Jesus sent out 12 apostles as His witnesses.

The big picture. Jesus sent the apostles to proclaim the kingdom of
God (Matthew 10:1-15; Mark 6:6-13; Luke 9:1-6). He warned them
they would be persecuted, but there was no need to fear. God sovereignly watches over all believers (Matthew 10:16-42). In response to
evangelism, some will accept Christ, others will reject Him (10:34).

Transformational truth. Jesus proclaimed, "Students are to be like
their teacher, and slaves are to be like their master" (Matthew 10:25).
In New Testament times, a disciple would always seek to be like his
teacher. The goal of every Christian is to be like Jesus. A practical means
of bringing this about is to walk daily in dependence on the Holy Spirit,
for the fruit of the Spirit is a perfect description of Jesus's character (see
Galatians 5:16-23).

A verse for meditation. "The harvest is great, but the workers are few.
So pray to the Lord who is in charge of the harvest; ask him to send
more workers into his fields" (Matthew 9:37-38).

A question to ponder. Are you personally involved in any form of
evangelism in your community?

JESUS PERFORMS MIRACLES

*Matthew 14:1-2,13-33; Mark 6:14-16,30-
52; Luke 9:7-17; John 6:1-21*

Yesterday we focused on Jesus sending out 12 apostles (Matthew 9:35–10:42; 14:3-12; Mark 6:6-13,17-29; Luke 9:1-6). Today we turn our attention to more miracles done by Jesus.

Key concept. Jesus performed two of His most incredible miracles, further attesting to His identity as the divine Messiah.

The big picture. Jesus had performed two remarkable miracles— feeding more than 5,000 (Matthew 14:21), and walking on water (Matthew 14:22-33; Mark 6:45-52; John 6:16-21). He repeatedly displayed a power over natural forces that could belong only to God, the author of these forces. This should not surprise us, for Christ Himself is the Creator (John 1:3; Colossians 1:16).

Transformational truth. God can turn something small into something great (John 6:8-9). A little boy gave what little food he had, and God (Jesus) multiplied it into enough food to feed 5,000 men and their families. You and I may sometimes feel that we are insignificant, and that we don't have much to offer God. But if you offer to God what little you have—your talents, your skills, your spiritual gifts, your time—God can turn these into something great.

A verse for meditation. "You have so little faith. Why did you doubt me?" (Matthew 14:31).

A question to ponder. Would you like to give what little you have to God so He can make something great out of it? What are you waiting for?

THE BREAD OF LIFE

Matthew 14:34 – 15:20; Mark 6:53 – 7:23; John 6:22-71

In the previous lesson, we explored two incredible miracles of Jesus (Matthew 14:1-2,13-33; Mark 6:14-16,30-52; Luke 9:7-17; John 6:1-21). Today we consider Jesus's claim to be the bread of life.

Key concept. Jesus is the bread of life. Appropriating Him brings eternal life.

The big picture. Jesus miraculously fed more than 5,000 men, along with their families, with just five barley loaves and two fish. He desired to satisfy not just their physical hunger but also their spiritual hunger. Jesus therefore taught that just as one must partake of physical food (such as bread) to sustain physical life, so one must spiritually appropriate Christ (the "bread of life") to have spiritual life: "I am the bread of life. Whoever comes to me will never be hungry again" (John 6:35). He gave this teaching in mid-AD 29.

Transformational truth. Jesus criticized the Jewish leaders for placing a higher priority on their human traditions than on the inspired Word of God (Matthew 15:1-9). Man-made traditions typically turn religion into a routine of mechanically going through the motions. How much better it is to focus on the living and supernatural Word of God.

A verse for meditation. "Why do you, by your traditions, violate the direct commandments of God?" (Matthew 15:3).

A question to ponder. How much do you think you have been influenced by man-made religious traditions?

MORE MIRACLES OF JESUS

Matthew 15:21–16:20; Mark 7:24–8:30; Luke 9:18-21

Yesterday we considered Jesus's claim to be the bread of life (Matthew 14:34–15:20; Mark 6:53–7:23; John 6:22-71). Today we focus on more miracles of Jesus and their significance.

Key concept. Jesus continued to confirm His identity as the divine Messiah by performing miracles.

The big picture. Christ engaged in further miraculous proofs of His identity as the divine Messiah. He healed the lame, the blind, the crippled, the mute, and those afflicted by demons (see Matthew 15:21-28; Mark 7:24-30). He also multiplied food to feed the masses. Jesus asked the disciples who they thought He was. Peter rightly responded that He is the Christ, the divine Messiah (Matthew 16:16).

Transformational truth. Always guard against hypocrisy in your life. Jesus often spoke against Pharisaic hypocrisy (Matthew 23:28; Mark 8:15; 12:15; Luke 12:1). Hypocrisy involves the pretense of having virtuous character, or moral/religious beliefs and principles, that one does not really possess (see Revelation 3:1). Don't be a faker; don't be a pretender.

A verse for meditation. "'Who do you say I am?' Simon Peter answered, 'You are the Messiah, the Son of the living God'" (Matthew 16:15-16).

A question to ponder. Have you ever noticed in your own life how hypocrisy can be like leaven, starting out small but increasing over time, if not purposefully resisted?

RADICAL COMMITMENT

Matthew 16:21–17:20; Mark 8:31–9:29; Luke 9:22-43

Yesterday we gave attention to the miracles of Jesus and their significance (Matthew 15:21–16:20; Mark 7:24–8:30; Luke 9:18-21). Today we turn our attention to radical commitment to Jesus.

Key concept. Jesus required radical commitment from His followers—commitment even to the point of death.

The big picture. The path of discipleship means turning from self and ambition to a life of sacrifice and total submission to Christ (Matthew 16:21-28; Mark 8:31–9:1; Luke 9:22-27). We might paraphrase Jesus's words this way: "If you want to follow Me, do not do so in word only, but put your life on the line and follow Me on the path of the cross—a path that will involve sacrifice, self-denial, and possibly even death for My sake."

Transformational truth. Jesus's disciples experienced defeat right after a mountaintop experience (Matthew 17:14-18). They had just witnessed Jesus transfigured—shining forth the very glory of God. As soon as they came down off the mountain, they could not deliver a person from a demon. This is an example of how people are vulnerable to defeat following a mountaintop experience. *Christian beware.*

A verse for meditation. "If any of you wants to be my follower, you must give up your own way, take up your cross, and follow me" (Mark 8:34).

A question to ponder. How do you think losing your life enables you to find it?

IMPORTANT SPIRITUAL LESSONS

Matthew 17:22 – 18:35; Mark 9:30-
50; Luke 9:43-50; John 7:1-9

Yesterday we focused on radical commitment to Jesus (Matthew 16:21–17:20; Mark 8:31–9:29; Luke 9:22-43). Today we turn our attention to some important spiritual lessons taught by Jesus.

Key concept. Jesus taught on humility, avoiding offense, thwarting personal sin, and forgiving others.

The big picture. Jesus continued to teach important spiritual lessons to His followers, including these: The path to greatness in the kingdom of God is becoming like a little child (Matthew 18:1-5; Mark 9:33-37; Luke 9:46-48). Avoid narrow exclusivism (Mark 9:38-41; Luke 9:49-50). Avoid causing any kind of offense that could bring temptation to others (Matthew 18:6-10; Mark 9:42-50). Forgive the sins of others (Matthew 18:21-35).

Transformational truth. We each need childlike faith (Matthew 18:2). This does not mean that adults should behave childishly. But adults need to have the same type of faith that little children exhibit. The most trusting people in the world are children. They have not acquired the obstructions to faith that often come with advanced education and exposure to the philosophies of the world. Children are trusting even in circumstances they do not understand. God delights in and responds to such faith.

A verse for meditation. "Anyone who becomes as humble as this little child is the greatest in the Kingdom of Heaven" (Matthew 18:4).

A question to ponder. Have you ever experienced difficulty in maintaining a childlike trust in God?

MIXED RESPONSES TO JESUS

Matthew 8:18-22; 19:1-2; Mark 10:1;
Luke 9:51-62; John 7:10 – 8:20

In the previous lesson, we explored some important spiritual lessons taught by Jesus (Matthew 17:22 – 18:35; Mark 9:30-50; Luke 9:43-50; John 7:1-9). Today we consider various responses people had to Jesus.

Key concept. Some people responded positively to Jesus; others negatively.

The big picture. Jesus continued to minister in mid- to latter AD 29. He was receiving a mixed response in His travels. Some accepted Him; others rejected Him (Matthew 19:1-2; Mark 10:1; Luke 9:51-56). Still others offered excuses (Matthew 8:18-22; Luke 9:57-62). His own unbelieving brothers mocked Him (John 7:1-5). The Pharisees tried to have Him arrested (John 7:32-53). Jesus had a polarizing effect on people.

Transformational truth. Jesus affirmed, "Anyone who believes in me may come and drink! For the Scriptures declare, 'Rivers of living water will flow from his heart.' (When he said 'living water,' he was speaking of the Spirit)" (John 7:38-39). For believers, the Holy Spirit is a continual and blessed source of joy, comfort, satisfaction, and a sense of the very presence of God.

A verse for meditation. "I am the light of the world. If you follow me, you won't have to walk in darkness, because you will have the light that leads to life" (John 8:12).

A question to ponder. Do you have a close relationship with the Holy Spirit?

THE GOOD SAMARITAN

Luke 10; John 8:21-59

Yesterday we considered various responses people had to Jesus (Matthew 8:18-22; 19:1-2; Mark 10:1; Luke 9:51-62; John 7:10–8:20). Today we focus on Jesus's teaching on the good Samaritan.

Key concept. Be a compassionate "good Samaritan" to other people around you.

The big picture. Jesus told the parable of the good Samaritan in late AD 29 to demonstrate the real meaning of showing compassion to a neighbor. In the parable, the people that one would naturally expect to show compassion to a man wounded by bandits—the priest and the Levite—showed no compassion at all. They were uncaring and apathetic. The one not expected to show compassion—the Samaritan (disliked by the Jews)—was full of compassion (Luke 10:25-37). As Christians, we ought to be like the good Samaritan.

Transformational truth. The truth that Jesus reveals to us sets us free from doctrinal error, self-deception, Satan's trickery, slavery to sin and self, and condemnation (John 8:32). As someone put it, Jesus set us free not so that we can do whatever we want, but rather to be free in following God. Following Jesus does not burden us with a hard yoke of legalism (Matthew 11:28).

A verse for meditation. "You will know the truth, and the truth will set you free" (John 8:32).

A question to ponder. Is there anyone in your social circle to whom you might be a good Samaritan this week?

SPIRITUAL HEALTH

Luke 11:1-13,33-54; 12:1-48

Yesterday we gave attention to the parable of the good Samaritan (Luke 10; John 8:21-59). Today we turn to Jesus's teachings on spiritual health.

Key concept. Jesus taught on prayer, religious hypocrisy, guarding against covetousness, trusting God in place of anxiety, maintaining an eternal perspective, and faithfulness.

The big picture. Jesus taught His followers all about spiritual health. He taught them how to pray (Luke 11:1-13). He drilled into them some of the spiritual dangers of hypocrisy, using the Pharisees and scribes as examples (11:37-54). He warned against being all show with no substance (12:1-12). He said we are to maintain an eternal perspective (12:13-34). He emphasized we should be steadfast in faithfulness to God (12:35-48).

Transformational truth. A person could easily give an outer appearance of respectability, when in reality his or her heart is far from God (Luke 12:1-2). This is hypocrisy. Hypocrisy wasn't just pervasive among the Pharisees and scribes; it's pervasive in the modern church as well. The church has plenty of pretenders, plenty of fakers, plenty of outer respectability with compromised hearts. If you're struggling with this, it's never too late to get on the right track.

A verse for meditation. "Guard against every kind of greed. Life is not measured by how much you own" (Luke 12:15).

A question to ponder. How can we make sure we are not a faker or a pretender?

THE GOOD SHEPHERD

Luke 12:49 – 13:17; John 9:1 – 10:21

Yesterday we focused on Jesus's teachings on spiritual health (Luke 11:1-13,33-54; 12:1-48). Today we turn our attention to Jesus as the Good Shepherd.

Key concept. Jesus is the Good Shepherd who gives His life for the sheep.

The big picture. Jesus as the Good Shepherd has an intimate relationship with His sheep, calling them by name. They listen to His voice, and follow and obey Him. He liberates His sheep so they are truly free and unfettered by the chains of any kind of bondage. He protects them from danger, and perpetually seeks their well-being. So much does the Good Shepherd love His sheep that He voluntarily laid down His life for them (John 10:1-21).

Transformational truth. Jesus came to give His followers "a rich and satisfying life" (John 10:10). The ESV translates it, "I came that they may have life and have it abundantly." The NIV puts it, "I have come that they may have life, and have it to the full." Jesus offers us a rich, full, vibrant, dynamic, and joyful life. He gives us a life better than anything we could possibly imagine.

A verse for meditation. "I am the good shepherd. The good shepherd sacrifices his life for the sheep" (John 10:11).

A question to ponder. What does it mean to you personally that Jesus is the Good Shepherd who watches over your life?

JEWISH REJECTION OF JESUS

Matthew 23:37-39; Luke 13:22–15:10; John 10:22-42

In the previous lesson, we learned about Jesus as the Good Shepherd (Luke 12:49–13:17; John 9:1–10:21). Today we consider the consistent Jewish rejection of Jesus.

Key concept. Jewish leaders and common folk often expressed open rejection of Jesus.

The big picture. Between late AD 29 and early AD 30, Jewish religious leaders sought to execute Jesus for claiming oneness with God (John 10:22-42). The Jewish inhabitants of Jerusalem consistently rejected Him (Matthew 23:37-39; Luke 13:31-35). The Jewish leaders criticized Him for healing a man on the Sabbath (Luke 14:1-6). Despite Jesus's repeated offer of the kingdom to Israel, Israel's inhabitants consistently rejected it (Luke 14:15-24).

Transformational truth. Jesus urged, "When you give a banquet, invite the poor, the crippled, the lame, the blind, and you will be blessed. Although they cannot repay you, you will be repaid at the resurrection of the righteous" (Luke 14:13-14 NIV). Proverbs 14:31 tells us that the person who is generous to the needy honors the Lord. Indeed, "whoever is generous to the poor lends to the LORD, and he will repay him for his deed" (19:17 ESV).

A verse for meditation. "If you want to be my disciple, you must, by comparison, hate everyone else—your father and mother, wife and children, brothers and sisters—yes, even your own life. Otherwise, you cannot be my disciple" (Luke 14:26).

A question to ponder. Do you love Jesus above all others?

THE PRODIGAL SON

Luke 15:11 – 17:10

Yesterday we considered the Jewish people's consistent rejection of Jesus (Matthew 23:37-39; Luke 13:22–15:10; John 10:22-42). Today we focus on Jesus's teaching on the prodigal son.

Key concept. God welcomes repentant sinners into His arms.

The big picture. Jesus taught on the prodigal son in early AD 30. In this parable, Jesus taught about God's boundless love toward those who are lost and turn to Him for forgiveness (Luke 15:11-32). We might loosely paraphrase the parable's meaning this way: "If you feel unworthy—if you feel alienated from God—turn to Him immediately, for *His arms are open wide.*"

Transformational truth. The prodigal son confessed his folly to his father (Luke 15:21). His father's heart was full of forgiveness, and he had his arms wide open to embrace his son. You and I are instructed to confess our sins to the Father when we become aware of them. The reason for this is that sin breaks our fellowship with God, and that fellowship is immediately restored through confession (John 1:9; see also Proverbs 28:13).

A verse for meditation. "No one can serve two masters. For you will hate one and love the other; you will be devoted to one and despise the other. You cannot serve God and be enslaved to money" (Luke 16:13).

A question to ponder. Do you ever feel down on yourself like the prodigal son? How has this lesson helped you in this regard?

JESUS IS THE RESURRECTION AND THE LIFE

Luke 17:11–37; John 11

Yesterday we gave attention to Jesus's parable of the prodigal son (Luke 15:11–17:10). Today we turn our attention to Jesus as the resurrection and the life.

Key concept. Jesus resurrected Lazarus from the dead to prove that He Himself is the resurrection and the life.

The big picture. When Jesus heard Lazarus was ailing, He affirmed to His followers that Lazarus's situation would bring glory to God (John 11:1-44). But upon receiving the news, Jesus did not depart immediately to be with him. By the time Jesus arrived, Lazarus had been dead four days. This made Christ's miracle of resurrection all the more impressive.

Transformational truth. Martha experienced a conflict between walking by sight and walking by faith (John 11:3-4,16). By sight, Martha recognized that Lazarus's body had been in the tomb four days. By sight, Martha knew that dead men tend to stay dead. By sight, Martha thought it was too late to help Lazarus. Walking by faith, however, looks beyond circumstances to the Lord of miracles. Lazarus's resurrection taught Martha to walk by faith.

A verse for meditation. "I am the resurrection and the life. Anyone who believes in me will live, even after dying" (John 11:25).

A question to ponder. Have you ever pondered what your resurrection body will be like—no more sickness, no more growing old, and no more death?

INSIGHTS ON CHRISTIAN LIVING

Matthew 19:3-30; Mark 10:2-31; Luke 18:1-30

Yesterday we focused on Jesus as the resurrection and the life (Luke 17:11-37; John 11). Today we turn our attention to Jesus's insights on Christian living.

Key concept. Jesus taught on persistence in prayer, the necessity of humility, avoiding legalism, and the dangers of wealth.

The big picture. Jesus taught on many relevant topics: Christians should be persistent in prayer (Luke 18:1-8). They should avoid self-righteousness, and pray humbly (Luke 18:9-14). God desires marriage to be permanent if possible (Matthew 19:3-12; Mark 10:2-12). Jesus loves little children (Matthew 19:13-15; Mark 10:13-16; Luke 18:15-17). No one can earn eternal life by keeping commandments (Matthew 19:16-30; Mark 10:17-31; Luke 18:18-30).

Transformational truth. It's hard for a rich person to turn to God because he has little sense of need for God (Luke 18:24-25). Of course, it's not wrong to be wealthy. But wealth can be a big distraction from spiritual things. A love of material things is a sure sign that a person is living according to a temporal perspective, not an eternal one (Luke 16:13; 1 Timothy 6:10; Hebrews 13:5). A love of money can lead to destruction (1 Timothy 6:9).

A verse for meditation. "I tell you the truth, it is very hard for a rich person to enter the Kingdom of Heaven" (Matthew 19:23).

A question to ponder. In what ways have you found yourself distracted from the things of God by the things of this world?

MORE TEACHINGS FROM JESUS

Matthew 20; Mark 10:32-52; Luke 18:31–19:10

In the previous lesson, we explored Jesus's insights on Christian living (Matthew 19:3-30; Mark 10:2-31; Luke 18:1-30). Today we consider more teachings from Jesus.

Key concept. Jesus taught about serving Him humbly, and spoke on the nature of true greatness in the kingdom.

The big picture. Jesus told a parable in which the workers labored for different lengths of time, yet all were paid the same at the end of the day (Matthew 20:1-16). The point: We should humbly serve the Lord without sticking up for personal rights. Jesus also indicated that the one who wants to be great in the kingdom must become a humble servant (Matthew 20:20-28; Mark 10:35-45).

Transformational truth. After Zacchaeus became a Christian, he told Jesus, "I will give half my wealth to the poor, Lord, and if I have cheated people on their taxes, I will give them back four times as much!" (Luke 19:8). Faith shows itself in good works. As James 2:17 put it, "Faith by itself isn't enough. Unless it produces good deeds, it is dead and useless." True faith in Christ will change your behavior.

A verse for meditation. "Whoever wants to be a leader among you must be your servant, and whoever wants to be first among you must become your slave" (Matthew 20:26-27).

A question to ponder. Have you ever noticed how some of Jesus's teachings seem to be counterintuitive?

HOSANNA IN THE HIGHEST

Matthew 21:1-11; 26:6-13; Mark 11:1-11;
14:3-9; Luke 19:11-40; John 12:1-19

Yesterday we considered some key teachings of Jesus (Matthew 20; Mark 10:32-52; Luke 18:31–19:10). Today we focus on Jesus riding a donkey into Jerusalem as the prophesied Messiah.

Key concept. Jesus is portrayed as the Jewish Messiah who fulfills Old Testament prophecy.

The big picture. Jesus rode into Jerusalem on a donkey and fulfilled prophecy in doing so (Matthew 21:1-11; Mark 11:1-11; Luke 19:28-40; John 12:12-19; Zechariah 9:9). This was the Sunday before crucifixion day. The people were jubilant, apparently thinking their moment of deliverance from Roman oppression had finally come. They were blind to Jesus's real mission—bringing spiritual salvation.

Transformational truth. The Lord desires that we optimally use our God-given gifts, talents, and time during earthly life (Luke 19:13). He wants us to "do good business" until that future day when there will be an accounting at the future judgment seat of Christ (Romans 14:10; 2 Corinthians 5:10). Every day we arise, our attitude should be, "Today I will serve the Lord with enthusiasm."

A verse for meditation. "Praise God! Blessings on the one who comes in the name of the LORD! Hail to the King of Israel!" (John 12:13).

A question to ponder. Does the future judgment seat of Christ motivate you to use your time and talents on His behalf?

CONFLICT WITH JEWISH LEADERS

Matthew 21:12-27; Mark 11:12-33;
Luke 19:41–20:8; John 12:20-50

Yesterday we gave attention to Jesus riding a donkey into Jerusalem as the prophesied Messiah (Matthew 21:1-11; 26:6-13; Mark 11:1-11; 14:3-9; Luke 19:11-40; John 12:1-19). Today we turn our attention to Jesus's increasing conflict with the Jewish leaders.

Key concept. The Jewish religious leaders were continuously offended by the words and works of Jesus.

The big picture. In the second quarter of AD 30, Jesus's conflict with the Jewish leaders continued. Jesus stated that because Jerusalem's inhabitants had rejected Him, the Jewish temple would soon be destroyed (Luke 19:41-44). He cleansed the temple of corrupt scribes and Pharisees on the Monday prior to crucifixion day (Mark 11:12-19).

Transformational truth. Jesus made a big deal about forgiving others. He said if you pray, and then remember you have something against someone, your top priority is to forgive that person (Mark 11:25-26). A lack of forgiveness shows that your heart is not right before God. In the New Testament, the Greek term for "forgiveness" (*aphiemi*) comes from a word that means "to let go." Forgiveness is a release, a letting go of self-destructive feelings such as anger and bitterness. Be a perpetual forgiver!

A verse for meditation. "When you are praying, first forgive anyone you are holding a grudge against, so that your Father in heaven will forgive your sins, too" (Mark 11:25).

A question to ponder. Can you think of any grudges that you need to let go of?

CONTINUED JEWISH REJECTION

Matthew 21:28 – 22:22; Mark 12:1-17; Luke 20:9-26

Yesterday we read about Jesus's increasing conflict with the Jewish leaders (Matthew 21:12-27; Mark 11:12-33; Luke 19:41 – 20:8; John 12:20-50). More of the same today.

Key concept. Jesus said that the Jewish leaders would one day be punished for their religious hypocrisy and their rejection of Him as the divine Messiah.

The big picture. At the beginning of the second quarter of AD 30, Jesus, in a parable, drew a stark contrast between the self-righteous, prideful Pharisees and repentant sinners (Matthew 21:28-32). Another parable pointed to how the Jewish leaders resisted and even killed God's prophets down through the centuries, and even His Son (Matthew 21:33-46; Mark 12:1-12; Luke 20:9-19). They would be held responsible for their rejection.

Transformational truth. Jesus instructed His followers to give to Caesar the things that belonged to him, and give to God the things that belong to Him (Luke 20:25). Underlying Jesus's statement is the reality that Christians have a dual citizenship—one earthly and one heavenly. Our heavenly citizenship is most important. We are pilgrims passing through on earth, on our way to another country, another land, another city (Hebrews 11:16). Our behavior on earth ought to be governed by our heavenly citizenship (see Philippians 1:27; 3:20).

A verse for meditation. "Give to Caesar what belongs to Caesar, and give to God what belongs to God" (Mark 12:17).

A question to ponder. In what ways should your heavenly citizenship motivate how you live?

THE GREATEST COMMANDMENT

Matthew 22:23 – 23:36;
Mark 12:18-44; Luke 20:27 – 21:4

In the previous lesson, we explored the continued Jewish rejection experienced by Jesus (Matthew 21:28 – 22:22; Mark 12:1-17; Luke 20:9-26). Today we consider Jesus's teaching on the greatest and second greatest commandments.

Key concept. The greatest commandment is to love God supremely.

The big picture. We've now arrived at Passion Week, near the beginning of the second quarter in AD 30. Because the crucifixion was drawing near, Christ provided some final teachings for His followers. Among the most important: The greatest commandment is to love God supremely with one's whole being (Deuteronomy 6:4-5). The second greatest commandment is to love one's neighbor (Leviticus 19:18; Matthew 22:34-40; Mark 12:28-34).

Transformational truth. Jesus taught that legalism is deadly, and it should be avoided at all costs (Matthew 23:13-36). A spirituality based on legalistic rules and regulations is doomed to failure. The backdrop to Jesus's teaching was the seemingly never-ending list of legalistic rules and regulations set forth by the scribes and Pharisees. Thanks be to God that our salvation is based on God's grace from beginning to end (Ephesians 2:8-9).

A verse for meditation. " 'You must love the Lord your God with all your heart, all your soul, and all your mind.' This is the first and greatest commandment. A second is equally important: 'Love your neighbor as yourself' " (Matthew 22:37-39).

A question to ponder. How do you assess your life in terms of the first and second greatest commandments?

THE END TIMES

Matthew 24; Mark 13; Luke 21:5-38

Yesterday we considered Jesus's teaching on the greatest and second greatest commandments (Matthew 22:23 – 23:36; Mark 12:18-44; Luke 20:27 – 21:4). Today we focus on Jesus's teachings about the end times.

Key concept. Jesus revealed the signs of the end of the age.

The big picture. The disciples asked, "What sign will signal your return and the end of the world?" The Olivet Discourse, delivered during Passion Week at the beginning of the second quarter of AD 30, is Jesus's response. Highlights include Jesus's prediction of the appearance of false Christs, wars, earthquakes, famines, and cosmic disturbances (Matthew 24:1-28; Mark 13:1-23; Luke 21:5-24). The climactic event of the end times is the second coming of Christ. Prior to His coming, people will be carousing about, just like they had in the days of Noah (Matthew 24:36-44).

Transformational truth. As Jesus addressed the end times, He warned about the rise of false teachers. He urged, "Don't let anyone mislead you" (Matthew 24:4). The only way to avoid deception is to be anchored in Scripture. We ought to test all truth claims against the Scriptures, like the Bereans (Acts 17:11). We ought to "test everything that is said" and "hold on to what is good" (1 Thessalonians 5:21).

A verse for meditation. "When the Son of Man returns, it will be like it was in Noah's day" (Matthew 24:37).

A question to ponder. Do you think we are living in the end times?

CHRIST'S JUDGMENT OF THE NATIONS

Matthew 25

Yesterday we considered Jesus's comments on the end times (Matthew 24; Mark 13; Luke 21:5-38). Today we focus on Christ's end-times judgment of the nations.

Key concept. Following His second coming, Christ will gather the people of all the nations and judge them.

The big picture. We are still in Passion Week. Jesus taught that the judgment of the nations will follow the second coming (Matthew 25:31-46). The nations are comprised of the "sheep" and the "goats"—the saved and the lost among the Gentiles. The basis of the judgment is how Christ's "brothers" were treated. The result of the judgment is two-fold: the righteous (sheep) will enter Christ's kingdom; the unrighteous (goats) will be cast into the lake of fire.

Transformational truth. We should each be engaged in faithful service to God as we anticipate Christ's coming (Matthew 25:21). We are to use our time, talents, and treasures in service to Him. We are reminded of James 2:17: "Faith by itself isn't enough. Unless it produces good deeds, it is dead and useless." The faithful servant will hear these words from the Lord: "Well done, my good and faithful servant" (Matthew 25:21).

A verse for meditation. "Well done, my good and faithful servant. You have been faithful in handling this small amount, so now I will give you many more responsibilities" (Matthew 25:21).

A question to ponder. Has today's lesson influenced your view on how we are to treat our Christian brothers and sisters?

PASSOVER CELEBRATION

*Matthew 26:1-5,14-25; Mark 14:1-2,10-
21; Luke 22:1-13; John 13:1-30*

Yesterday we focused on Christ's judgment of the nations (Matthew 25). Today we consider Jesus's last celebration of the Passover.

Key concept. Jesus washed the disciples' feet to illustrate the need for humility and self-denial among the disciples. He then predicted Judas's betrayal.

The big picture. Jesus celebrated the Passover on Thursday, April 2, AD 30, the night before the crucifixion. This Passover would have been especially meaningful to Jesus because the time of His death was imminent (Matthew 26:17-19; Mark 14:12-16; Luke 22:7-13). During the celebration, Jesus taught the disciples about humility and self-denial (John 13:1-20), and predicted His betrayal (Matthew 26:20-25; Mark 14:17-21; John 13:21-30).

Transformational truth. Jesus is the highest authority in the universe, and yet He engaged in the humble act of washing the disciples' feet (John 13:1-17). Great men of God have often combined authority with humility. Examples include King David (2 Samuel 7:18-21) and the apostle Paul (1 Timothy 1:15-16). God desires humility of each of us. God's people should "show true humility to everyone" (Titus 3:1-2). Peter exhorted, "Dress yourselves in humility as you relate to one another" (1 Peter 5:5-6). After all, "God opposes the proud but gives grace to the humble" (James 4:6).

A verse for meditation. "Since I, your Lord and Teacher, have washed your feet, you ought to wash each other's feet" (John 13:14).

A question to ponder. What should you do when you find yourself struggling with pride?

A PREDICTION AND
FINAL TEACHINGS

*Matthew 26:26-35; Mark 14:22-31;
Luke 22:14-34; John 13:31 – 14:31*

In the previous lesson, we looked at Jesus's last celebration of the Passover (Matthew 26:1-5,14-25; Mark 14:1-2,10-21; Luke 22:1-13; John 13:1-30). Today we consider Jesus taking care of final business before His crucifixion.

Key concept. Jesus informed the disciples of key things they would need to know following His crucifixion.

The big picture. Jesus was now taking care of final business on Thursday, April 2, AD 30, the night before the crucifixion. He knew He would soon die. He therefore gave crucial instruction to the disciples: *Love one another* (John 13:31-35 NIV). He also instituted the Lord's Supper (Matthew 26:26-29), foretold Peter's denial (Mark 14:26-31), and gave them a promise about the Holy Spirit (John 14:15-31).

Transformational truth. After Jesus informed the disciples they would all stumble, an overconfident Peter said no way (Mark 14:29-31). The rest is history. Peter denied Jesus three times. Every Christian needs to cautiously avoid overconfidence. This brings to mind 1 Corinthians 10:12, where the apostle Paul warned: "If you think you are standing strong, be careful not to fall." No one is invulnerable to falling. Christian beware.

A verse for meditation. "Just as I have loved you, you should love each other. Your love for one another will prove to the world that you are my disciples" (John 13:34-35).

A question to ponder. Can you think of someone who needs to experience your love today?

MORE FINAL INSTRUCTIONS

John 15 – 17

Yesterday we considered Jesus's taking care of final business before His crucifixion (Matthew 26:26-35; Mark 14:22-31; Luke 22:14-34; John 13:31–14:31). More of the same today.

Key concept. Jesus is the true vine, and the Holy Spirit will be the divine Helper of all believers.

The big picture. It is still Thursday, April 2, AD 30, the night before the crucifixion. Jesus's final teachings to the disciples included these: Christians ("branches") must be plugged into Jesus ("the vine") so they'll bear fruit (John 15:1-17). Followers of Jesus will be hated by the world (15:18-26). Once He was in heaven, Jesus would send the Holy Spirit to believers to be their Helper (16:1-33). Jesus would soon die, but not to worry. He would rise again (16:16-23).

Transformational truth. Jesus said, "I have told you these things so that you will be filled with my joy. Yes, your joy will overflow" (John 15:11). The "things" Jesus spoke relate to Christians being branches plugged into the Vine (Jesus). Our joy comes from our close connection with Jesus. The more we are plugged in to Jesus, the greater our joy (see also John 16:33).

A verse for meditation. "I will send you the Advocate—the Spirit of truth. He will come to you from the Father and will testify all about me" (John 15:26).

A question to ponder. How do you think the Holy Spirit testifies about Jesus Christ?

THE BETRAYAL OF JESUS

Matthew 26:36-56; Mark 14:32-52;
Luke 22:35-53; John 18:1-14

Yesterday we considered some final instructions from Jesus (John 15–17). Today we focus on the betrayal and arrest of Jesus.

Key concept. Jesus prayed in Gethsemane as He pondered what lay ahead at the cross. He was betrayed by Judas and arrested.

The big picture. It is still Thursday, April 2, AD 30, the night before the crucifixion. In Gethsemane, Jesus experienced distress as never before. Jesus wanted the disciples to pray, but they fell asleep (Matthew 26:36-46). Judas, in a monumental betrayal, led the temple guards straight to Gethsemane. He identified Christ with a kiss, and Jesus was arrested (John 18:1-14).

Transformational truth. Jesus preferred to skip the agony of the cross. But He prayed, "My Father! If it is possible, let this cup of suffering be taken away from me. Yet I want your will to be done, not mine" (Matthew 26:39). Jesus is our example in complete obedience to God. Jesus elsewhere affirmed, "I have come down from heaven to do the will of God who sent me, not to do my own will" (John 6:38).

A verse for meditation. "'Abba, Father,' he cried out, 'everything is possible for you. Please take this cup of suffering away from me. Yet I want your will to be done, not mine'" (Mark 14:36).

A question to ponder. What degree of suffering did Christ endure for you?

JESUS'S TRIAL BEFORE CAIAPHAS

Matthew 26:57-75; Mark 14:53-72;
Luke 22:54-71; John 18:15-27

Yesterday we focused on the betrayal and arrest of Jesus (Matthew 26:36-56; Mark 14:32-52; Luke 22:35-53; John 18:1-14). Today we turn our attention to Jesus's trial before Caiaphas.

Key concept. Jesus stood trial, and Peter denied Him three times.

The big picture. Jesus was tried before Caiaphas and the council on crucifixion Friday, April 3, AD 30. Jesus knew that Caiaphas and the others would one day stand before Him at His tribunal, and He would be the sovereign Judge (Matthew 26:57-68). The tables would be turned in that future day. Meanwhile, Peter denied Christ, and afterward broke down in sorrow (Luke 22:54-65).

Transformational truth. Following Peter's third denial, Jesus looked into Peter's eyes (Luke 22:61). Some believe Jesus looked at Peter to remind him of His prediction of the denial. I don't think so. Jesus loved Peter. And Jesus, as God, knows how frail we all are. The Lord "knows how weak we are; he remembers we are only dust" (Psalm 103:14). I suspect that the Lord looked into Peter's eyes with compassion and forgiveness.

A verse for meditation. "You will see the Son of Man seated in the place of power at God's right hand and coming on the clouds of heaven" (Mark 14:62).

A question to ponder. Have you ever thought about how Christ will one day be the Judge instead of being the accused?

FURTHER TRIALS OF JESUS

Matthew 27:1-26; Mark 15:1-15;
Luke 23:1-25; John 18:28 – 19:16

In the previous lesson, we explored Jesus's trial before Caiaphas (Matthew 26:57-75; Mark 14:53-72; Luke 22:54-71; John 18:15-27). Today we consider the further trials of Jesus.

Key concept. Judas hanged himself in remorse for his betrayal. Jesus then underwent further trials.

The big picture. It is crucifixion Friday, April 3, AD 30. Judas was filled with remorse over betraying innocent blood, and ended up committing suicide (Matthew 27:3-10). Meanwhile, the Jewish council took Jesus to Pilate, the governor of Judea, and brought false accusations against Him. Pilate subsequently sent Jesus to Herod. Herod interrogated Jesus, but Jesus was silent. He sent Jesus back to Pilate without a verdict. Pilate affirmed he saw no crime in Jesus and wanted to release Him. The crowds shouted, "Crucify him!" Pilate finally consented (Matthew 27:15-26).

Transformational truth. Jesus informed Pilate He indeed was a King: "My Kingdom is not an earthly kingdom…My Kingdom is not of this world" (John 18:36-37). Jesus's kingdom is a spiritual kingdom where people are redeemed and lives are forever changed. You and I ought to live as loyal subjects of His kingdom during our short time on earth. His reign will be eternal (see Revelation 19:16).

A verse for meditation. "My Kingdom is not an earthly kingdom… My Kingdom is not of this world" (John 18:36).

A question to ponder. Is there room for growth in your loyalty to Christ the King?

JESUS WAS CRUCIFIED

Matthew 27:27-44; Mark 15:16-32;
Luke 23:26-43; John 19:17-30

Yesterday we considered the further trials of Jesus (Matthew 27:1-26; Mark 15:1-15; Luke 23:1-25; John 18:28–19:16). Today we will focus on the crucifixion of Jesus.

Key concept. Jesus was mocked, ridiculed, and crucified.

The big picture. It is crucifixion Friday, April 3, AD 30. The Roman soldiers stripped Jesus, put a scarlet robe on Him, forced a crown of thorns on His head, put a staff in His hand, mocked Him, spat on Him, struck Him, and led Him away to be crucified (Matthew 27:27-31; Mark 15:16-20). Upon arriving at Golgotha, Jesus was offered a first-century painkilling narcotic, but refused it. He then suffered Roman crucifixion (Matthew 27:33-44; Mark 15:22-32; Luke 23:33-43; John 19:17-30).

Transformational truth. Jesus loves you so much it hurts. Roman crucifixion involved a slow and torturous death. It was not only painful, but also caused the victim to slowly suffocate. Jesus willingly suffered through all this because He loves you: "I am the good shepherd. The good shepherd sacrifices his life for the sheep" (John 10:11). "There is no greater love than to lay down one's life for one's friends" (15:13).

A verse for meditation. "Jesus said, 'Father, forgive them, for they don't know what they are doing'" (Luke 23:34).

A question to ponder. Can you think of any greater example of forgiveness and love than that displayed in Luke 23:34?

JESUS'S DEATH AND BURIAL

*Matthew 27:45-66; Mark 15:33-47;
Luke 23:44-56; John 19:31-42*

Yesterday we considered the crucifixion of Jesus (Matthew 27:27-44; Mark 15:16-32; Luke 23:26-43; John 19:17-30). Today we focus on the moment of Jesus's death and His subsequent burial.

Key concept. Following His death on the cross, Jesus was buried in a tomb, and Roman soldiers were posted to guard the tomb.

The big picture. Following Jesus's death on the cross, His body was buried in a tomb owned by Joseph of Arimathea. An extremely large stone was then rolled, by means of levers, against the entrance (Matthew 27:57-61; Mark 15:42-47; Luke 23:50-56; John 19:38-42). Roman guards were stationed at the tomb (Matthew 27:62-66).

Transformational truth. When Jesus died, "the curtain in the sanctuary of the Temple was torn in two, from top to bottom" (Matthew 27:51). This thick curtain blocked all humans, except the high priest (once a year), from entering into the Most Holy Place. The torn curtain symbolically indicated that we now have unhindered access to God through Jesus: "Let us come boldly to the throne of our gracious God. There we will receive his mercy, and we will find grace to help us when we need it most" (Hebrews 4:16).

A verse for meditation. "When the Roman officer who stood facing him saw how he had died, he exclaimed, 'This man truly was the Son of God!'" (Mark 15:39).

A question to ponder. Why do you think Jesus said, "My God, my God, why have you abandoned me?" (Matthew 27:46)?

THE RESURRECTION OF JESUS

Matthew 28:1-15; Mark 16:1-13;
Luke 24:1-35; John 20:1-18

Yesterday we focused on Jesus's death and burial (Matthew 27:45-66; Mark 15:33-47; Luke 23:44-56; John 19:31-42). Today we turn our attention to Christ's resurrection from the dead.

Key concept. Jesus rose from the dead, and made many convincing appearances to His followers.

The big picture. It is now resurrection Sunday, April 5, AD 30. An angel revealed to Mary Magdalene, "the other Mary," and Salome that Jesus had resurrected from the dead. The tomb was thus empty. They were instructed to tell the disciples the good news. Jesus then made many resurrection appearances (Matthew 28:1-10; Mark 16:1-11; Luke 24:1-12; John 20:1-18).

Transformational truth. The two disciples on the road to Emmaus said to each other, "Did not our hearts burn within us while he talked to us on the road, while he opened to us the Scriptures?" (Luke 24:32 ESV). Jesus showed them all the Old Testament verses that spoke about Him. Jesus elsewhere claimed to be the theme of the entire Old Testament (Matthew 5:17; Luke 24:27,44; John 5:39; Hebrews 10:7). That same burning heart is the birthright of every Christian. Stay excited about the Lord!

A verse for meditation. "He isn't here! He is risen from the dead, just as he said would happen. Come, see where his body was lying" (Matthew 28:6).

A question to ponder. What difference does it make to you personally that Jesus is alive and well?

MORE RESURRECTION APPEARANCES

*Matthew 28:16-20; Mark 16:14-20;
Luke 24:36-53; John 20:19 – 21:25*

In the previous lesson, we explored Christ's resurrection from the dead (Matthew 28:1-15; Mark 16:1-13; Luke 24:1-35; John 20:1-18). Today we consider further resurrection appearances, as well as Christ's Great Commission.

Key concept. Jesus made further resurrection appearances to prove He really had risen from the dead.

The big picture. It is now AD 30, sometime after resurrection Sunday. Jesus made further resurrection appearances (John 20:24-31; 21:1-14) and charged His disciples with the Great Commission (Matthew 28:16-20; Mark 16:14-18; Luke 24:36-49; John 20:19-23). He then restored a bruised Peter (John 21:15-19) and ascended into heaven (Mark 16:19-20; Luke 24:50-53).

Transformational truth. Peter denied Jesus three times. That's bad. Notice, however, that Jesus sought him out to restore him. In the process, He asked Peter three times if he loved Him. It is obvious that Peter loved Him (see John 21:7). Peter went on to become a powerful leader in the early church (John 21:15-19; see the book of Acts). Likewise, the Lord can use you, even with all your flaws.

A verse for meditation. "Go and make disciples of all the nations, baptizing them in the name of the Father and the Son and the Holy Spirit. Teach these new disciples to obey all the commands I have given you" (Matthew 28:19-20).

A question to ponder. Have you been an active participant in fulfilling Christ's Great Commission, or are you on the sidelines?

ERA 9: THE EARLY CHURCH
AD 30 – 95

Acts Through Revelation

Today we begin our study of a new biblical era—titled "The Early Church." Bible books pertinent to our study of this era include Acts, Romans, 1 Corinthians, 2 Corinthians, Galatians, Ephesians, Philippians, Colossians, 1 Thessalonians, 2 Thessalonians, 1 Timothy, 2 Timothy, Titus, Philemon, Hebrews, James, 1 Peter, 2 Peter, 1 John, 2 John, 3 John, Jude, and Revelation. This last era covers a lot of territory.

We noted in the previous section that the New Testament is a collection of 27 books composed over a 50-year period by a number of different authors. The primary personality of the New Testament is Jesus Christ. The primary theme is salvation in Jesus Christ, based on the new covenant.

Following the four Gospels is the historical book of Acts, which focuses on how Christianity spread following the death and resurrection of Christ. Though the book is traditionally called the Acts of the Apostles, it is probably more appropriately called the Acts of the Holy Spirit, for truly it is the Holy Spirit who seems to be active in just about every chapter of the book.

Following the book of Acts are the epistles or letters. Approximately one-third of the New Testament is made up of epistles. Epistles served as a very important form of communication in the ancient Greek-speaking world. These letters typically included an introduction (the sender's name and some form of greeting), the body, and a conclusion. They were not delivered by a postal system, but rather were generally hand-delivered by a messenger.

Many of the New Testament epistles or letters were written to brand new churches that had just been formed and had certain problems or issues that needed to be addressed (1 and 2 Thessalonians are examples). The apostle Paul also wrote letters to churches as follow-ups to his missionary work among them, as he did with the Ephesians. Hence, Paul's letters were very personal in nature. In some cases, he gave advice to the leader of a particular church, as was the case with 1 and 2 Timothy. Other times he addressed the church as a whole, as he did with the Philippians.

Some New Testament epistles are categorized as "general epistles" because they were not directed at specific churches, but were rather circulated to a number of churches and dealt with general concerns. These are primarily the non-Pauline epistles and include 1 and 2 Peter, as well as 1, 2, and 3 John.

Though all these letters were directed at first-century churches and believers, they also have tremendous relevance for Christians today. The issues dealt with in the epistles apply to every generation.

The final book of the New Testament is Revelation, which is an apocalyptic book about the prophetic future. This book was written to persecuted believers to give them hope, inspiration, and comfort so they would be able to patiently endure the persecution and struggle they were facing. The book demonstrates that God wins in the end, and we will one day live face to face with Him forever in a new heavens and a new earth.

In the coming chapters, we will journey through Acts, all the epistles, and Revelation as we learn interesting details about the era of the early church. The following dates provide a helpful chronological orientation:

> AD 30 (May 24) — The Day of Pentecost, the day the church was born.
>
> AD 37 — The apostle Paul met with James and Peter on his first visit to Jerusalem after his conversion.
>
> AD 40 — Peter witnessed to Cornelius.
>
> AD 44 — James became the leader of the church at Jerusalem.
>
> AD 44–49 — James wrote his epistle to Jewish Christians.

AD 47 – 49 — Paul, Barnabas, and John Mark went on their first missionary journey.

AD 49 — Paul confronted Peter about not eating with Gentiles; Peter, Paul, Titus, and Barnabas travelled to Jerusalem to attend the Jerusalem Council.

AD 49 – 50 — Timothy joined Paul and Silas as they journeyed through north Galatia to Troas; Paul wrote his epistle to the Galatians to rescue them from a false gospel of legalism.

AD 49 – 52 — Paul and Silas went on their second missionary journey.

AD 50 — Paul and his companions visited Philippi during their second missionary tour and planted a church; Paul, Silas, and Timothy preached in Thessalonica; the church at Thessalonica was founded.

AD 50 – 51 — Paul travelled to Corinth and spent 18 months planting a church there.

AD 51 — Paul had a hearing before the proconsul Gallio in Corinth; Paul wrote his first and second epistles to the Thessalonians a number of months after his ministry among them.

AD 52 — Paul travelled through Ephesus on his second missionary tour; Apollos was mentored by Aquila and Priscilla in Ephesus.

AD 53 – 57 — Paul went on his third missionary journey.

AD 54 — Paul returned to Ephesus and ministered there for a few years.

AD 54 – 68 — Nero reigned in Rome.

AD 55 — Paul wrote his first epistle to the Corinthians from Ephesus.

AD 56 — Paul wrote his second epistle to the Corinthians

from Ephesus; he sent Titus to mediate a conflict between Paul and the Corinthian church.

AD 57 — Paul wrote Romans while in Corinth; he revisited Philippi to collect funds for the church at Jerusalem.

AD 60 — Luke wrote his Gospel.

AD 60–61 — Paul travelled to Rome.

AD 61 — Luke wrote Acts.

AD 61 — Paul was imprisoned in Rome; he wrote Ephesians and Colossians while in prison.

AD 62 — James was stoned to death.

AD 62–63 — Paul was released from prison.

AD 62–64 — Paul wrote his epistle to Titus; he commissioned Titus to train elders for churches in Crete; he also wrote his first epistle to his young apprentice Timothy.

AD 63 — Paul was taken to Rome and imprisoned again; he wrote his epistle to the Philippians while imprisoned; he also encountered Onesimus, a runaway slave, in prison; he then wrote his short epistle to Philemon on behalf of Onesimus.

AD 63–64 — Peter wrote his first epistle.

AD 64 — Nero blamed Christians for the great fire in Rome and persecuted them.

AD 66 — Peter was crucified upside-down.

AD 67 — John joined other Christians in relocating to Ephesus, prior to Jerusalem's fall in AD 70; Paul wrote 2 Timothy, recognizing his death was near; soon after, Paul was martyred.

AD 67–68 — Jude wrote his short epistle as a protective measure for his readers.

AD 68 — Hebrews was written by an anonymous writer.

AD 70—Jerusalem and its temple were destroyed by Titus and his Roman warriors.

AD 81–96—Domitian, the emperor of Rome, demanded emperor worship, a crisis faced by John's readers.

AD 90—Early gnostic heresies emerged, another crisis faced by John's readers; John wrote three letters to instruct believers in the crises they faced—1, 2, and 3 John.

AD 95—John was exiled to the isle of Patmos, in the Aegean Sea, for the "crime" of sharing the message about Jesus Christ (Revelation 1:9). The book of Revelation was written.

AD 97—John returned to Ephesus.

AD 98–100—John died at Ephesus.

Preview: On Day 322, we'll focus on Jesus's ascension into heaven, as well as the Holy Spirit's descent on the Day of Pentecost.

JESUS ASCENDS, THE HOLY SPIRIT DESCENDS

Acts 1 – 3

Yesterday we introduced Era 9, titled "The Early Church," dated AD 30 – 95. Today we turn our attention to the ascension of Jesus into heaven and the descent of the Holy Spirit at Pentecost.

Key concept. Jesus ascended into heaven. Not long after, the Holy Spirit fell upon believers on the Day of Pentecost.

The big picture. The risen Lord had instructed His followers to stay in Jerusalem so the promise concerning the Holy Spirit could be fulfilled. Christ ascended into heaven on Thursday, May 14, AD 30. The Day of Pentecost was later that month, on May 24, AD 30. The disciples became supernaturally empowered by the Holy Spirit (Acts 2). Filled with new courage, the disciples boldly proclaimed the message of the resurrected Lord.

Transformational truth. The indwelling presence and empowerment from the Holy Spirit enables Christ's followers to be bold and effective witnesses (Acts 1:8; see also 2:4; 1 Corinthians 6:19-20; Ephesians 3:16,20). Ephesians 5:18 says we are to be perpetually "filled" with — or controlled by — the Holy Spirit.

A verse for meditation. "You will receive power when the Holy Spirit comes upon you. And you will be my witnesses, telling people about me everywhere — in Jerusalem, throughout Judea, in Samaria, and to the ends of the earth" (Acts 1:8).

A question to ponder. Does Acts 1 – 3 make you want to learn more about the Holy Spirit?

MINISTRY OF THE APOSTLES

Acts 4 – 7

In the previous lesson, we explored the ascension of Jesus into heaven and the descent of the Holy Spirit at Pentecost (Acts 1 – 3). Today we consider the ministry of the apostles in the early church.

Key concept. The miracles done by the apostles attested to the truth of their message.

The big picture. In AD 30, the Jewish Sanhedrin interrogated Peter and John regarding a man's healing. Peter and John affirmed that the resurrected Christ had healed him. The Sadducees were perturbed at this claim because they denied the doctrine of the resurrection. The Sanhedrin warned them to speak no further in Jesus's name. They replied they were compelled to obey God rather than men (Acts 4).

Transformational truth. The apostles were persecuted for their witness of Christ (Acts 5:41). We know that the godly will suffer persecution (2 Timothy 3:12). Because the world hated Christ, it should not surprise us that it will likewise hate Christians (1 John 3:13). Christians ought to rejoice in being counted worthy to suffer while standing for Christ (Acts 5:41; see also Matthew 5:10-11).

A verse for meditation. "Let me clearly state to all of you and to all the people of Israel that he was healed by the powerful name of Jesus Christ the Nazarene, the man you crucified but whom God raised from the dead" (Acts 4:10).

A question to ponder. Like the apostles, have you ever had to disobey humans in order to obey God?

SAUL'S CONVERSION AND PETER'S GENTILE MINISTRY

Acts 8–11

Yesterday we considered the ministry of the apostles in the early church (Acts 4–7). Today we focus on Saul's conversion to Christ and Peter's ministry among Gentiles.

Key concept. The gospel was not for Jews only, but also for the Gentiles.

The big picture. Today's Scripture reading spans from AD 36 to the early 40s. Jesus appeared to Saul on the road to Damascus. Saul became a believer, and quickly turned into a powerful witness for Jesus Christ. Because he was to be an apostle to the Gentiles, he primarily went by his Greco-Roman name Paul (Acts 9:1-43). Meanwhile, Jesus taught Peter that Gentiles were now welcome to God's salvation (9:32–11:18).

Transformational truth. Before becoming a Christian, Saul (Paul) was a persecutor of the church: "Authorized by the leading priests, I caused many believers there to be sent to prison. And I cast my vote against them when they were condemned to death" (Acts 26:10). By the grace of God, however, the greatest persecutor of the church became the greatest missionary. Even the worst of sinners can be redeemed and transformed.

A verse for meditation. "Saul is my chosen instrument to take my message to the Gentiles and to kings, as well as to the people of Israel" (Acts 9:15).

A question to ponder. How miraculous was Saul's conversion to Christ?

PAUL AND BARNABAS PREACH

Acts 12 – 15:35

Yesterday we gave attention to Saul's conversion to Christ and Peter's ministry among the Gentiles (Acts 8 – 11). Today we turn our attention to the gospel preaching of Paul and Barnabas.

Key concept. Paul and Barnabas spread the gospel in various cities. The Jerusalem Council declared that Gentile believers did not need to be circumcised.

The big picture. Today's Scripture reading spans AD 44 – 49. Persecution increased against the early church. James (the brother of John) was executed. Peter was thrown in jail, but God arranged an angelic jailbreak (Acts 12). Paul and Barnabas continued ministering as traveling missionaries in various cities (Acts 13:1 – 14:28). Meanwhile, the Jerusalem Council affirmed that Gentile converts should not be required to adopt the ceremonial requirements of Judaism (Acts 15).

Transformational truth. During his missionary tours, Paul didn't just travel from city to city in random fashion. Rather, he purposefully visited major Roman capitals that were easily reached by existing trade routes. This strategy resulted in the gospel spreading out to other areas of the world through these trade routes (Acts 13 – 14). It is wise to develop strategies for the spread of the gospel.

A verse for meditation. "The Holy Spirit said, 'Appoint Barnabas and Saul for the special work to which I have called them'" (Acts 13:2).

A question to ponder. What do you learn about the Holy Spirit from Acts 13:2 above?

OBEDIENCE AND FAITH

The Book of James

Yesterday we focused on the gospel preaching of Paul and Barnabas (Acts 12–15:35). Today we turn our attention to lessons on obedience and faith in the book of James.

Key concept. Be a *doer* of God's Word, not just a *hearer.*

The big picture. The Jerusalem Council—addressed in yesterday's lesson—met in AD 49. James was written the same year. It is therefore appropriate to pause our study of Acts and parenthetically address James. James was the oldest half-brother of Jesus and leader of the Jerusalem church (Acts 12:17; Galatians 2:9). He wrote to Jewish Christians in danger of giving nothing but lip service to Jesus—perhaps as a result of increased Jewish persecution. James therefore emphasized that true faith in Jesus results in outward works.

Transformational truth. James made the important point that while faith alone saves a person, that faith ought to show itself in the way one lives. Faith should have very practical effects. Our faith should impact how we relate to God and other people, our sense of social justice, and our commitment to personal ethics (James 2:14-26).

A verse for meditation. "Don't just listen to God's word. You must do what it says. Otherwise, you are only fooling yourselves" (James 1:22).

A question to ponder. In what areas of your life would you like to improve as a "doer" of God's Word?

THE TRUE GOSPEL

Galatians 1–3

In the previous lesson, we explored teachings on obedience and faith in the book of James. Today we consider the nature of the true gospel.

Key concept. Don't fall for a false gospel of works. The true gospel is by grace through faith.

The big picture. The Jerusalem Council met in AD 49. James was written the same year. Galatians was then written in AD 50. Judaizers who infiltrated some of Paul's congregations (such as the church in Galatia) claimed Paul made the gospel more appealing to Gentiles by removing Jewish legal requirements (Acts 15:24; 20:29-30). They tried to add works to grace, and Paul would not have it (4:20). He emphasized that salvation is a grace-gift received solely by faith in Christ (3:6-9).

Transformational truth. Avoid the trap of thinking you need to "do this" and "do that" in order to receive salvation. You are saved by *grace alone* through *faith alone* (Ephesians 2:8-9). Paul warned that if anyone proclaimed to the church any other gospel than the one previously handed down (which was a *saved-by-grace* gospel), they were accursed before God (Galatians 1:8).

A verse for meditation. "Even if we or an angel from heaven should preach to you a gospel contrary to the one we preached to you, let him be accursed" (Galatians 1:8 ESV).

A question to ponder. Do you ever slip into the mentality that you need to do things to make God like you more?

FREE FROM THE YOKE OF SLAVERY

Galatians 4 – 6

Yesterday we considered the nature of the true gospel (Galatians 1 – 3). Today we focus on being free from any yoke of slavery.

Key concept. We have liberty in Christ. Good-bye to any and all yokes of slavery.

The big picture. The Galatians started out fine. They trusted in the gospel of grace. But then they became enslaved to the idea that they had to observe Jewish rituals to continue pleasing God. Paul said *no way.* The greatest single enemy to Christian liberty is legalism (Galatians 5:1-12). That said, believers must also be cautious not to fall into lawlessness (5:13 – 6:10). Christians are set free not only from bondage to the law, but also bondage to sin (5:16-26).

Transformational truth. We gain victory over sin by walking in dependence upon the Holy Spirit. The word "walk" in this verse is a present-tense verb, indicating continuing action. We are to persistently and continually walk in dependence upon the Holy Spirit. As we do this, we will live in a way that is pleasing to God. Walking in the Spirit also produces an abundance of spiritual fruit in our lives (Galatians 5:16-26).

A verse for meditation. "Christ has truly set us free. Now make sure that you stay free, and don't get tied up again in slavery to the law" (Galatians 5:1).

A question to ponder. Are there any "yokes of slavery" in your life right now?

PAUL'S CONTINUED EVANGELISM

Acts 15:36 – 18:11

Yesterday we gave attention to being free from any yoke of slavery (Galatians 4–6). Today we turn our attention to Paul's continued evangelism in various cities.

Key concept. Paul proclaimed the gospel in multiple cities.

The big picture. Following our study of James (written AD 49) and Galatians (written AD 50), we now return to Acts, focusing on events that took place between AD 50 and 51. During his second missionary tour, Paul visited Syria, Cilicia, Derbe, Lystra, Philippi, Thessalonica, Berea, and Corinth. A pattern emerged in these cities: (1) Paul preached, (2) the Jews resisted, and (3) persecution broke out. Paul worked with some fine Christians, including Silas, young Timothy, and Lydia. Through it all, the Holy Spirit guided Paul's steps (Acts 15:36–18:11).

Transformational truth. In these days of religious deception, we ought to follow the example of the Bereans and test all truth claims against Scripture. We guard ourselves from false doctrine by consulting Scripture, which is our barometer of truth (Acts 17:11; 1 Thessalonians 5:21).

A verse for meditation. "The people of Berea were more open-minded than those in Thessalonica, and they listened eagerly to Paul's message. They searched the Scriptures day after day to see if Paul and Silas were teaching the truth" (Acts 17:11).

A question to ponder. Do you think the *test-all-things* policy of the Bereans is even more relevant today than it was back in Bible times?

JESUS WILL ONE DAY COME FOR US

1 Thessalonians

Yesterday we focused on Paul's continued evangelism in various cities (Acts 15:36–18:11). Today we turn our attention to Paul's teaching that Jesus will one day come for us.

Key concept. Paul taught that at the rapture, we will experience a reunion with Christian loved ones.

The big picture. The events we addressed yesterday in Acts 15:36–18:11 spanned AD 50 to 51. Today we turn our attention to 1 Thessalonians, written in early AD 51. Among other things, Paul taught the Thessalonians that at the rapture both dead and living Christians will be raised and caught up to meet the Lord in the air. From that point forward, they will be with the Lord forever (1 Thessalonians 4:13-17). Christians are urged to comfort one another with this truth (verse 18).

Transformational truth. The imminence of the rapture should motivate us to live in purity and righteousness. Those expecting the Lord's return "will keep themselves pure, just as he is pure" (1 John 3:2-3). In view of the prophetic future, we are exhorted to live "holy and godly lives" (2 Peter 3:10-14; see also Romans 13:11-14; 1 Thessalonians 4:1-12).

A verse for meditation. "Always be joyful. Never stop praying. Be thankful in all circumstances, for this is God's will for you who belong to Christ Jesus" (1 Thessalonians 5:16-18).

A question to ponder. In what ways can prophecy make a difference in the way you live your life?

THE DAY OF THE LORD

2 Thessalonians

In the previous lesson, we explored Paul's teaching that Jesus will one day come for us (1 Thessalonians). Today we consider Paul's teaching on the future Day of the Lord.

Key concept. Unbelievers will one day be judged during the Day of the Lord.

The big picture. Following Paul's writing of 1 Thessalonians in early AD 51, he wrote 2 Thessalonians later that same year to further explain and clarify God's program of events relating to the future Day of the Lord and Christ's second coming. He debunked the idea that the Day of the Lord had already begun, as was apparently being taught by some phony epistles. Paul also encouraged the Thessalonians to correct the disorders remaining among them. He emphasized the proper attitude Christians should have in awaiting the Lord's coming: (1) Be ready by living righteously; (2) don't be idle.

Transformational truth. Believers ought to avoid idleness and remain committed to work as they await the Lord's coming (2 Thessalonians 3:6-13; see also Romans 12:11; Hebrews 6:12). In keeping with this, Romans 12:11 exhorts believers to "never be lazy, but work hard and serve the Lord enthusiastically."

A verse for meditation. "The Lord is faithful; he will strengthen you and guard you from the evil one" (2 Thessalonians 3:3).

A question to ponder. If the Lord came for you today, would you feel spiritually ready to meet Him?

AVOID DIVISIONS

Acts 18:12 – 19:22; 1 Corinthians 1 – 4

Yesterday we considered Paul's teaching on the future Day of the Lord (2 Thessalonians). Today we will focus on Paul's instructions to do away with divisions in the church.

Key concept. In Acts, we find Priscilla and Aquila training Apollos. According to 1 Corinthians, significant divisions had erupted in the Corinthian church. These needed immediate attention.

The big picture. The events described in Acts 18:12 – 19:22 occurred around AD 53. First Corinthians was then written in AD 55. Paul said the Corinthians needed to get rid of their divisions (1 Corinthians 1). They needed to understand God's Word (2) and build on the foundation of Jesus Christ alone, not on human leaders (3). The leaders of the church must find their true purpose in using their spiritual gifts to serve Christ alone (4).

Transformational truth. At the future judgment seat of Christ, our works will be examined and tested against the fire of Christ's holiness (1 Corinthians 3:11-15). If our works are built with good "materials" — Christ-honoring motives, godly obedience, and integrity — our works will stand. If our works are built with useless "materials" — carnal attitudes, sinful motives, pride-filled actions, and selfish ambition — they will burn up.

A verse for meditation. "No one can lay any foundation other than the one we already have — Jesus Christ" (1 Corinthians 3:11).

A question to ponder. Does the future judgment seat of Christ scare you or motivate you?

CHRISTIAN ETHICS

1 Corinthians 5 – 7

Yesterday we gave attention to Paul's instructions to do away with divisions in the church (Acts 18:12–19:22; 1 Corinthians 1–4). Today we turn our attention to applying Christian ethics to specific issues in the church.

Key concept. Paul addressed two ethical issues: (1) sexual immorality in the Corinthian church; (2) lawsuits against other members in the church.

The big picture. A man in the Corinthian church engaged in incest, and yet the church had done nothing about it. Paul chastised the church for this. He instructed that the sexual offender be ousted from fellowship until he repented (1 Corinthians 5). Paul then urged church members to stop taking legal action against each other (6).

Transformational truth. Paul instructed that all Christians should flee fornication (1 Corinthians 6:13,18). Joseph in the Old Testament is an example of such fleeing. He literally "ran from the house" when the wife of an Egyptian official tried to seduce him (Genesis 39:12). Fornication should not even be named or spoken of among Christians (Ephesians 5:3).

A verse for meditation. "Don't you realize that your body is the temple of the Holy Spirit, who lives in you and was given to you by God? You do not belong to yourself, for God bought you with a high price. So you must honor God with your body" (1 Corinthians 6:19-20).

A question to ponder. Is your life characterized by the pursuit of purity?

AVOIDING OFFENSE

1 Corinthians 8 – 11:1

Yesterday we focused on applying Christian ethics to specific issues in the church (1 Corinthians 5–7). Today we turn our attention to avoiding offense with other Christians.

Key concept. Christians must make efforts not to offend the consciences of weaker brothers and sisters.

The big picture. Avoiding offense to other Christians was an important matter to Paul. He said that while a particular action might be permissible for a Christian, it is best to avoid that action if it would injure the conscience of another (1 Corinthians 8). He emphasized that he accommodated himself to the needs and characteristics of others in order to evangelize among them more effectively (see 9:22). He also warned that Christians must stay away from idolatry in all its forms (10-11:1).

Transformational truth. Idolatry involves worshipping other things in the place of God. It can take many forms—money, materialism, the pursuit of fame, sexual immorality, and more. The New Testament consistently urges Christians to avoid all forms of idolatry (1 Corinthians 5:11; 2 Corinthians 6:16; Galatians 5:20; Colossians 3:5; 1 John 5:21). This would have been an important instruction for Christians in idolatrous Corinth.

A verse for meditation. "Whether you eat or drink, or whatever you do, do it all for the glory of God" (1 Corinthians 10:31).

A question to ponder. Do you think it might be life-transforming to adopt the attitude that *everything* you do in life is for the glory of God?

THE LORD'S SUPPER, SPIRITUAL GIFTS, AND RESURRECTION

1 Corinthians 11:2 – 16:24

In the previous lesson, we learned about avoiding offense with other Christians (1 Corinthians 8 – 11:1). Today we consider three important matters: the Lord's Supper, spiritual gifts, and the future resurrection.

Key concept. Paul provided a correct perspective on three important doctrinal issues.

The big picture. Paul taught that the Lord's Supper should be celebrated with respect, not as a gluttonous feast (1 Corinthians 11:2-34). He taught that the Holy Spirit gives a spiritual gift (or gifts) to all believers so they can mutually edify the body of Christ (12). He also emphasized that because Christ resurrected from the dead, we too shall be resurrected (15).

Transformational truth. Spiritual gifts are special abilities bestowed by the Holy Spirit upon individual believers so they can edify other church members. Every Christian has at least one spiritual gift. These gifts include teaching, pastoring, evangelizing, the message of wisdom, the message of knowledge, faith, healing, miraculous powers, prophecy, distinguishing between spirits, speaking in different tongues, and the interpretation of tongues (Romans 12:3-8; 1 Corinthians 12:8-10; Ephesians 4:7-13). These gifts surface in the process of participating in ministry.

A verse for meditation. "A spiritual gift is given to each of us so we can help each other" (1 Corinthians 12:7).

A question to ponder. Do you know what your spiritual gift is? How are you using it?

COMFORT AND FORGIVENESS

Acts 19:23 – 20:1; 2 Corinthians 1:1 – 2:13

Yesterday we considered the Lord's Supper, spiritual gifts, and the future resurrection (1 Corinthians 11:2–16:24). Today we will focus on comforting and forgiving others.

Key concept. God comforts us so that we may then comfort others. Repentant sinners should be forgiven by those in the church.

The big picture. We completed our study of 1 Corinthians, written in AD 55. The events in Acts 19:23-41 took place in AD 55–56. Second Corinthians was written in AD 56. Here, Paul speaks of a "chain reaction" of comfort. God comforts us, and then we can be used by God to comfort others (2 Corinthians 1:1-11). Paul also requested the Corinthians to graciously restore a repentant sinner to fellowship (2 Corinthians 2:5-13).

Transformational truth. Each of us can be a channel of comfort through which God's own comfort can flow to a suffering brother or sister (2 Corinthians 1:3-4). The church is full of people who are hurting. Because they are hurting, church members who have been through specific hurts are admonished to help others who are going through similar hurts. *We need each other!*

A verse for meditation. "God...comforts us in all our troubles so that we can comfort others. When they are troubled, we will be able to give them the same comfort God has given us" (2 Corinthians 1:3-4).

A question to ponder. Is there someone who needs your comfort today? What can you do?

MINISTER OF THE NEW COVENANT

2 Corinthians 2:14 – 7:16

Yesterday we gave attention to comforting and forgiving others (Acts 19:23 – 20:1; 2 Corinthians 1:1 – 2:13). Today we turn our attention to Paul as a minister of the new covenant, and the blessings of that covenant.

Key concept. Paul considered it a glorious honor to be a minister of the new covenant of grace.

The big picture. When it came to proclaiming the new covenant of grace, Paul compared himself to a clay pot filled with a treasure — the glory of the gospel (2 Corinthians 4). He affirmed that in the future, our resurrection bodies will be powerful and permanent (unlike our present bodies). We have Jesus to thank, whom God sent to reconcile sinners to Himself.

Transformational truth. Paul warned against being unequally yoked with unbelievers (2 Corinthians 6:14-15). This was important for the Corinthians, for they were surrounded by paganism on every side. First Timothy 5:22 urges, "Do not share in the sins of others. Keep yourself pure." Ephesians 5:11 likewise exhorts, "Take no part in the worthless deeds of evil and darkness; instead, expose them."

A verse for meditation. "We don't look at the troubles we can see now; rather, we fix our gaze on things that cannot be seen. For the things we see now will soon be gone, but the things we cannot see will last forever" (2 Corinthians 4:18).

A question to ponder. How does 2 Corinthians 4:18 affect your worldview?

PAUL DEFENDS HIS APOSTLESHIP

2 Corinthians 8 – 13

Yesterday we focused on Paul as a minister of the new covenant, and the blessings of that covenant (2 Corinthians 2:14 – 7:16). Today we turn our attention to the poor Jerusalem church and Paul's apostleship.

Key concept. Paul first gave instructions regarding a collection for the poor at the church in Jerusalem. He then vindicated his apostleship.

The big picture. Paul desired that the Corinthians make a generous donation in support of the poor Christians in Jerusalem. He said their generosity would be rewarded by God (2 Corinthians 8 – 9). He then vindicated his apostolic authority and credentials. This was necessary because some church members at Corinth had challenged him (10 – 13).

Transformational truth. Paul taught a paradox based on his own experience: The weaker the human vessel, the greater that God's strength and grace shines forth (1 Corinthians 12:8). Paul elsewhere affirmed, "We ourselves are like fragile clay jars containing this great treasure. This makes it clear that our great power is from God, not from ourselves" (2 Corinthians 4:7). We need not be dismayed by our weaknesses. They provide opportunity for God's great power to work!

A verse for meditation. "My grace is all you need. My power works best in weakness" (2 Corinthians 12:9).

A question to ponder. Do you ever feel weak in the face of life's difficulties? What have you learned in this lesson that can help you?

ALL STAND GUILTY

Romans 1:1 – 3:20

In the previous lesson, we considered the poor at the church in Jerusalem and Paul's apostleship (2 Corinthians 8–13). Today we look at how all people stand guilty before God.

Key concept. *All* are guilty before God—no exceptions.

The big picture. Yesterday we completed our study of 2 Corinthians, written in AD 56. The next book chronologically is Romans, written in AD 57. Paul declared that the Gentiles stood condemned before God because they had suppressed the knowledge of God and had turned to idolatry and paganism (Romans 1:18-32). The Jews also stood condemned before God because they had failed to live up to His infinitely righteous standards and had failed to believe God's Word (Romans 2:1–3:8). The conclusion is obvious: *All* stand guilty before God (Romans 3:9-20).

Transformational truth. Paul said he was not ashamed of sharing the good news about Jesus with people everywhere (Romans 1:16-17). Far from being something to be ashamed about, the gospel ought to be shouted from every rooftop. After all, the word *gospel* means "good news," and everyone needs to hear it.

A verse for meditation. "I am not ashamed of this Good News about Christ. It is the power of God at work, saving everyone who believes—the Jew first and also the Gentile" (Romans 1:16).

A question to ponder. Do you ever feel ashamed about sharing the good news about Christ?

RIGHTEOUSNESS IMPUTED AND IMPARTED

Romans 3:21 – 8:39

Yesterday we considered how all people stand guilty before God (Romans 1:1 – 3:20). Today we will focus on the imputation and impartation of righteousness.

Key concept. Paul doctrinally addresses both justification (the imputation of righteousness) and sanctification (the impartation of righteousness).

The big picture. No one has it within themselves to attain the righteousness that leads to salvation. God's solution is justification. This involves not just acquitting the believing sinner of all sin, but also imputing the very righteousness of Christ to his or her account. It cannot be earned. It is entirely of God's grace (Romans 3:21 – 5:21). Moreover, the Holy Spirit indwells and empowers every believer so that the sanctified lifestyle becomes possible in this life (Romans 6:1 – 8:39).

Transformational truth. Paul affirmed in Romans 8:28 that God has the unique ability to bring good out of evil in any situation. Example: Paul was thrown into prison in Rome. While imprisoned, God provided "time off" for Paul to write Ephesians, Philippians, Colossians, and Philemon. Paul also shared the gospel with his prison guards.

A verse for meditation. "We know that God causes everything to work together for the good of those who love God and are called according to his purpose for them" (Romans 8:28).

A question to ponder. Can you think of a time when God brought good out of evil in your life?

GOD'S PLAN FOR ISRAEL

Romans 9 – 11

Yesterday we gave attention to the imputation and impartation of righteousness (Romans 3:21 – 8:39). Today we turn our attention to God's sovereign plan for Israel.

Key concept. God sovereignly elected Israel in the past. Israel is currently in a state of unbelief. Yet there is a future salvation for Israel.

The big picture. In Romans 9 – 11, Paul addressed the salvation of the Jews, God's chosen people. He spoke of the past election and spiritual privileges of Israel (9), Israel's present state of unbelief (10), and Israel's future prospect of restoration and salvation (11). There is yet a future for Israel, and Israel will be regrafted into its place of promised blessing, thus fulfilling God's covenant promises.

Transformational truth. Paul loved his fellow Jews so much that he was willing to give up his life on their behalf (Romans 9:1-3). This brings to mind the words of Jesus: "There is no greater love than to lay down one's life for one's friends" (John 15:13). Jesus, of course, demonstrated His great love for us by dying on our behalf (John 3:16-17; 1 John 2:2).

A verse for meditation. "Oh, how great are God's riches and wisdom and knowledge! How impossible it is for us to understand his decisions and his ways" (Romans 11:33).

A question to ponder. Do you think you would ever be willing to make the supreme sacrifice, and give your life for another?

LIVING RIGHTEOUSLY

Romans 12 – 16

Yesterday we focused on God's sovereign plan for Israel (Romans 9–11). Today we turn our attention to what it means to live righteously before God.

Key concept. Christians are called to live righteously.

The big picture. Romans 12 instructs believers to surrender themselves to God as living sacrifices, and experience transformation through the renewing of the mind. Romans 13 teaches that because all authority comes from God, believers must submit to their government. Believers must also show love to their neighbor, for love comes from God. Romans 14–16 says that strong Christians need to give consideration to their weaker brothers and sisters so that they do not offend or injure them in any way.

Transformational truth. Paul urged Christians to not allow themselves to be molded by the world, but rather, to seek to be renewed in the mind (Romans 12:2). The word "world" here refers not to planet Earth but to an anti-God, satanic philosophical system. The renewing of minds can happen only through the ministry of the Holy Spirit as believers read and digest God's Word (Psalm 119:11; Philippians 4:8; Colossians 1:28; 3:10,16).

A verse for meditation. "Don't copy the behavior and customs of this world, but let God transform you into a new person by changing the way you think" (Romans 12:2).

A question to ponder. How strongly do you think your mind has been influenced and conditioned by the things of this world?

PAUL CONTINUES EVANGELIZING

Acts 20 – 24

In the previous lesson, we explored what it means to live righteously before God (Romans 12 – 16). Today we consider Paul's continued evangelism.

Key concept. Paul continued his ministry of sharing the gospel, and continued to experience Jewish resistance.

The big picture. Yesterday we completed our study of Romans, written in AD 57. We now turn to events in Acts 20:1 – 24:27, dated in late AD 57 – 58. Paul continued his ministry as a traveling evangelist. Upon arriving in Jerusalem, he was apprehended by a mob of angry Jews for a perceived offense, but Roman soldiers rescued him (Acts 21). Paul was put in a Roman jail for protection. While there, he revealed he was a Roman citizen, thereby necessitating fair treatment (22). The Jews were trying to charge Paul with blasphemy. He ended up in a Caesarian prison (24).

Transformational truth. The apostle Paul affirmed, "I have done the Lord's work humbly" (Acts 20:19). Scripture exhorts all of God's people to be clothed with humility (Colossians 3:12; 1 Peter 5:5-6), to be humble and gentle (Ephesians 4:2), and to walk humbly with our God (Micah 6:8). Other servants of God who walked in humility include John the Baptist (John 3:30) and the Old Testament prophet Daniel (Daniel 2:27-28).

A verse for meditation. "I always try to maintain a clear conscience before God and all people" (Acts 24:16).

A question to ponder. Do you always try to possess a clear conscience before God and before all people?

PAUL'S DEFENSE

Acts 25 – 28

Yesterday we considered Paul's continued evangelism and subsequent imprisonment (Acts 20 – 24). Today we will focus on Paul's defense.

Key concept. Paul defended himself before the Roman authorities.

The big picture. The events in Acts 25 – 28 took place in AD 59 – 60. Paul defended himself before Festus, the Roman provincial governor of Judea. Not wanting to be tried before the Jewish Sanhedrin, Paul — with Roman rights — appealed his case to Caesar. Before being sent to Rome, another Roman ruler, Herod Agrippa II, wanted to hear Paul's story (Acts 25). Paul made an able defense before both Festus and Agrippa. They agreed he was innocent (26). After a brief detour in Malta, Paul eventually made it to Rome, where he was put under house arrest (27 – 28).

Transformational truth. At the close of Acts, Paul was forced to live within the confines of a rented house, not free to go about as he desired (Acts 28:30). While in confinement, Paul not only wrote Ephesians, Philippians, Colossians, and Philemon, but he also preached the Word of God to any who were around him. God thereby brought good out of evil (see Romans 8:28). God can bring good out of evil in our lives too.

A verse for meditation. "He welcomed all who visited him, boldly proclaiming the Kingdom of God and teaching about the Lord Jesus Christ" (Acts 28:30-31).

A question to ponder. What do you think was the secret of Paul's boldness for the Lord?

CHRIST IS PREEMINENT

Colossians; Philemon

Yesterday we gave attention to Paul's defense before Roman authorities (Acts 25–28). Today we learn about Christ's preeminence and full sufficiency.

Key concept. Christ is preeminent over all things, and is fully sufficient for all our needs.

The big picture. We concluded our study of events in Acts 25–28, dated at AD 59–60. Today we explore Philemon and Colossians, both written in AD 61. Philemon was a prominent man whose slave Onesimus escaped, became a believer after encountering Paul, and was now returning under Paul's counsel. Paul, in a letter, appealed to Philemon to set Onesimus free so he could aid Paul in ministry. Paul also wrote to the Colossians, seeking to correct some of their doctrinal errors. He strongly emphasized Christ's supremacy and full sufficiency.

Transformational truth. Because God has forgiven us, we should forgive others (Philemon 1:17). The Pharisees said one should forgive another person two times. When Peter asked Jesus about forgiving seven times, he thought he was being generous. Jesus said to forgive 70 times 7. In other words, *forgive without limit* (Matthew 18:21-22).

A verse for meditation. "Just as you accepted Christ Jesus as your Lord, you must continue to follow him" (Colossians 2:6).

A question to ponder. Do you consider Christ to be fully sufficient for your every need?

BLESSINGS IN CHRIST

Ephesians 1–3

Yesterday we focused on the preeminence and supremacy of Christ (Colossians; Philemon). Today we turn our attention to the many blessings we have in Christ.

Key concept. We have rich spiritual blessings in the heavenlies.

The big picture. We completed our study of Philemon and Colossians, both written in AD 61. Today we study Ephesians, also written in AD 61. Paul made a number of highly relevant doctrinal points in Ephesians 1–3, such as these: God's eternal purposes include the redemption of believers (Ephesians 1:1-14); believers have many blessings in Christ (1:15-23); salvation is solely by grace, with no works involved (2:1-10); Jews and Gentiles become one in union with Christ (2:11-22; 3:1-13); and Christ's love is immeasurable (3:14-21).

Transformational truth. Even though we live in different cities here on earth, we are more fundamentally citizens of heaven—"citizens along with all of God's holy people" (Ephesians 2:19). "We are citizens of heaven, where the Lord Jesus Christ lives" (Philippians 3:20). We should therefore behave here below as citizens of heaven above. We should live *now* in view of *then*. We need to keep our eyes on heaven (Colossians 3:1-2).

A verse for meditation. "All praise to God, the Father of our Lord Jesus Christ, who has blessed us with every spiritual blessing in the heavenly realms because we are united with Christ" (Ephesians 1:3).

A question to ponder. Have you ever thought about your spiritual wealth in Jesus Christ?

RELATIONSHIPS AND HOLINESS

Ephesians 4 – 6

In the previous lesson, we explored the many blessings we have in Christ (Ephesians 1–3). Today we consider Paul's spiritual insights on relationships and walking in godliness.

Key concept. One's walk with Christ affects all personal relationships as well as one's commitment to godliness.

The big picture. Paul demonstrated how doctrine affects duty. In view of what we learned in chapters 1–3—more specifically, because we are in union with Christ—we are now to walk for Christ as we continue to live on earth. We must walk in unity (4:1-16), in holiness (4:17-32), in love (5:1-6), in the light (5:7-14), in wisdom (5:15 – 6:9), and in victory (6:10-20).

Transformational truth. Believers are sealed by the Holy Spirit unto the day of redemption (Ephesians 1:13; 4:30). This divine seal guarantees we will be delivered into eternal life. In keeping with this, we are secure in the Father's hand (John 10:29). God has the power to keep us "from falling away" (Jude 24). Those who have trusted in Christ "will never be condemned for their sins" (John 5:24). Because our salvation is secure, we can now live in joyful anticipation of heaven (Psalm 100:4; Philippians 4:6).

A verse for meditation. "Always be humble and gentle. Be patient with each other, making allowance for each other's faults because of your love" (Ephesians 4:2).

A question to ponder. Do you ever have doubts about your salvation? How has this lesson helped you in this regard?

JOY IN CHRIST

Philippians

Yesterday we considered Paul's spiritual insights on relationships and walking in godliness (Ephesians 4–6). Today we focus on joy in Christ.

Key concept. We can have joy in Christ, regardless of our circumstances.

The big picture. After Paul wrote Ephesians in AD 61, he wrote Philippians in AD 63 to correct certain problems in the church relating to rivalries, legalism, and worldliness. He also communicated some exciting spiritual truths: We can have joy in the midst of adverse circumstances (Philippians 1:12-26). Departing this life means to be with Christ in heaven (1:21-23). Humility among church members is foundational to church unity (2:1-4). True righteousness is rooted not in external obedience to the law, but is received through faith in Christ (3). As we cast our anxieties upon God, we experience indescribable peace (4:6-7).

Transformational truth. Like the apostle Paul, we can experience joy in every circumstance (Philippians 4:4). He affirms that God's "peace will guard your hearts and minds as you live in Christ Jesus" (verse 7).

A verse for meditation. "Always be full of joy in the Lord. I say it again—rejoice!" (Philippians 4:4).

A question to ponder. Is your life characterized by the type of joy Paul spoke about? If not, what have you learned in this lesson that might help you?

LIVING IN LIGHT OF GOD'S AWESOME GRACE

1 Peter

Yesterday we gave attention to joy in Christ (Philippians). Today we turn to our living hope and the call to holiness.

Key concept. Believers are born again to a living hope and are called to be holy.

The big picture. Soon after Paul wrote Philippians, Peter wrote 1 Peter in AD 63. He wrote to encourage and strengthen his brethren. Among his key points were these: The believer's future hope in heaven gives them strength as they suffer trials (1 Peter 1:1-9). Submissiveness is Christlike (2:13–3:8). If believers must suffer, it ought to be for the sake of righteousness and not because of sin (3:17). Christians should avoid lust, pursue love, pursue humility, pray, resist the devil, and stay strong in the faith (4–5).

Transformational truth. Peter said Christians are temporary residents on earth (1 Peter 1:1). Our time on this planet is relatively short. But our time in heaven will be very long (eternal). We are presently headed toward our "heavenly homeland" (Hebrew 11:16; see also Philippians 3:20). We should therefore live our short earthly lives in view of what awaits us in our long heavenly future!

A verse for meditation. "Stay alert! Watch out for your great enemy, the devil. He prowls around like a roaring lion, looking for someone to devour" (1 Peter 5:8).

A question to ponder. Have you ever experienced severe spiritual warfare?

SOUND DOCTRINE

Titus

Yesterday we focused on living in light of God's awesome grace (1 Peter). Today we turn our attention to the teaching and defense of sound doctrine.

Key concept. Sound doctrine must be taught and defended in the church.

The big picture. Titus was written in AD 64, not long after 1 Peter. Paul wrote this letter to "Titus, my true son in the faith" (Titus 1:4). Titus was a young pastor and leader of the church in Crete. He was one of Paul's trusted inner circle of friends and ministry associates (2 Corinthians 8:23). Paul's main points included: Church elders must meet high standards (Titus 1:5-9). Church elders were to protect the congregation against false teachers (1:5-9). False teachers were to be silenced (1:10-16). We are to pursue sound doctrine and good works (1:9; 2:1–3:11). Good doctrine naturally leads to good behavior (3).

Transformational truth. Titus speaks of good works, but these works rest on the foundation of God's grace (Titus 2:11-13; 3:5-7). Works are not the condition of our salvation, but a consequence of it. While we are saved by grace through faith, we are saved for good works. Good works are a by-product of salvation (Matthew 7:15-23; 1 Timothy 5:10,25).

A verse for meditation. "We should live in this evil world with wisdom, righteousness, and devotion to God" (Titus 2:12).

A question to ponder. Can you think of any television preachers who do not set forth sound doctrine?

PAUL INSTRUCTS TIMOTHY

1 Timothy 1 – 3

In the previous lesson, we explored the teaching and defense of sound doctrine (Titus). Today we consider Paul's instructions to Timothy, his young ministry associate.

Key concept. Beware of false teachers. Fight the good fight.

The big picture. Paul wrote 1 Timothy in AD 64. Timothy was a young and trusted colleague of Paul. Paul, in this letter, spoke as a more mature, experienced pastor to a younger, inexperienced pastor (Timothy). Key teachings include these: Church leaders must take a stand against false teachers (1 Timothy 1:1-11), fight the good fight (1:12-20), pray for government officials (2:1-8), and maintain good character (3:1-13). Timothy took all this to heart.

Transformational truth. Paul informed Timothy that Jesus "has given me strength to do his work" (1 Timothy 1:12). This is a common theme in the New Testament. Paul elsewhere affirmed, "I can do everything through Christ, who gives me strength" (Philippians 4:13). Conversely, Jesus warned His followers, "I am the vine; you are the branches. Those who remain in me, and I in them, will produce much fruit. For apart from me you can do nothing" (John 15:5). Stay plugged into Jesus!

A verse for meditation. "Cling to your faith in Christ, and keep your conscience clear. For some people have deliberately violated their consciences; as a result, their faith has been shipwrecked" (1 Timothy 1:19).

A question to ponder. Do you make it a high priority to keep a clear conscience?

FIGHT THE GOOD FIGHT

1 Timothy 4 – 6

Yesterday we considered Paul's instructions to Timothy, his young ministry associate (1 Timothy 1–3). Today we continue our look at Paul's instructions to Timothy, focusing specifically on the importance of fighting the good fight in the work of ministry.

Key concept. Apostasy will emerge in the latter times. Meanwhile, be a committed servant of Christ and focus on good doctrine. Fight the good fight of faith.

The big picture. Paul urgently warned Timothy as a church pastor to beware of false teachers and to watch his doctrine closely. Good doctrine produces a healthy spirituality. Bad doctrine is spiritually injurious (1 Timothy 4). Paul also warned about the unbiblical idea that godliness results in material blessing (6:3-16). Paul urged: Be content with what you have.

Transformational truth. Paul informed Timothy that "godliness with contentment is itself great wealth" (1 Timothy 6:6). Because of our relationship with Christ, we can be content in all circumstances: "I have learned how to be content with whatever I have. I know how to live on almost nothing or with everything" (Philippians 4:11-12). You may wish to consult these verses: Psalm 90:14; Proverbs 19:23; Ecclesiastes 5:10,18; Hebrews 13:5.

A verse for meditation. "True godliness with contentment is itself great wealth. After all, we brought nothing with us when we came into the world, and we can't take anything with us when we leave it" (1 Timothy 6:6-7).

A question to ponder. Has this lesson adjusted your attitude regarding personal wealth?

STAND FOR TRUTH

2 Timothy

Yesterday we gave attention to the importance of fighting the good fight in the work of ministry (1 Timothy 4–6). Today we focus on the importance of taking a stand for God's truth.

Key concept. Paul urged Timothy as a soldier of Christ to stand strong for God's truth.

The big picture. Paul wrote 2 Timothy in AD 67. Knowing his death was near, Paul urged Timothy: Stand firm in the power of the gospel. Don't give way to fear, intimidation, or shame (2 Timothy 1:1-18). Preach and teach, be single-minded, patiently endure, work diligently, pursue righteousness, and avoid youthful lusts (2). Stand strong in defending the Word of God (3:1-17). Preach the Word (4:1-5).

Transformational truth. Paul instructed Timothy to "run from anything that stimulates youthful lusts" (2 Timothy 2:22). This reminds us of 1 Corinthians 6:18, where Paul warned, "Run from sexual sin." The Amplified Bible renders it this way: "Run away from sexual immorality [in any form, whether thought or behavior, whether visual or written]."

A verse for meditation. "All Scripture is inspired by God and is useful to teach us what is true and to make us realize what is wrong in our lives. It corrects us when we are wrong and teaches us to do what is right" (2 Timothy 3:16).

A question to ponder. Why do you think so many Christians do not spend much time reading God's Word today?

BEWARE OF FALSE TEACHERS

2 Peter and Jude

Yesterday we focused on the importance of taking a stand for God's truth (2 Timothy). Today we turn our attention to watching out for false teachers.

Key concept. Both books stress the danger of false teachers, and the importance of persevering in the truth.

The big picture. Not long after 2 Timothy was written, 2 Peter and Jude were written around AD 67–68. Second Peter teaches that believers ought to avoid worldly corruption, pursue Christian virtues (2 Peter 1:5-11), and beware of false teachers (2:1-22). Moreover, the reality of Christ's future coming should motivate righteousness (3:11-18). Meanwhile, Jude teaches that every Christian ought to contend for "the faith" delivered to believers (Jude 1-4), and resist turning Christian grace and liberty into a license to sin (5-16). They should also beware of false teachers and apostasy (17-25).

Transformational truth. After revealing what the future holds, 2 Peter 3:11 urges, "What holy and godly lives you should live" (see also Titus 2:11-13). *Holy* behavior is that which is set apart from sin and set apart unto righteousness. *Godly* behavior refers to living in such a way that you honor and reverence God by your very lifestyle (see also Romans 13:11-14; 1 John 3:2-3).

A verse for meditation. "Defend the faith that God has entrusted once for all time to his holy people" (Jude 3).

A question to ponder. Are you a defender of Christian truth?

JESUS IS SUPREME

Hebrews 1:1–4:13

In the previous lesson, we explored the danger of false teachers (2 Peter; Jude). Today we consider how Jesus is supreme in every way.

Key concept. Because Jesus is supreme, Jewish believers must not drift back into Jewish teachings, practices, and rituals.

The big picture. Hebrews was written in AD 68, two years before Jerusalem and the temple were overrun by Rome (AD 70). The backdrop is that any Jew who converted to Christ in the first century was immediately branded as a blemish to the Jewish nation. He was expelled from the synagogue. He lost his job. He was sometimes thrown in jail (Hebrews 10:33-34). These circumstances caused some Jewish believers to wane in their outward commitment to Christ and consider drifting back into the external observances of Judaism to get the Jewish high priest off their back. The author of Hebrews said *don't do it, because Jesus is supreme.*

Transformational truth. Scripture warns of the possibility of Christians developing calloused hearts (Hebrews 3:8; 4:7; Psalm 95:8). Just as calloused skin is insensitive, so a calloused heart is insensitive to the things of God. The best remedy: Regular exposure to God's Word (Psalm 119) combined with obedience (John 14:21; 1 John 5:3).

A verse for meditation. "We must listen very carefully to the truth we have heard, or we may drift away from it" (Hebrews 2:1).

A question to ponder. Do you sometimes pay too little attention to God's Word?

MOVE ON TO MATURITY

Hebrews 4:14 – 7:28

Yesterday we considered how Jesus is supreme in every way (Hebrews 1:1–4:13). Today we will focus on the importance of moving on to maturity.

Key concept. Don't spiritually stagnate. Move on to spiritual maturity in Jesus Christ.

The big picture. Christ's priesthood is superior to the Levitical priesthood (Hebrews 4:14–5:10). Levitical priests were tainted by sin, offered countless animal sacrifices, and eventually died. Christ was sinless, offered Himself as a once-for-all sacrifice, and lives forever. These Jewish believers should therefore cease drifting back into Judaism and move on to maturity in Christ. They should render absolute commitment to the faithful High Priest, Jesus Christ (5:11–6:12). Christ removed sin forever by His one sacrifice at Calvary (6:13–7:28).

Transformational truth. Hebrews thoroughly establishes that Jesus is superior to the prophets (Hebrews 1:1-4), the angels (1:5–2:18), and Moses (3:1-6). He is therefore a supreme object of faith (3:7–4:16). Because Jesus is supreme in all things, He must also be supreme at the throne of our own hearts. Let us hold nothing back. Let us submit to His sovereign rule in all things.

A verse for meditation. "Let us come boldly to the throne of our gracious God. There we will receive his mercy, and we will find grace to help us when we need it most" (Hebrews 4:16).

A question to ponder. Can you think of any specific needs to bring before the throne of grace and mercy today?

A BETTER COVENANT

Hebrews 8:1–10:18

Yesterday we gave attention to the importance of moving on to maturity (Hebrews 4:14–7:28). Today we turn to how Jesus is the High Priest of a better covenant.

Key concept. Jesus is the High Priest of a better covenant. This better covenant is based on the once-for-all sacrifice of Christ upon the cross of Calvary.

The big picture. Christ's new covenant brings about the forgiveness of sins and yields a personal relationship with God (Hebrews 8:1-13). This covenant is based on Christ's superior sacrifice (9:1–10:18). Christ's *once-for-all* sacrifice enabled Him to completely remove sin and attain eternal redemption for all of God's people. No further sacrifice is necessary.

Transformational truth. Jesus is our High Priest. He represents God the Father to us and represents us to God the Father. He is our go-between. He is the bridge between God and us: "There is one God and one Mediator who can reconcile God and humanity—the man Christ Jesus" (1 Timothy 2:5). As our High Priest, Jesus also prays for us (Hebrews 7:25). And His prayers are always answered!

A verse for meditation. "He is the one who mediates a new covenant between God and people, so that all who are called can receive the eternal inheritance God has promised them" (Hebrews 9:15).

A question to ponder. How does it make you feel to know that an eternal inheritance awaits you?

ASSURANCE OF FAITH

Hebrews 10:19 – 13:25

Yesterday we focused on Jesus as the High Priest of a better covenant (Hebrews 8:1 – 10:18). Today we turn our attention to how we can have an assurance of faith in God's wondrous promises.

Key concept. Faith gives us assurance in God's promises. Faith is the assurance of things hoped for, the conviction of things not seen.

The big picture. Jesus has completed the work of salvation on our behalf (Hebrews 10:19-39). It remains for us only to trust in Him. Hebrews 11 inspires us to trust all of God's promises, for He is faithful. Hebrews 12 instructs that believers ought to fix their eyes on Jesus. Hebrews 13 tells us that our faith should show itself in the way we live our lives (such as not succumbing to high priestly pressure).

Transformational truth. When things seem at their most hopeless, the God of miracles can come through in ways we would never have fathomed. That's why it's important to always maintain a strong faith in God (Hebrews 11:1). Examples include Daniel's rescue in the lions' den (Daniel 6) and David's victory over Goliath (1 Samuel 17). Keep your faith in God strong (Proverbs 3:5-6).

A verse for meditation. "Faith shows the reality of what we hope for; it is the evidence of things we cannot see" (Hebrews 11:1).

A question to ponder. Are you presently facing any hard circumstances that you need to hand over to God in faith?

FELLOWSHIP

1, 2, 3 John

In the previous lesson, we explored how we can have an assurance of faith in God's wondrous promises (Hebrews 10:19–13:25). Today we zero in on fellowship with God and with one another.

Key concept. Christians are to walk in the light and love one another. This leads to fellowship with God and with one another.

The big picture. John wrote 1, 2, and 3 John around AD 90. John said we must walk in the light in order to spiritually fellowship with Christ (1 John 1:5-7). If we sin, we must confess it to God so that fellowship may be restored (1 John 1:8-10). Fellowship with God shows itself in one's life (1 John 2:28–5:3). Jesus, in the incarnation, came in a real human body (2 John 7-13). Some believers are godly and generous (3 John 1-8), while others are prideful and ambitious (3 John 9-14).

Transformational truth. Our vertical relationship with God affects our horizontal relationships with other people: "If anyone claims, 'I am living in the light,' but hates a fellow believer, that person is still living in darkness" (1 John 2:9; see also 4:8).

A verse for meditation. "Do not love this world nor the things it offers you, for when you love the world, you do not have the love of the Father in you" (1 John 2:15).

A question to ponder. Do you ever struggle with loving the things of this world?

JESUS AND THE CHURCHES

Revelation 1–4

Yesterday we considered fellowship with God and one another (1, 2, 3 John). Today we will focus on how Jesus is sovereign over the churches.

Key concept. Jesus is the Lord of glory who is sovereign over the churches.

The big picture. John wrote Revelation around AD 95. John emphasizes that Jesus is the Lord of glory (Revelation 1:5,7,8,17,18). Revelation 1:19 outlines the book: John was to write about what he had seen (chapter 1), the things "that are now happening" (2–3), and the things "that will happen" (4–22). Christ commended the churches where He could (Revelation 2:2-3,6,9,13,19; 3:4,8), but also rebuked them where He had to, calling for repentance (2:4-5,14-16,20-23; 3:1-3,15-20). God's throne room is glorious (Revelation 4).

Transformational truth. A failure to repent of sin always brings God's discipline in a believer's life. That's what happened to David following his sin with Bathsheba (Psalm 32:3-5; 51). It can happen to us too (Hebrews 12:5-11). It makes good sense to have a lifestyle of repentance before God. As 1 Corinthians 11:31 puts it, "If we would examine ourselves, we would not be judged by God in this way."

A verse for meditation. "You don't love me or each other as you did at first! Look how far you have fallen! Turn back to me and do the works you did at first" (Revelation 2:4-5).

A question to ponder. Do you think you love Jesus as much as you used to?

JUDGMENT FALLS

Revelation 5–8

Yesterday we gave attention to how Jesus is sovereign over the churches (Revelation 1–4). Today we turn to how judgment falls upon the world from the "Lamb," who is Jesus the divine Messiah.

Key concept. The seal judgments and the first four trumpet judgments are unleashed upon the earth.

The big picture. Only the Lamb—Jesus, the divine Messiah—is worthy to open the scroll and its seven seals. As Jesus breaks each respective seal, a new divine judgment is unleashed on earth. God's 144,000 Jewish witnesses on earth are supernaturally protected as they evangelize. The seventh seal judgment brings about the trumpet judgments. All of heaven becomes silent—soberly aware of what now lies ahead.

Transformational truth. God remains on the throne, bringing about His eternal purposes, even when the world around us seems tumultuous (Revelation 5:13). "Everything I plan will come to pass, for I do whatever I wish" (Isaiah 46:10; see also Deuteronomy 10:14; 1 Chronicles 29:12; 2 Chronicles 20:6; Job 42:2; Psalms 33:8-11; 47:2; John 14:1-3; Ephesians 1:20-22).

A verse for meditation. "The Lamb on the throne will be their Shepherd. He will lead them to springs of life-giving water. And God will wipe every tear from their eyes" (Revelation 7:17).

A question to ponder. Do you ever struggle with trusting God in a world where evil is running rampant and fear of the Lord seems absent?

THE TWO PROPHETIC WITNESSES

Revelation 9 – 12

Yesterday we focused on how judgment falls upon the world from the "Lamb," who is Jesus the divine Messiah (Revelation 5 – 8). Today we turn our attention to God's two prophetic witnesses.

Key concept. God's two prophetic witnesses give a powerful testimony of the true God, even as war breaks out on earth and in heaven.

The big picture. Revelation 11 speaks of God's two witnesses who will testify about God with miraculous acts during the first half of the tribulation period. After their ministry is complete, the antichrist will kill them. Three days later, they will resurrect from the dead and ascend into heaven. Revelation 12 speaks of how Satan sought to kill Jesus upon birth, but he was unsuccessful. Jesus ascended into heaven following His resurrection (Acts 1:9; 2:33; Hebrews 1:1-3; 12:2).

Transformational truth. Christians are called to live in reverent fear of God (Revelation 11:18). Fearing the Lord involves showing reverence to Him (Proverbs 2:5; Deuteronomy 32:6; Hosea 11:1; Isaiah 1:2; 63:16; 64:8). Such reverence naturally leads to obedience to God and motivates the desire to serve him (Deuteronomy 6:13). Conversely, the person who feels free to disobey God typically has no fear of God.

A verse for meditation. "I will give power to my two witnesses, and they will…prophesy during those 1,260 days" (Revelation 11:3).

A question to ponder. Does Bible prophecy frighten you or comfort you?

THE ANTICHRIST, THE FALSE PROPHET, AND MORE JUDGMENTS

Revelation 13 – 17

In the previous lesson, we looked at God's two prophetic witnesses (Revelation 9 – 12). Today we consider the antichrist, the false prophet, and further judgments on the world.

Key concept. The antichrist and false prophet emerge, and God's judgments continue.

The big picture. The antichrist will come on the scene and will be energized by Satan. He will attain world dominion. His right-hand man will be the false prophet (Revelation 13). The seven bowl judgments will finally be unleashed, and they will go from bad to worse (Revelation 15). The false religion of the end times will be destroyed, and the antichrist will demand to be the sole object of worship (Revelation 17).

Transformational truth. The 144,000 Jewish witnesses will be committed to "following the Lamb wherever he goes" (Revelation 14:4). No matter what the cost, they will remain committed. You and I, too, are called to follow Christ regardless of the cost: "If any of you wants to be my follower, you must give up your own way, take up your cross, and follow me" (Matthew 16:24; see also John 12:26; 14:15).

A verse for meditation. "Blessed are those who die in the Lord from now on. Yes, says the Spirit, they are blessed indeed, for they will rest from their hard work; for their good deeds follow them!" (Revelation 14:13).

A question to ponder. Do you ever ponder what life will be like in heaven?

THE SECOND COMING

Revelation 18 – 20

Yesterday we considered the antichrist, the false prophet, and further judgments on the world (Revelation 13–17). Today we will focus on the second coming of Jesus Christ and His glorious kingdom.

Key concept. Christ's second coming will be a glorious event, followed by the setting up of His glorious millennial kingdom. The wicked will be judged at the great white throne judgment.

The big picture. Christ's second coming will be glorious and majestic (Revelation 19). On His head are many diadems, representing total sovereignty and royal kingship. He will come as the King of kings and Lord of lords. The glorious kingdom He will set up will feature an enhanced physical environment, plenty of food for all, harmony with the animal kingdom, longevity among humans, illnesses removed, prosperity, and joy (Revelation 20).

Transformational truth. Jesus is King of kings and Lord of lords (Revelation 19:16). He sovereignly oversees all that comes into our lives. No matter what we may encounter, the knowledge that our sovereign King of kings is in control of everything anchors us in the midst of life's storms. Because Christ is sovereign, we are never victims of our circumstances.

A verse for meditation. "On his robe at his thigh was written this title: King of all kings and Lord of all lords" (Revelation 19:16).

A question to ponder. What does it mean to you personally that Christ is the supreme authority in all the universe?

THE ETERNAL STATE

Revelation 21–22

Yesterday we gave attention to the second coming of Jesus Christ and His glorious kingdom (Revelation 18–20). Today we focus on the eternal state.

Key concept. God will create new heavens and a new earth. The New Jerusalem is the eternal city of the redeemed that will rest upon the new earth.

The big picture. The present (old) heavens and earth will one day pass away (Psalm 102:25-26; Isaiah 51:6). God will create new heavens and a new earth. The New Jerusalem is the eternal city we will one day inhabit on the new earth. God will live directly with redeemed humankind (Revelation 21).

Transformational truth. We will recognize all of our Christian loved ones in heaven (Revelation 21–22). The Thessalonian believers were concerned about their believing loved ones who had died. Paul informed them they would be reunited in heaven—implying they would recognize each other (1 Thessalonians 4:13-17). David knew he would be reunited with his deceased son in heaven, and had no doubt about recognizing him (2 Samuel 12:23). The rich man, Lazarus, and Abraham all recognized each other in the afterlife (Luke 16:19-31).

A verse for meditation. "God's home is now among his people! He will live with them, and they will be his people. God himself will be with them" (Revelation 21:3).

A question to ponder. Are you motivated to maintain a top-down perspective—that is, a heavenly one?

POSTSCRIPT

When a person goes on a well-organized tour, there is always a sense of gratification when the tour is complete. There's a sense of "Wow, that was interesting. I feel good about what I learned."

Having sojourned through the entire Bible from Genesis to Revelation, we have every reason to feel good about what we have learned. After all, the Bible is brimming with applicable truths that are uplifting and life-transforming.

I have chosen to close our tour by sifting a key applicable truth from each book of the Bible, from Genesis to Revelation. May the Lord bless you as you contemplate these life-changing truths:

Genesis—Because God is our Creator, we ought to daily show creaturely respect toward Him.

Exodus—God can engage in tremendous miracles in delivering you from challenging circumstances.

Leviticus—God's holiness has profound implications for how you and I live.

Numbers—God is a promise-keeper.

Deuteronomy—Reviewing God's Word on a consistent basis will keep you on track.

Joshua—Regular meditation on the Word of God brings success in life.

Judges—God continues to remain faithful, even when His children are unfaithful.

Ruth—Treat others with kindness, and kindness will be returned upon you.

1 Samuel—Human beings tend to fixate on people's external features, but the Lord looks at the heart.

2 Samuel—Fear of the Lord is the beginning of wisdom.

1 Kings—A person can be "wholly true to the Lord," and yet still fall into sin.

2 Kings—Bad leadership can bring a nation down—and *keep* a nation down.

1 Chronicles—Avoid idolatry at all costs. God hates it.

2 Chronicles—Obedience to God brings blessing, just as disobedience brings chastisement.

Ezra—Count on it: God's mercy always exceeds His anger.

Nehemiah—Every believer ought to take a stand for social justice.

Esther—God has the sovereign ability to place His people in strategic positions of authority.

Job—Good people can encounter difficult circumstances in life, but God always has a purpose in allowing it.

Psalms—Our Lord is worthy to be praised. Make it a daily habit.

Proverbs—Living according to biblical wisdom leads to the good life.

Ecclesiastes—God has put within each of our hearts a yearning for the eternal. We ought therefore to maintain an eternal perspective.

Song of Solomon—The marital love between a man and a woman involves the deepest of bonds, just as God intended.

Isaiah—No matter what you face in life, fear not. The Lord is with you.

Jeremiah—A lack of repentance brings God's disciplinary judgment.

Lamentations—There are always consequences to our choices. Make wise choices.

Ezekiel—Beware: You may not have as long as you think to repent.

Daniel—Let us resolve to always be people of integrity.

Hosea—When God's Word is marginalized in a society, sin can run rampant.

Joel—Blessing from God follows obedience to Him.

Amos—Take whatever steps you need to avoid spiritual complacency and lethargy in your life. They are deadly.

Obadiah—Pride goes before destruction.

Jonah—The Lord can bring us down; the Lord can lift us up.

Micah—True religion is not just about rituals. It's about showing love, justice, mercy, and faithfulness.

Nahum—God is a jealous God—He desires His people to be faithful. Avoid infidelity!

Habakkuk—Father knows best! Always trust that God's plan is the best plan for your life.

Zephaniah—Continued unrepentant sin is like a judgment magnet. Repentance, by contrast, repels judgment.

Haggai—Future blessing from God hinges on present commitment to God.

Zechariah—God does not like empty ritualism. He likes when people authentically relate to Him and live according to His instructions.

Malachi—Never doubt God's love, even when things seem to be going haywire in your life.

Matthew—Jesus, the messianic King, teaches us what we

need to know about rightly relating to God, rightly relating to each other, and how to live a God-honoring life.

Mark—Jesus is our one and only true source of spiritual rest. Come to Him now.

Luke—Don't be hypocritical, judgmental, or prideful. Those traits don't sit well with Jesus.

John—The gist of God's law comes down to this: Love the Lord with all your being, and love your neighbor as yourself.

Acts—The Holy Spirit is an ever-present source of spiritual power and blessing for the believer.

Romans—We are justified not by works but by faith alone. No one can earn God's salvation, so don't even try.

1 Corinthians—Believers will one day face Christ at the judgment seat of Christ. Live your life accordingly.

2 Corinthians—God comforts us in our afflictions so that we may in turn comfort others.

Galatians—Rejoice: You and I are made right with God by *faith alone* in *Christ alone*.

Ephesians—Our salvation rests on God's amazing grace. Works play no role.

Philippians—You can have joy even in the midst of life's most difficult circumstances.

Colossians—God's Word is not just to provide us with *information*, but to bring about personal *transformation*.

1 Thessalonians—We can look forward to a glorious reunion with all our Christian loved ones in heaven.

2 Thessalonians—It is best to maintain a balanced and discerning perspective on life as we await the coming of the Lord.

1 Timothy—Don't ever give up. Fight the good fight.

2 Timothy—Be single-minded in your service to the Lord.

Titus—Plan your life according to your full lifetime expectancy, but live your life as if Christ could come today.

Philemon—Faith in Christ shows itself in how one lives.

Hebrews—If you want to know what God is like, then look at Jesus.

James—Faith shows itself in being a "doer of the Word."

1 Peter—We derive our spiritual nourishment by daily feeding upon God's Word.

2 Peter—There's a new world coming. Hold tight to an eternal perspective.

1 John—When we sin, Jesus is our defense attorney—and He never loses a case in God's court. Our fellowship with God is thereby protected.

2 John—Don't play games with a lip-service kind of love for God. Make your love for Him obvious in the way you live your life.

3 John—Doing good to others is an "I.D. card" that proves we are members of God's family.

Jude—Beware: God's forgiveness is not a license for Christians to live in immorality without fear of judgment.

Revelation—You and I will have resurrected bodies and live in a resurrected city (the New Jerusalem) that rests upon a resurrected earth (a new earth) in a resurrected universe (new heavens)—and we will live face to face with God forever (Revelation 21–22). Rejoice in this!

> *All Scripture is inspired by God*
> *and is useful to teach us what is true*
> *and to make us realize what is wrong in our lives.*
> *It corrects us when we are wrong*
> *and teaches us to do what is right.*
> *God uses it to prepare and equip his people*
> *to do every good work.*
>
> 2 Timothy 3:16-17

Other Great Harvest House Books by Ron Rhodes

BOOKS ABOUT THE BIBLE

40 Days Through Genesis
The Big Book of Bible Answers
Bite-Size Bible® Answers
Bite-Size Bible® Charts
Bite-Size Bible® Definitions
Bite-Size Bible® Handbook
Commonly Misunderstood Bible Verses
The Complete Guide to Bible Translations
Find It Fast in the Bible
The Popular Dictionary of Bible Prophecy
Understanding the Bible from A to Z
What Does the Bible Say About…?

BOOKS ABOUT THE END TIMES

8 Great Debates of Bible Prophecy
40 Days Through Revelation
Cyber Meltdown
The End Times in Chronological Order
Northern Storm Rising
Unmasking the Antichrist

BOOKS ABOUT OTHER IMPORTANT TOPICS

5-Minute Apologetics for Today
1001 Unforgettable Quotes About God, Faith, and the Bible
Answering the Objections of Atheists,
Agnostics, and Skeptics
Christianity According to the Bible
The Complete Guide to Christian Denominations
Conversations with Jehovah's Witnesses
Find It Quick Handbook on Cults and New Religions
The Truth Behind Ghosts, Mediums, and Psychic Phenomena
Secret Life of Angels
What Happens After Life?
Why Do Bad Things Happen If God Is Good?
Wonder of Heaven

To learn more about Harvest House books and
to read sample chapters, visit our website:

www.harvesthousepublishers.com

HARVEST HOUSE PUBLISHERS
EUGENE, OREGON